The Heritage of Literature Series

SECTION B NO. 53

TWENTIETH CENTURY PROSE
1940-1960

The Heritage of Literature Series
General Editor: E. W. Parker, M.C.

A series that will lead to wider horizons
by awakening a love of good books, and
by providing a key to the treasures of the
world's best thought.

TRAVEL AND ADVENTURE

ESSAYS AND BELLES LETTRES

DRAMA

FICTION

MYTHS AND FOLK LORE

HISTORY

LIFE AND LETTERS

POETRY

Twentieth Century Prose

1940-1960

Selected with an Introduction
and Notes by

A. C. WARD

LONGMANS

LONGMANS, GREEN AND CO LTD
48 GROSVENOR STREET, LONDON W1
RAILWAY CRESCENT, CROYDON, VICTORIA, AUSTRALIA
AUCKLAND, KINGSTON (JAMAICA), LAHORE, NAIROBI

LONGMANS SOUTHERN AFRICA (PTY) LTD
THIBAULT HOUSE, THIBAULT SQUARE, CAPE TOWN
JOHANNESBURG, SALISBURY

LONGMANS OF NIGERIA LTD
W. R. INDUSTRIAL ESTATE, IKEJA

LONGMANS OF GHANA LTD
INDUSTRIAL ESTATE, RING ROAD SOUTH, ACCRA

LONGMANS GREEN (FAR EAST) LTD
443 LOCKHART ROAD, HONG KONG

LONGMANS OF MALAYA LTD
44 JALAN AMPANG, KUALA LUMPUR

ORIENT LONGMANS LTD
CALCUTTA, BOMBAY, MADRAS
DELHI, HYDERABAD, DACCA

LONGMANS CANADA LTD
137 BOND STREET, TORONTO 2

First published in the Heritage of Literature Series 1962
This edition © Longmans, Green and Co Ltd 1962

PRINTED IN GREAT BRITAIN BY
NORTHUMBERLAND PRESS LIMITED
GATESHEAD ON TYNE

CONTENTS

*Most of the headings used have been provided by the
editor. With the exception of Sir Winston Churchill's,
the passages are arranged in order of publication dates.*

ACKNOWLEDGMENTS

We are indebted to the following for permission to reproduce copyright material:

George Allen & Unwin Ltd. for material from *Portraits from Memory* by Bertrand Russell; Edward Arnold (Publishers) Ltd. for material from *Two Cheers for Democracy* by E. M. Forster; the author's agents for material from *The Silence of the Sea* by Hilaire Belloc, published by Cassell & Company Ltd.; The Trustees of the Joyce Cary Estate for material from *The Horse's Mouth*, published by Michael Joseph Ltd.; Cassell & Company Ltd. and Houghton Mifflin Company for material from *The Second World War* Vol. 1 by Sir Winston Churchill; the author's agents for material from *Two Quiet Lives* by Lord David Cecil, published by Constable & Co Ltd.; Chatto & Windus Ltd. for material from *The Flame Trees of Thika* by Elspeth Huxley, and *Under the Net* by Iris Murdoch; William Collins Sons & Co Ltd. for material from *The World My Wilderness* by Dame Rose Macaulay; Mr. T. S. Eliot for material from *On Poetry and Poets*, published by Faber & Faber Ltd.; The English Universities Press Ltd. for material from *Life on Other Worlds* by Sir Harold Spencer Jones; Mr. Christopher Fry for material from *An Experience of Critics*; Victor Gollancz Ltd. for material from *Elizabeth the Great* by Elizabeth Jenkins; Rupert Hart-Davis Ltd. for material from *The Drunken Forest* by Gerald Durrell; Mr. L. P. Hartley and Putnam & Co Ltd. for material from *The Shrimp and the Anemone*; The Estate of Richard Hillary, Macmillan & Co Ltd. and The Macmillan Company of Canada Ltd. for material from *The Last Enemy*; William Heinemann Ltd. for material from *Over the Bridge* by Richard Church, and ' From Bloomsbury to Bayswater ' from *Mainly on Air* by Sir Max Beerbohm; Hutchinson & Co (Publishers) Ltd. for material from *Seal Morning* by Rowena Farre; Michael Joseph Ltd. for material from *Still Digging* by Sir Mortimer Wheeler; Longmans, Green & Co Ltd. for material from *Gone to the Cricket* by John Arlott, *English Social History* by G. M. Trevelyan, *He That Plays the*

King by Kenneth Tynan, and *Bernard Shaw* by A. C. Ward; MacGibbon & Kee Ltd. for material from *Memories* by Sir Desmond MacCarthy; John Murray (Publishers) Ltd. for 'Happiness' from *Perseus in the Wind* by Freya Stark; Mr. F. D. Ommanney for material from *The House in the Park*, published by Longmans, Green & Co. Ltd.; Oxford University Press for material from *Selected Speeches from H.R.H. The Prince Philip*; Mr. J. B. Priestley for material from *Thoughts in the Wilderness*, published by William Heinemann Ltd; the author's agents for material from *Annals of Innocence and Experience* by Sir Herbert Read, published by Faber & Faber Ltd.; The Public Trustee and The Society of Authors for *Producing a Play* by Bernard Shaw; the author's agents for material from *Left Hand, Right Hand* by Sir Osbert Sitwell, published by Macmillan & Co Ltd.; *The Times* for 'The Lost Umbrella' from the September 28th 1959 issue, and 'No Room for Books' from the June 6th 1960 issue, all rights reserved ©; Miss Winifred Thompson for material from *Still Glides the Stream* by Flora Thompson; the author's representatives for material from *The King's Peace* by C. V. Wedgwood, published by William Collins Sons & Co Ltd.; Mr. Leonard Woolf for 'Ellen Terry' from *The Moment and Other Essays* by Virginia Woolf; and Mr. John Wyndham for 'Wild Flower' from *The Seeds of Time*, published by Michael Joseph Ltd.

INTRODUCTION

EVERYONE WRITES prose; only a gifted few write poetry; therefore prose is easier to write than poetry. That is a fallacy to which most people would mistakenly assent. Let us look at the facts.

When the Royal Society for Improving Natural Knowledge was founded in 1660, 'natural knowledge' meant the unified body of learning which has since branched into the two groups of studies now separately named Philosophy and Science. Science was then called Natural Philosophy.

The Royal Society long ago became the world's most famous fellowship of scientists, and election to its ranks, with the right to add F.R.S. to his name (or her name, for women can now be elected), is a rare distinction and the highest a scientist can achieve, apart perhaps from the Nobel Prize. Only scientists and mathematicians are now admitted as Fellows of the Royal Society, but at first it included authors, and all were desired to have a careful regard for the English language by developing 'a close, naked, natural way of speaking; positive expressions, clear senses, a native easiness'.

Among the earliest to be enrolled in the Royal Society was John Dryden, poet, playwright, and essayist, who has been called the Father of English Prose. He had command of an English prose style which observes the principles laid down by the Society, and though it is not to be supposed that he would have written less well if the Society had never come into being, his prose *is* 'close' (economical, i.e. it wastes no words), 'naked' (free from deliberate ornamentation), positive, clear, and easy. These are qualities we might expect all prose writers to have; but in fact, while sixteenth and seventeenth century poets had a fine and confident command of language, much prose of those times was either tangled and hard to unravel, or so elaborate that it attracts more by artificial splendour than by ease of understanding. In the middle of the sixteenth century (1553) a statesman named Thomas Wilson wrote a book called *The Art of Rhetoric* in which he urged other writers to avoid stiff pedantic language and foreign phrases. This is an example of his own prose style (the spelling is modernized here):

> Some seek so far for outlandish English, that they forget alto-gether their mother's language. And I dare swear this, if some of their mothers were alive, they were not able to tell what they say: and yet these fine English clerks will say, they speak in their mother tongue, if a man should charge them for counter-feiting the King's English. Some far journeyed gentlemen at their return home, like as they love to go in foreign apparel, so they will powder their talk with oversea language. He that cometh lately out of France, will talk French English and never blush at the matter. Another chops in with English Italianated, and applieth the Italian phrase to our English speaking, the which is, as if an Orator that professeth to utter his mind in plain Latin, would needs speak Poetry, and far fetched colours of strange antiquity.

This passage is by no means as 'outlandish' as some of the prose this writer's contemporaries were accustomed to use, but it can scarcely be claimed that Wilson's own prose is close, naked, or natural, or that it is notable for 'positive expressions, clear senses, a native easiness'.

If we turn onward rather more than a century, and look at the writings of Thomas Traherne, a shoemaker's son who became a clergyman, we find such prose as this:

> The dust and stones of the street were as precious as gold: the

gates were at first the end of the world. The green trees when I
saw them first through one of the gates transported and
ravished me, their sweetness and unusual beauty made my
heart to leap, and almost mad with ecstasy, they were such
strange and wonderful things.

This is very beautiful, and English literature would be
the poorer if Traherne's prose had been lost to us, as it
nearly was,[1] but it certainly is not close, naked, or natural.

Traherne's contemporary, John Bunyan, was also a
contemporary of John Dryden. Both Dryden and Bunyan
were writing in the Restoration period, and it may sometimes surprise us to remember that the Puritan Bunyan
wrote nearly all his great works in the reign of Charles II.
The most famous, *The Pilgrim's Progress*, came out in
1678. It is unlikely that Bunyan knew anything about
the Royal Society's views on prose style, expressed eigh-
teen years before, but the Society could have found little
fault with most of Bunyan's prose—such as:

My sword I give to him that shall succeed me in my pil-
grimage, and my courage and skill to him that can get it. My
marks and scars I carry with me, to be a witness for me, that
I have fought His battles who will now be my rewarder.

Yet that is still, like Traherne's, *religious* prose, concerned with heavenly matters. What the Royal Society
was concerned about was, much more, prose dealing with
human knowledge and capable of rendering in plain
terms the particular branch—scientific knowledge—which
was then developing fast. In this connection it has to
be remembered that the seventeenth century in England was a great age of scientific progress; through

[1] His best poetry and prose was not published until 1903 and
1908, the manuscripts having then been found by a London
bookseller.

the work of Sir Isaac Newton and others an age as important and remarkable then as the present is to us. What was needed then, as now, was the development of a prose style capable of conveying—positively, clearly, and easily—knowledge of the new scientific discoveries and ideas.

Though Dryden was not a scientist, prose like his *was* capable of being used for all manner of practical purposes. The title of his *Essay of Dramatic Poesy* does not suggest that it would also be an essay in the use of plain English. It begins with a description of a trip on the river Thames from London towards Greenwich while the guns of the Dutch fleet were making thunder in the air. On their journey the four friends in the boat discussed not the war with the Dutch and the peril close at hand, but the comparative merits of English and French poetic drama—a fine example of that imperturbability in time of crisis which has brought England through greater perils. The real names of the friends who were with Dryden that day are known, but he disguised them under classical pseudonyms. When their discussion had run its course and they came back up the river in the evening, one of the company was still arguing and oblivious of his surroundings:

Neander was pursuing this discourse so eagerly that Eugenius had called to him twice or thrice, ere he took notice that the barge stood still, and that they were at the foot of Somerset Stairs, where they had appointed it to land. The company were all sorry to separate so soon, though a great part of the evening was already spent; and stood awhile looking back on the water, upon which the moonbeams played, and made it appear like floating quicksilver: at last they went up through a crowd of French people, who were merrily dancing in the open air, and nothing concerned for the noise of the guns which had alarmed the town that afternoon.

We cannot pause here to do more than remark on the straightforwardness of Dryden's style, which is precise in regard both to time and place. But it is also worth noting that the only image he uses is a scientific one: the moonlight on the river made the water look like floating quicksilver. This image could only be a recollection of a personally observed fact, and the purpose of scientific prose is to record, for the information of others, facts which have been observed by the writer.

It is one of the unavoidable shortcomings of this anthology—a shortcoming regretted by the editor—that it contains little that can be called scientific prose. That such prose is not available is all the more regrettable because the majority of people nowadays feel themselves to belong to a different order of humanity from the scientists who govern so much of life—govern it and at the same time threaten it. A long-standing complaint is that scientists, however great, are rarely able to communicate understandably with ordinary people, people who would very much like to know what the scientists are up to with their new sources of energy, and what is man's future in competition with computers. It would no doubt reduce the membership of the Royal Society to a sparse company if no one were admitted as a Fellow until he had written a book or pamphlet in language easily comprehended by non-scientific readers whose intelligence is not below G.C.E. level. That this is a reasonable requirement is shown by the writings in the recent past of such eminent scientists and thinkers as Sir James Jeans and Sir Arthur Eddington, both of whom wrote popular, understandable books without objectionable vulgarization of their subjects. Jeans and Eddington died in the 1940s and their books were published before that decade began, so nothing by them qualified for inclusion here.

In defence of present-day scientists it can be said that their work is increasingly a matter of mathematical formulæ and symbols capable of being expressed on paper only algebraically and diagrammatically and beyond the scope of intelligible prose. However inevitable this may be—if it is inevitable—it is extremely and unhappily limiting for the populace at large whose lives are in the hands of men with whom they have no channel of communication.

This is for us, however, a negative approach to the matter of the present book. What we are to consider is not what cannot be conveyed in English prose, but the manner in which what can be conveyed has been conveyed.

This anthology ends at 1960, just three hundred years after the Royal Society's beginnings. To attempt to follow even in bare outline the progress of English prose through those three centuries would make far too long a story here. We can only note in passing that the ease and clarity of Dryden's prose was succeeded in the eighteenth century by a good deal of formality and not a little pomposity, and in the nineteenth century by a congested variety. There is nothing in common in the prose of Dickens, Ruskin, Carlyle, Matthew Arnold, Robert Louis Stevenson and Thomas Hardy, to name only a very few of the many eminent writers of the past century.

Towards the end of that century much attention was given to the Art of Writing. *What* was written tended in some minds to be overshadowed by *how* it was written. Essays on Style were composed by Stevenson, Walter Pater, and Sir Walter A. Raleigh (an Oxford Professor) in the last twenty years of the nineteenth century; and if we agree that the true purpose of prose is to convey meaning as directly as possible, we must also agree that devotion to Style and the Art of Writing is apt to be a handicap and a barrier if it interposes some element between the writer and the reader, interrupting or slowing down communication. What is produced by Style or Art in prose may be superficially beautiful in sound and sensation, but it cannot be considered good prose unless it is meaningful, conveying its idea or information intelligibly and in an attention-compelling manner.

Every writer has a style of some sort, good or bad; it is the stamp of the writer's mind and personality. Sloppy minded people will write sloppy prose; precise clear-minded people will write clear and precise prose, expressing exactly what they mean with simplicity and brevity. Stevenson and Pater and Raleigh thought of Style with a capital S. The product was often pleasing in sound and in its summoning up of verbal pictures, but it was too consciously dressed-up. In 'An Apology for Idlers', an essay in the volume called *Virginibus Puerisque* (1881) Robert Louis Stevenson has this account of the idler:

His way takes him along a by-road, not much frequented, but very even and pleasant, which is called Commonplace Lane, and leads to the Belvedere of Common-sense. Thence he shall command an agreeable, if no very noble prospect; and while others behold the East and West, the Devil and the Sunrise, he will be contentedly aware of a sort of morning hour upon all sublunary things, with an army of shadows, running speedily and in many different directions into the great daylight of Eternity. The shadows and the generations, the shrill doctors and the plangent wars, go by into ultimate silence and emptiness; but underneath all this, a man may see, out of the Belvedere windows, much green and peaceful landscape; many fire-lit parlours; good people laughing, drinking, and making love as they did before the Flood or the French Revolution; and the old shepherd telling his tale under the hawthorn.

This is fine-sounding 'literary' prose. It is pleasant, if one is a poetry-lover, to catch in the final phrase an echo of Milton's lines in *L'Allegro*:

> And every shepherd tells his tale
> Under the hawthorn in the dale;

but it would be a hard task to extract and express the plain meaning of Stevenson's prose in this passage. It is a kind of verbal music, and as an exercise in the Art of Writing it permits Art to override Sense, as even Stevenson himself would not have allowed it to be overridden in, say, *Treasure Island*, where he is telling a story, not playing with words. The more he tried to be an artist in words the less he made words in prose do their primary job of saying something plainly.

One of the topics discussed by Sir Walter Raleigh in his short book on *Style* (1897) is the use of slang, which he divides into Good Slang and Bad Slang. The words invented to express or describe technical and scientific ideas and apparatus for which no language terms existed before, he puts into the category of Good Slang (a more recent word for it would be *jargon*). Raleigh continues:

But there is another kind that goes under the name of slang, the offspring rather of mental sloth, and current chiefly among those idle, jocular classes to whom all art is a bugbear and a puzzle. There is a public for every one; the pottle-headed lout who in a moment of exuberance strikes on a new sordid metaphor for any incident in the beaten round of drunkenness, lubricity, and debt, can set his fancy rolling through the music-halls, and thence into the street, secure of applause and a numerous sodden discipleship.

Here we have a writer who, we feel as we read, gradually lets words take command of him instead of keeping them under his own command; the words go to his head and lead him into a fit of verbal drunkenness.

Let us not overlook, however, that such prose as has been quoted here from Stevenson and Raleigh, and a great deal that might be quoted from Walter Pater and Oscar Wilde, was much admired in their time and can still be admired when we are in an appropriate mood and more susceptible to sound than to sense.

Meanwhile two World Wars have changed the current of thought and taste and habit for millions of men and women and accustomed them to a rough informality inconsistent with a prose style which formerly paid much attention to a fine literary *art* of writing. Whereas fifty to a hundred years ago dressed-up prose was much admired, today there is a strong tendency to admire under-dressed prose: the crude has displaced the precious. Each age has its fashion in prose as well as in verse. It is one of the misfortunes of the present age that so much of the prose read by millions is fabricated by journalists with an impoverished vocabulary, and by advertisers whose main concern is to turn the public into fashion-fodder for the enrichment of those who tell us what we should eat, what we should wear, what we should read, and even what we should think.

Good prose, like good wine, matures slowly. Though there have been more good young poets than good old ones, it is otherwise with prose. Young men feel more; older men think more. Prose is the literary medium for thought and meditation, poetry of emotion and sensation (but not of sensation in the newspaper-placard sense). There is, of course, much intellectualized philosophical poetry, some of it among the greatest; yet it is not what most readers expect poetry to be and it is usually hard to take, particularly by younger readers. In the long run we can hardly help but agree with the proposition that prose is a thinking form, poetry a feeling form. But thinking does not exclude fun, and fun is present in a fair proportion of the passages in this book, which offers a representative view of what people were thinking and doing and at what they were working and playing from 1940 to 1960.

In the following pages there is much about young people and their doings, about animals, about the theatre, about history, about distant places and near places. When we examine the prose style (or styles) of the various writers, we find dignified and stately writing in the passages by Winston Churchill, G. M. Trevelyan, Bertrand Russell, Bernard Shaw, T. S. Eliot, and others, and prose with a lighter touch in as many more. What will not be found is prose designed purely as fine writing, nor prose which brutalizes life and degrades ourselves. All the writers are concerned first with having something to say that is worth reading, and among the nearly forty authors represented there is none that would be rejected by critics brought up on original Royal Society standards and requiring 'a close, naked, natural way of speaking; positive expressions, clear senses, a native easiness'.

A. C. WARD

1

The Day our Age began

Certain days in the history of the world have marked the opening of a new epoch. For our own age, a turning point in history was reached on the day described below by Winston Churchill. The Second World War started at the beginning of September 1939 with the German invasion of Poland, an attack which drew Britain, Poland's ally, into the conflict. After Poland had been swiftly and brutally crushed, the war (in which France was also involved) remained in a passive phase—the so-called ' phony war '—until the Spring of 1940, when Germany invaded Denmark and Norway on the pretext that it was necessary to forestall an alleged similar intention by Britain. A few weeks later Hitler's armies launched their long-planned full scale offensive in the West, and it can be said that from that day—the 10th of May 1940—the world was never to be the same again. The terrible events of the war led at length to the manufacture of the atom bomb and the subsequent development of the other nuclear weapons which may either destroy mankind or compel the abandonment of active warfare, according to whether the leaders of the nations choose to be governed by fear and madness or by sanity.

Winston Churchill's history of the Second World War shares with Julius Cæsar's Commentaries *the distinction of being the record of world-changing events written not by armchair authors but by men upon whose shoulders rested in their time the destiny of the world.*

This, then, is the true prelude to the twenty years of

varied writings from which the present anthology is selected.

SIR WINSTON CHURCHILL

THE MORNING of the tenth of May [1940] dawned, and with it came tremendous news. Boxes with telegrams poured in from the Admiralty, the War Office and the Foreign Office. The Germans had struck their long-awaited blow. Holland and Belgium were both invaded. Their frontiers had been crossed at numerous points. The whole movement of the German Army upon the invasion of the Low Countries and of France had begun.

At about ten o'clock Sir Kingsley Wood came to see me, having just been with the Prime Minister. He told me that Mr. Chamberlain was inclined to feel that the great battle which had broken upon us made it necessary for him to remain at his post. Kingsley Wood had told him that, on the contrary, the new crisis made it all the more necessary to have a National Government, which alone could confront it, and he added that Mr. Chamberlain had accepted this view. At eleven o'clock I was again summoned to Downing Street by the Prime Minister. There once more I found Lord Halifax. We took our seats at the table opposite Mr. Chamberlain. He told us that he was satisfied that it was beyond his power to form a National Government. The response he had received from the Labour leaders left him in no doubt of this. The question therefore was whom he should advise the King to send for after his own resignation had been accepted. His demeanour was cool, unruffled, and seemingly quite detached from the personal aspect of the affair. He looked at us both across the table.

I have had many important interviews in my public life, and this was certainly the most important. Usually I

talk a great deal, but on this occasion I was silent. Mr.
Chamberlain evidently had in his mind the stormy scene
in the House of Commons two nights before, when I had
seemed to be in such heated controversy with the Labour
Party. Although this had been in his support and
defence, he nevertheless felt that it might be an obstacle
to my obtaining their adherence at this juncture. I do
not recall the actual words he used, but this was the implication. His biographer, Mr. Feiling, states definitely
that he preferred Lord Halifax. As I remained silent, a
very long pause ensued. It certainly seemed longer than
the two minutes which one observes in the commemora-
tions of Armistice Day. Then at length Halifax spoke.
He said that he felt that his position as a Peer, out of
the House of Commons, would make it very difficult for
him to discharge the duties of Prime Minister in a war
like this. He would be held responsible for everything,
but would not have the power to guide the Assembly
upon whose confidence the life of every government
depended. He spoke for some minutes in this sense, and
by the time he had finished it was clear that the duty
would fall upon me—had in fact fallen upon me. Then,
for the first time, I spoke. I said I would have no communication with either of the Opposition Parties until I
had the King's Commission to form a Government. On
this the momentous conversation came to an end, and
we reverted to our ordinary easy and familiar manners
of men who had worked for years together and whose
lives in and out of office had been spent in all the friend-
liness of British politics. I then went back to the Admiralty, where, as may well be imagined, much awaited me.

The Dutch Ministers were in my room. Haggard and
worn, with horror in their eyes, they had just flown over
from Amsterdam. Their country had been attacked with-

out the slightest pretext or warning. The avalanche of fire and steel had rolled across the frontiers, and when resistance broke out and the Dutch frontier guards fired, an overwhelming onslaught was made from the air. The whole country was in a state of wild confusion; the long-prepared defence scheme had been put into operation; the dykes were opened; the waters spread far and wide. But the Germans had already crossed the outer lines, and were now streaming across the causeway which enclosed the Zuyder Zee. Could we do anything to prevent this? Luckily, we had a flotilla not far away, and this was immediately ordered to sweep the causeway with fire, and take the heaviest toll possible of the swarming invaders. The Queen was still in Holland, but it did not seem she could remain there long.

As a consequence of these discussions, a large number of orders were dispatched by the Admiralty to all our ships in the neighbourhood, and close relations were established with the Royal Dutch Navy. Even with the recent overrunning of Norway and Denmark in their minds, the Dutch Ministers seemed unable to understand how the great German nation, which, up to the night before, had professed nothing but friendship, should suddenly have made this frightful and brutal onslaught. Upon these proceedings and other affairs an hour or two passed. A spate of telegrams pressed in from all the frontiers affected by the forward heave of the German armies. It seemed that the old Schlieffen plan, brought up to date with its Dutch extension, was already in full operation. In 1914 the swinging right arm of the German invasion had swept through Belgium but had stopped short of Holland. It was well known then that had that war been delayed for three or four years, the extra army group would have been ready, and the railway terminals and communications adapted, for a movement through Holland. Now the famous movement had been launched with all these facilities and with every circumstance of surprise and treachery. But other developments lay ahead. The decisive stroke of the enemy was not to be a turning movement on the flank, but a break through the main front. This none of us or the French, who were in responsible command, foresaw. Earlier in the year I had, in a published interview, warned these neutral countries of the fate which was impending upon them and which was evident from the troop dispositions and road and rail development, as well as from the captured German plans. My words had been resented.

In the splintering crash of this vast battle the quiet conversations we had had in Downing Street faded or fell back in one's mind. However, I remember being told that Mr. Chamberlain had gone, or was going, to see the King, and this was naturally to be expected. Presently a message arrived summoning me to the Palace at 6 o'clock. It only takes two minutes to drive there from the Admiralty along the Mall. Although I suppose the evening newspapers must have been full of the terrific news from the Continent, nothing had been mentioned about the Cabinet crisis. The public had not had time to take in what was happening either abroad or at home, and there was no crowd about the Palace gates.

I was taken immediately to the King. His Majesty received me most graciously and bade me sit down. He looked at me searchingly and quizzically for some moments, and then said: 'I suppose you don't know why I have sent for you?' Adopting his mood, I replied: 'Sir, I simply couldn't imagine why.' He laughed and said: 'I want to ask you to form a Government.' I said I would certainly do so.

The King had made no stipulation about the Government being National in character, and I felt that my commission was in no formal way dependent upon this point. But in view of what had happened, and the conditions which had led to Mr. Chamberlain's resignation, a Government of National character was obviously inherent in the situation. If I found it impossible to come to terms with the Opposition Parties, I should not have been constitutionally debarred from trying to form the strongest Government possible of all who would stand by the country in the hour of peril, provided that such a Government could command a majority in the House of Commons. I told the King that I would immediately send for the leaders of the Labour and Liberal Parties, that I proposed to form a War Cabinet of five or six Ministers, and that I hoped to let him have at least five names before midnight. On this I took my leave and returned to the Admiralty.

Between seven and eight, at my request, Mr. Attlee called upon me. He brought with him Mr. Greenwood. I told him of the authority I had to form a Government and asked if the Labour Party would join. He said they would. I proposed that they should take rather more than a third of the places, having two seats in the War Cabinet of five, or it might be six, and I asked Mr. Attlee to let me have a list of men so that we could discuss particular offices. I mentioned Mr. Bevin, Mr. Alexander, Mr. Morrison and Mr. Dalton as men whose services in high office were immediately required. I had, of course, known both Attlee and Greenwood for a long time in the House of Commons. During the eleven years before the outbreak of war, I had in my more or less independent position come far more into collision with the Conservative and National Governments than with the Labour and Liberal

Oppositions. We had a pleasant talk for a little while, and they went off to report by telephone to their friends and followers at Bournemouth, with whom of course they had been in the closest contact during the previous forty-eight hours.

I invited Mr. Chamberlain to lead the House of Commons as Lord President of the Council, and he replied by telephone that he accepted and had arranged to broadcast at nine that night, stating that he had resigned, and urging everyone to support and aid his successor. This he did in magnanimous terms. I asked Lord Halifax to join the War Cabinet while remaining Foreign Secretary. At about ten, I sent the King a list of five names, as I had promised. The appointment of the three Service ministers was vitally urgent. I had already made up my mind who they should be. Mr. Eden should go to the War Office; Mr. Alexander should come to the Admiralty; and Sir Archibald Sinclair, Leader of the Liberal Party, should take the Air Ministry. At the same time I assumed the office of Minister of Defence, without however attempting to define its scope and powers.

Thus then, on the night of the tenth of May, at the outset of this mighty battle, I acquired the chief power in the State, which henceforth I wielded in ever-growing measure for five years and three months of world war, at the end of which time, all our enemies having surrendered unconditionally or being about to do so, I was immediately dismissed by the British electorate from all further conduct of their affairs.

During these last crowded days of the political crisis my pulse had not quickened at any moment. I took it all as it came. But I cannot conceal from the reader of this truthful account that as I went to bed at about 3 a.m., I was conscious of a profound sense of relief. At last I had the authority to give directions over the whole scene. I felt as if I were walking with destiny, and that all my past life had been but a preparation for this hour and for this trial. Eleven years in the political wilderness had freed me from ordinary Party antagonisms. My warnings over the last six years had been so numerous, so detailed, and were now so terribly vindicated, that no one could gainsay me. I could not be reproached either for making the war or with want of preparation for it. I thought I knew a good deal about it all, and I was sure I should not fail. Therefore, although impatient for the morning, I slept soundly and had no need for cheering dreams. Facts are better than dreams.

SIR WINSTON CHURCHILL: from *The Second World War* (Vol. I. 1948).

2

An Awful Prospect

*One of the most important human values threatened
during the period preceding the Second World War is
dealt with in this essay by E. M. Forster. The glorifica-
tion of brutality in the totalitarian countries was compressed into a phrase by Hitler's lieutenant in the Nazi
dictatorship, Hermann Goering: 'When I hear the word
"culture" I reach for my revolver.' It is an unhappy
fact that those who value the fine things that human intelligence and human goodness create can always be shot
down by a barbarian with a gun; but civilization and the
worthwhile things of life which it is the duty and privilege of civilization to protect and foster must be made
to triumph over the new barbarism. Barbarians with or
without guns are dedicated to destruction and are therefore the deadly enemies of culture, art, and beauty.
Under the name of Culture, E. M. Forster includes most
of the genuinely good things which mark the difference
between civilized persons and barbarians. At least for
the present, Culture is no longer threatened by guns;
yet it still has enemies, and the barbarians in our midst,
though they may no longer shoot, have not ceased to
sneer.*

E. M. FORSTER

Culture is a forbidding word. I have to use it, knowing
of none better, to describe the various beautiful and
interesting objects which men have made in the past, and

9

handed down to us, and which some of us are hoping to hand on. Many people despise them. They argue with force that cultural stuff takes up a great deal of room and time, and had better be scrapped, and they argue with less force that we live in a new world which has been wiped clean by science and cannot profit by tradition. Science will wipe us clean constantly, they hope, and at decreasing intervals. Broadcasting and the cinema have wiped out the drama, and quite soon we may hope for some new invention which will wipe out the cinema industry and Broadcasting House. In this constant scrubbing, what place can there be for the Brandenburg Concertos, or for solitary readings of Dante, or for the mosaics of Santa Sophia, or for photographs of them? We shall rush forward doing our work and amusing ourselves during the recreation hour with whatever gives least bother.

This prospect seems to me so awful that I want to do what I can against it, without too much attempt at fair-mindedness. It is impossible to be fair-minded when one has faith—religious creeds have shown this—and I have so much faith in cultural stuff that I believe it must mean something to other people, and anyhow want it left lying about. Faith makes one unkind: I am pleased when culture scores a neat hit. For instance, Sir Richard Terry, the organist of Westminster Cathedral, once made a remark which gave me unholy joy: speaking to some young musicians at Blackpool, he told them that they could be either men or crooners when they grew up, but not both. A storm in a cocktail resulted. The bands of Mr. Jack Payne and Mr. Henry Hall fizzed to their depths, and the less prudent members in them accorded interviews to the press. One crooner said that he and his friends could knock down Sir Richard and his friends any day, so they must be men. Another crooner said that he and his friends made more money than Sir Richard's friends, so they must be musicians. The pretentiousness and conceit of these amusement-mongers came out very strikingly. They appeared to be living in an eternal *thé dansant* which they mistook for the universe, and they couldn't bear being teased. For my own part, I don't mind an occasional croon or a blast in passing from a Wurlitzer organ, and Sir Richard Terry's speciality, madrigals, bore me; nevertheless, the music represented by him and his peers is the real thing; it ought to be defended and it has the right occasionally to attack. As a rule, it is in retreat, for there is a hostility to cultural stuff to-day which is disquieting.

Of course, most people never have cared for the classics, in music or elsewhere, but up to now they have been indifferent or ribald, and good-tempered, and have not bothered to denounce. 'Not my sort, bit tame', or 'sounds like the cat being sick, miaou pussy', or 'Coo, he must have felt bad to paint them apples blue'— these were their typical reactions when confronted with Racine, Stravinsky, Cézanne. There was no to-do—just 'not my sort'. But now the good-humour is vanishing, the guffaw is organized into a sneer, and the typical reaction is 'How dare these so-called art-chaps do it? *I'll* give them something to do.' This hostility has been well analysed by Mrs. Leavis, in her study of the English novel. She shows that though fiction of the best-seller type has been turned out for the last two hundred years, it has only lately realized its power, and that the popular novelist of to-day tends to be venomous and aggressive towards his more artistic brethren—an attitude in which he is supported by most of the press, and by the cheap libraries. Her attitude leads to priggishness; but it is better to be superior than to kow-tow. There was once a curious incident, which occupied several inches on a prominent page of *The Times*. A popular comedian had been faded out on the air, and the B.B.C., generally so stiff-necked, were grovelling low in apology, and going into all kinds of detail in extenuation of their grave offence. When they had done, the comedian's comment was printed; he professed himself appeased and consented to broadcast in the future. I wonder how much fuss a poet or a philosopher would have made if his talk had been cut short, and how many inches of regret he would have been given.

Incidents like this, so trivial in themselves, suggest that the past, and the creations that derive from the past, are losing their honour and on their way to being jettisoned. We have, in this age of unrest, to ferry much old stuff across the river, and the old stuff is not merely books, pictures and music, but the power to enjoy and understand them. If the power is lost the books, etc., will sink down into museums and die, or only survive in some fantastic caricature. The power was acquired through tradition. Sinclair Lewis, in *Babbitt*, describes a civilization which had no tradition and could consequently only work, or amuse itself with rubbish; it had heard of the past, but lacked the power to enjoy it or understand. There is a grim moment at a mediumistic séance, when Dante is invoked. The company knew of Dante as the guy who got singed, so he duly appears in this capacity and returns to his gridiron after a little banter, with a pleased smirk. He has become a proper comic. And it would seem that he is having a similar if less extreme experience in Soviet Russia. He has been ferried across there, but he is condemned as a sadist; that is to say the power to understand him has been left behind. Certainly Dante wrote over the gates of Hell that they were made by the power, wisdom and love of God: . . . and neither the Middle West nor the Soviets nor ourselves can be expected to agree with that. But there is no reason why we should not understand it, and stretch our minds against his, although they have a different shape. The past is often uncongenial as far as its statements are concerned, but the trained imagination can surmount them and reach the essential. Dante seems to me a test case. If people are giving him up it is a sign that they are throwing culture overboard, owing to the roughness of the water, and will reach the further bank sans Dante sans Shakespeare and sans everything.

Life on that further bank, as I conceive it, is by no means a nightmare. There will be work for all and play for all. But the work and the play will be split; the work will be mechanical and the play frivolous. If you drop tradition and culture you lose your chance of connecting work and play and creating a life which is all of a piece. The past did not succeed in doing that, but it can help us to do it, and that is why it is so useful. Crooners, best-sellers, electrical-organists, funny-faces, dream-girls, and mickey-mice cannot do it—they throw the weight all to one side and increase the split. They are all right when they don't take themselves seriously. But when they begin to talk big and claim the front row of the dress-circle and even get to it, something is wrong. Life on that further bank might not be a nightmare, but some of us would prefer the sleep that has no dreams.

E. M. FORSTER: 'Does Culture Matter' (1940), from *Two Cheers for Democracy*.

3

The Flower of Cities

*Among the delights of literature is that it can preserve
in words for all time memories of places that are swept
away by natural processes of decay and by changing
human needs. Some five hundred years ago a Scottish
poet, William Dunbar (about 1460-1520), wrote what still
ranks as one of the finest poems ever written on London,
there described as 'the flower of cities all'. Though
London is ever-changing, and though many people
declare that modern buildings are robbing it of its former
attraction, London nevertheless remains for those who
have known it from their childhood—and probably for
innumerable visitors also—'the flower of cities'.*

*Sir Max Beerbohm, after living in Italy for many years,
talked enchantingly about London present and past in
several essays and radio broadcasts, and through his eyes
we are still able to glimpse London in several aspects.*

SIR MAX BEERBOHM

In August 1935, it seemed that we might at any moment
be at war with Italy, a country in which I had resided for
many years. Accordingly I returned to the land of my
birth and heart; and the stormy petrel, partly by chance,
and partly for good reasons of economy, folded its wings
in Bloomsbury, and was there for rather more than a
year.

Tavistock Square is not so fine a place as Bedford

Square or Brunswick Square; but it is (as you will already have guessed) a Square, and has therefore much to be said for it. Very greatly did I enjoy the charm of seeing through my two large windows on the ground-floor the gradual turn of the leaf, the yellowing and the browning of it, its fall, its wind-swept eddying along the road; and the austere nakedness of the great old trees, offering a distant view of the houses on the other side, and of the omnibuses that passed incessantly along that unhappy other side and blessedly couldn't be heard on ours; and in due time the clean snow upon the grass and upon the soot-black but noble branches; and later the small green buds that are so much stranger than on country trees; and gradually the disappearance of the inaudible omnibuses and of the windows of the unblest; and then again the yellowing and the browning, the falling and the eddying. It is in a city, surely, that the lover of Nature finds deepest pleasure in watching her old round of phases.

Nevertheless, he prefers the country; and I am sure that in the eighteenth century I should have wished to murder that Duke of Bedford who for purposes of pelf had his great house demolished, and his park and his fields innumerable built over by a bright young architect and surveyor. I should not have realized that the architecture was good. I should have taken its manner as a matter of course. The spaciousness and solidity and homely grandeur of it all, the generous width of its doors and door-steps and of its areas, would have won no word of praise from my pursed-up lips. Nor would the correspondingly generous width of the roads and of the pavements have surprised and mollified me. One lives and learns. One lives another century and a half and begins to appreciate.

In my youth Bloomsbury meant little to me. It didn't —it doesn't even now—appeal to the historic sense. Such places as St. James's and Westminster and Mayfair had always had shining inmates: such places were of the centre, and near the rose. Bloomsbury in its day was much favoured by eminent lawyers, and by their wives and families. And outside their courts lawyers mostly burn with but a dim light. Moreover, they had deserted Bloomsbury before I was born, leaving their houses to the letters of lodgings and to the keepers of boarding-houses, or even to emptiness and darkness, or even to disrepute. If Bloomsbury had vanished utterly, my young heart would not have mourned it. But now it *is* beginning to vanish little by little. Many of the Squares and Streets have been more or less vandalized. All of them are threatened. I gather that the arch-threatener is the University of London. I understand that there are no limits to its desire for expansion of that bleak, blank, hideous and already vast white sepulchre which bears its name. Simultaneous tens of thousands of youths and maidens yet unborn will in the not so very far distant future be having their minds filled there and their souls starved there. Poor things! (And I'm sorry for the dons too.)

To them, perhaps, what may remain of the present Bloomsbury will have that historic interest which for us it lacks. They may say to one another, 'In that small brown house yonder, Henry Smith wrote his immortal "Snarls",' and 'In that one, Philip Robinson painted some of the most exquisitely unsightly of his dissignifica-tions.' For of course, since 1918 or so, Bloomsbury has got into inverted commas, and has (though Philip Robin-son will blame me for using the word) a meaning. It has become an intellectual centre, or, as it would call itself (for it is very Russian in its leanings), a focus of the intelligentsia. I myself am not *very* Russian, and to me the term 'intelligentsia' seems less modest and less apt than 'mental underworld'. Dostoievsky, their god, was a man of genius, certainly, and gave beautifully poignant expression to his spinelessness. But he is altogether alien to our rough island race; and laborious little imitations of his inspired maunderings cut no ice, and win scant patience from the average reader, even if they are contrived in all deep reverence to the memory of Karl Marx, and in fond though violent indigestion of the theories of Dr. Freud. But here I am presuming an average reader able to elucidate those tricksy snippets of dry prose in which the poetry of the West Central young is written. Here I am forgetting that intelligibility is as darkly frowned on by these young as are those stuffy old fads of the Victorian bourgeoisie, beauty, harmony, movement, development, and similar rot that had been handed down from the dark ages of Periclean Athens and had loathsomely imposed itself on generation after craven generation of the cloddish human race, and was seen through and discarded only as a result of the European War of 1914-18.

Certainly that war was a bad time to be born in, and the subsequent years must have been unhappy ones to grow up in. I daresay that were I a young man of the period I too should be disgruntled. I was fortunate in the (almost pre-historic) date of my birth. Even so, however, I was foolish enough in my youth, as is the way of young men. But I wonder whether if I were young now, I should be quite such a fool as to suppose that literary or graphic artists can advantageously forgo the influence of tradition and start with quite clean slates. The world has been going on for ever so long, with ever so many gifted people in it. Anything that is worth doing has been done frequently. Things hitherto undone should be given, I suspect, a wide berth. Let the young rise in revolt, from time to time, by all means. But, to be fruitful, their revolts must be, in another sense, from time to time; from the present to the past. In the nineteenth century there were two movements of importance; one of them a revolt from the formalism of the previous century, the other from the current fashions of academic art. But Romance was, after all, an old and familiar affair; nor were Giotto and his kind imaginary figures. The only novelty was the style in which the old ways were handled and developed and extended in the new period. The Impressionists? For the moment, I was forgetting them. But they are no snag. None of my Chelsea friends of the 'nineties supposed Manet to have been a phœnix. Steer and Sickert, MacColl and Will Rothenstein, were all vocally aware of kings before Agamemnon—Spanish, Italian, and other kings.

I wonder that the Chelsea of those days could have slipped my memory, so obvious is the contrast of it with the Bloomsbury of these!—so fresh and tonic was the air of it; so gay were the artists of that village (for village it still seemed to be) by the riverside. Why hasn't Bloomsbury a river?—a cheering, strong-flowing river, washing things away to the sea. I feel sure that even in the inter-bella period a river would have done Bloomsbury no end of good. Regent's Park is very airy, and isn't very far away from Bloomsbury; but it is a smug, urban expanse, and, such as it is, can be reached only by walking along the Euston Road, awfullest of thoroughfares, and is therefore valueless for the purpose of bracing up the spirits of the Bloomsburyites and giving them that lively faith in themselves and in their works which is

just what, in my daily rovings around the district, and
in my observings of the passers-by, they seemed to me
to lack. The passers-by were never many. The inhabitants didn't seem to take much exercise. They seemed to
be mostly at home and at work all day. And it may be
that none of the young men and women who passed by
me was a poet or a painter, or even a critic. But some of
them, I thought, must be something of that kind. And I
wished they would bear themselves more proudly. I did
not demand of them defiance. I merely craved an air
of young self-confidence—a pleasant touch of juvenile
swagger. Their work was treated with deep respect by
most of the elderly reviewers (terrified of not seeming
abreast of the times). But they seemed to be not elated
by the timorous eulogies that were heaped on them.
Their eyes lacked lustre. Their cigarettes drooped almost
vertically from between lips that never broke into a
smile. And sometimes, I noted, they were wearing very
muddy shoes though the sun had for several days been
shining brilliantly. But there was one of them (and he
a foreigner, I was told) who stood out distinctly from the
rest: he was a tall, thin, keen-faced man with short
side-whiskers; and he wore a kind of tam-o'-shanter, a
brick-coloured cloak, a long robe to match, and a pair of
sandals; and his brown hair fell to the back of his waist,
and in windy weather streamed out behind him with
immense vivacity. He attracted great attention always,
and comment too, of course. The best comment on
him that I overheard was made by one of two coster-
mongers whom he had just passed by. 'Well, Bill,' said
the one to the other, who was grinning widely, 'at any
rate 'e's got more courage than wot *we*'ve got.'

These words, so typical of cockney wisdom and toler-
ance, impressed me deeply. And perhaps it was they that

caused me, me too, to become courageous. I had read in letters to the press many hostile references to 'the Old School Tie', as a symbol of snobbish devotion to an individuality-crushing old horrid system, and had thought to myself, 'What nonsense!' It had never occurred to me to exercise my right to wear such a tie. But now, here, in the heart of Bloomsbury, I felt that I would belatedly do so, and I went to my hosier and ordered two Old Carthusian ties. Do you know the colours? They are three: bright crimson, salmon pink, and royal blue. They are dangerous to the appearance of even a quite young man. To that of an old man they are utterly disastrous. Nevertheless, I, without faltering, wore one of my pair until my sojourn in Bloomsbury came to its end.

This was in October 1936. The Anglo-Italian horizon had cleared. I returned to my home in Italy. In August of the next year but one, that horizon was again dark. One didn't know at what moment Hitler might strike, nor whether Mussolini wouldn't strike with him. Behold me again upon this isle!—but, this time, in Bayswater, where, indeed, I had been born and had lived (barring school-terms) until I was sixteen. A touching picture. The return of the old native.

There, in Inverness Terrace, I abode for some months, remembering Bloomsbury, and marvelling how two districts with but a few miles between them could have inhabitants so immeasurably different.

Bayswater! Is there no magic for you, reader, in that name? There had been none in it for me. But I'm not at all sure that it won't be found graven on my heart—graven there by the feeble hand of Bloomsbury.

Is it the climate that makes the difference? Bayswater is on a higher level, certainly. Or is it the soil? Bloomsbury, I am sure, is on clay, and Bayswater on gravel. Or is it the presence of Kensington Gardens? As is the river to Chelsea, so is (or are?) Kensington Gardens to Bayswater—exhilarating, purging, cobweb-preventing, spirit-of-village preserving. Even in the darkest days of the autumnal crisis the mien of the inhabitants was suggestive of Merrie England. Swinging was their gait, bright were their eyes, clear their complexions, obviously high their spirits. The scene was Arcadian, the scene seemed vernal. The young women hadn't masked their faces with make-up nor plucked out their eyebrows, and weren't smoking, and were mostly wheeling perambulators with babies in them. The young men accompanying them seemed not to have a care in the world, and were mostly wearing Old School Ties. And the old people looked quite young. Time does not age the people of Bayswater.

SIR MAX BEERBOHM: 'From Bloomsbury to Bayswater' from *Mainly on the Air* (1940).

4

Comfortable Words

Sometimes because they wish not to hurt the feelings of others, and sometimes (if they are politicians or advertisers) because plain words are inconvenient or unprofitable for their purposes, men will speak and write in terms that soften what they have to say or convey an impression that is deceptive. That is to say, they use euphemisms, defined by the dictionary as the 'substitution of mild or vague expressions for harsh or blunt ones'. In this essay Hilaire Belloc, not without irony, presents arguments for and against euphemism and indirectly poses for his readers a problem both moral and literary: 'Should I always say exactly what I mean and mean exactly what I say?'

HILAIRE BELLOC

THE EUPHEMISM is a little creature deserving the closest attention. Its origin is always of interest, its youth and early growth of still greater interest, its struggle to maturity absorbing. Even when it has worn smooth in age and become a commonplace it is still a much better subject of study than the contemporaries of its youth might imagine. The Euphemism as a species is probably as old as human speech: and how old that is nobody knows, least of all the philologists. The Euphemism is born of that social sense without which man would not be man, and because it is so true a child of that sense it reflects from every facet characters of *Homo Civis*, Man the Citizen.

The Euphemism is a recognition by man of man's own imperfection, and at the same time a recognition by man that he belongs to better things. It is play acting, but none the worse for that. It is a false word substituted for the true word in order to soften the shock of reality.

A man stands on a platform. He is about to address a packed audience of Swindlers, Cowards, Bounders, Painted Harridans, and Trulls. He opens his mouth to address them. What does he say? He says: 'Ladies and gentlemen.' Human language should be packed with Euphemisms. It is, indeed, proof that man was meant to live with his fellows, and proof also of how difficult it is for man to carry on that task without inordinate friction. It testifies also to the ingenuity of man himself, for we must note that the Euphemism ninety-nine times out of a hundred rises up from the masses; it has no one author, or if it has, that author is rarely known.

* * *

Take the commonest of the Euphemisms, the use of the second or third person in the place of the first. We say 'You' instead of 'Thou' because (Heaven knows how long ago!) it was thought more polite to pretend that the person addressed was too grand to be treated as a mere individual. He might not be a monarch, but it was only decent to give him the title of one. It is very pretty to see that in the transition towards the Dark Ages both the second person plural and the third person singular came into use for courteous address, and we keep up the habit to this day for the better conduct of human affairs. We write to an ambassador, 'Your Excellency will hardly have failed to observe,' where brute nature

would have written, 'Don't sham ignorance.' It is all to
the good so to soften the edges of life. But, in connection
with this useful and honourable human habit, remark
that the Euphemism sometimes avenges itself. When it
finds it is being overworked it revives with added force an
original simple use which it was supposed to supplant.
Thus the French express both insult and affection by
saying 'Thou' instead of 'You', and in English we use
'Thou' for adoration.

The Euphemism is sometimes killed at birth and often
killed in early youth. The wealthy and the powerful are
always suspicious of it. A new Euphemism is nearly
always Middle Class; usually it has to fight hard to get
accepted. I could quote half a dozen which I have seen
in my own lifetime either done to death or thrust down
into the lower ranks of society to which they have, ever
since their fall, been inexorably condemned. The use
of 'homely' as a Euphemism for ugly is an example in
point; others, far more striking, I forbear to record
through the respect I owe you.

Among Euphemisms thus ruthlessly exiled from the
great world, never to re-enter it, are 'mansion' and
'approach'. Both of them were originally of a very
roundabout grandeur. Mansion (which is *mansio*) simply
meant the place where you stop, and Approach was just
approach: the way by which you got near to a place.
But hardly had they taken on the air of grandeur when
the wealthier classes came out against them to do battle
and thrust them back into obscurity. But in doing so
they again transformed them. Mansion became one of
fifty ways of saying (in the plural) a town flat, while
Approach after lingering painfully, licking its wounds
for half a century, died—round about the seventies or
eighties I think. At any rate, it is well dead now. We

know 'Drive' or 'Avenue', but 'Approach' is forgotten. 'Villa' is another glorious specimen. A 'Villa' was a country estate of the Roman rich: a village community with the lord's great house in the midst. The word was then borrowed to save the face of the suburbs. Now it has a disdainful sound. You may hear a rich woman say of some habitation she despises: 'Oh no! nothing of that sort! Just a villa.'

*   *   *

It is sadly true of the Euphemism that when it has got itself well rooted and established it dies in another way: not by losing its body, but by losing its soul. It becomes a commonplace word like any other. We come to use it straightforwardly, as though it had never been a Euphemism at all. A Judge in Chambers, Chamber Music, the Upper Chamber, all the hundred uses of that word, come from the late Latin for a vault. It was thought more polite to allude to a man's room as his 'vault' because the great Roman palaces would be vaulted where the little Roman houses had plain flat floors and roofs. When you talk of the 'camber' of the road, you are using the same word but in quite another sense. And, what is amusing, you talk of the camera in photography with no sort of relation to any vault at all, nor even to any house, but to a box.

Euphemisms grow unnaturally and dangerously by competition, very much as do advertisements, superlatives, and words of emphasis. One Euphemism will supplant another in a few years and then be destroyed again in its turn, like the outlaw of the Nemi wood, by a supplanter. A neat case of this which has happened almost within a lifetime is the Euphemism for madhouse. A madhouse is something unpleasant; so, man being a social animal, he must give it a name pleasanter than the true one. He began early by calling it a Bethlehem, from a charitable foundation dedicated to the Nativity and coming to function as a refuge for the afflicted. Hence Bedlam. When Bedlam had ceased to be even tolerably polite, we invented Asylum. Asylum is a very beautiful word. It should by rights be full of repose and peace, for it means a secure refuge. But Asylum wore thin in less than a century. We have got by now to 'Mental Hospital'; and it is a sad tribute to the divine intelligence of man that 'mental' already means with the poor (and perhaps in time will mean with the rich) a person of distracted mind. What Euphemism will men use when they have grown frightened of 'Mental Hospital'?

*　　*　　*

We never know what the next Euphemism will be. It comes up out of the depths and steals upon us unawares. I doubt whether a locution which is a favourite with the leisured English will ever take final root, though I confess I am very fond of it myself because it always reminds me of that high genius in whose writings I first found it: P. G. Wodehouse. I mean the term 'loonybin'. It is admirable, it is first-rate, therefore it will go down the dark way which all the best things in this world must tread: the road to oblivion: the unreturning way. Perhaps it will not die in my time, but if it does I shall mourn it sincerely.

And so much for Euphemism. Do not attempt to live without it in a fit of straightforwardness, for if you do you will pass an unhappy manhood and a lonely old age. Not that I care.

HILAIRE BELLOC: 'On Euphemism'
from *The Silence of the Sea* (1941).

5

Fiddler Dick

Parents can never foresee what seed they are sowing in their children's minds by little acts of kindness and affection. When the father of the Brontë children took home a box of toy soldiers he little knew that there would spring from his gift such masterpieces as Emily Brontë's Wuthering Heights *and her sister Charlotte's* Jane Eyre. *When Herbert Read's father bought his son a musical box he may have laid in the child's mind the foundations of a love of music, but also, through that one particular art, the love and profound knowledge of Art in general which was to make Herbert Read in later years one of his generation's foremost interpreters of modern painting and sculpture.*

SIR HERBERT READ

ONE day my Father brought a delightful toy back from Northallerton: it was a small musical box which played 'For there's nae luck about the house'. But my Mother, perhaps then, or perhaps shortly afterwards, when there was sufficient cause, thought the tune was ominous. My only sister was a baby then, between two and three years old. Our Farm was called the Grange, and though it had no moat, this daughter was christened Mariana. Perhaps that too was ominous, for a sad song goes by her name. Mariana was fair as sunlight, and smiled to the tinkle of the musical box. And that is all I remember

27

of her, for that Spring I was suddenly sent away. A few days later my Aunt told me that Mariana had become an angel, and the next time we went to Kirkdale I was taken to see the unmeaning mound that covered her body.

Apart from this fatal musical box, the only other music I ever heard in my childhood was Fiddler Dick's. Every year the young horses bred on the Farm had to be 'broken in', and this was work for a specialist, who, like the blacksmith, paid us periodical visits. Fiddler Dick was a natty little man, with a hot swarthy complexion and waxed moustaches—probably he was of gipsy blood. He would stay a few days at the Farm, sleeping in the loft above the saddle-room. He always brought his fiddle with him, and after dinner, or in the evening, he used to play to a wondering audience. I was fascinated by this man—fascinated when he stood in the Cow Pasture, his neat leggings winking in the sunshine, a wild young colt galloping, trotting, walking in a circle at the end of a long rope, controlled by Fiddler Dick's flicking whip— still more fascinated when the brown fiddle came out of its box and a sound, never imagined before, was conjured out of the air. Now, I had seen, in a chest in the attic, just such a brown fiddle, and one day when Fiddler Dick was at the Farm, I brought it down and asked him to teach me to make such music. But some of the strings were broken, and the bow had no horse-hair. Some untwisted binder-band served to repair the bow, and we got some cat-gut from the nearest cobbler for the strings. Fiddler Dick rejoiced in the word cat-gut, and cats took on a new significance for me. I cannot now believe that the sounds which issued from this improvised instrument bore any resemblance to the plaintive voice of a violin, but I retained my longing to play. Later, when I went away to school, I persuaded my Mother to let me take music as an extra subject, and she consented. But I was put to the piano, which had no charm for me, no urgency of aspiration. I could not rival Fiddler Dick on such an instrument! Besides, instead of Fiddler Dick, I had for a teacher a fierce Dutchman, bristling with long hair and a silk bow-tie, flashing with rings. At the end of the year my enthusiasm had so waned that I could not urge my Mother to pay the extra fees for music. But I still clung to the old violin, with the vague hope that I might one day learn to play it. It was still in my possession at the beginning of the War, but my Mother died at this time, and in the subsequent confusion the violin disappeared. I had expected to find it among the few possessions I had stored in a cellar against my return, but it was not there. I should perhaps never have given it another thought but for an experience of several years later. I came late one evening, after a walk along a forest road in Bavaria, the moon staring at me through the cage-bars of the trees, to a large castle where many guests were being entertained. Supper was finished and there was not a soul to be seen, except a porter who took my bag, and told me that everyone was in the music-room—even the servants—and that I had better make my way there and wait for the end. I was directed to a small balcony, which I could enter without disturbing the audience. The room was in darkness, except for an electric lamp at the far end of the room, above the dais where the music was being played. It was a violin sonata, and I was immediately held, not so much by the music as by the image which came into my mind as I gazed at the woman playing the violin. Her slender body was like a stem on which nodded, to the rhythm of the music, a strange exotic flower. The corolla of this flower was a human face, very white beneath an arch of raven black hair, and it seemed to brood over the coiled tawny petals of the instrument, preserving an essential stillness in the midst of the force that agitated them. The notes of the piano, to whose rise and fall it seemed bound in some inevitable way, might have been the voice of a stream urging its way past the resisting stem of the flower which swayed above its swift current.

All my early fascination for this instrument, awakened long before by Fiddler Dick and long dormant, awoke again at this moment with a glow in which there was no longer any sense of aspiration or self-directed interest, a fire of renunciation and surrender. Once more an early impulse had found its fulfilment, its transformation, to become a conscious interest in my life.

SIR HERBERT READ: from *Annals of Innocence and Experience* (1941).

6

Portrait of an Actress[1]

*Ellen Terry was born (in 1847) into a theatrical family
and began to act in Shakespeare (as Mamillius in* The
Winter's Tale*) when she was only nine. She had a varied
stage experience during her girlhood, but after marrying
G. F. Watts the Victorian painter she left the stage. Although the marriage was a failure and she returned for a
while to acting, it was not until after another interval of
retirement that she became famous as Henry Irving's leading lady at the Lyceum Theatre in London from 1878 to
1902, during which time she played many great Shakespearean parts. It has often been said that (before sound
recording and film making were perfected) the fame of
actors and actresses ceased with their death. Ellen Terry's
greatness lay as much in her character and personality
as in her genius as an actress. She had no formal education, yet she became the intellectual equal of outstanding
men of her period, as is shown in particular by her many
letters to Bernard Shaw (*Ellen Terry and Bernard Shaw:
A Correspondence, *published in 1930). She was the most
eminent, fascinating and lovable of the Terrys, who
through several generations have been one of the great
English stage families. Her genius and that of his father,
Edward Godwin (architect and stage designer), were in-
herited by her son Gordon Craig (1872-   ), whose influence on play production and scenic design and costume
has been worldwide.*

[1] This account of Ellen Terry was written in 1941 but did not
appear in book form until 1947.

31

VIRGINIA WOOLF

WHEN SHE came on to the stage as Lady Cicely in *Captain Brassbound's Conversion*, the stage collapsed like a house of cards and all the limelights were extinguished. When she spoke it was as if someone drew a bow over a ripe, richly seasoned 'cello; it grated, it glowed, and it growled. Then she stopped speaking. She put on her glasses. She gazed intently at the back of a settee. She had forgotten her part. But did it matter? Speaking or silent, she was Lady Cicely—or was it Ellen Terry? At any rate, she filled the stage and all the other actors were put out, as electric lights are put out in the sun.

Yet this pause when she forgot what Lady Cicely said next was significant. It was a sign not that she was losing her memory and past her prime, as some said. It was a sign that Lady Cicely was not a part that suited her. Her son, Gordon Craig, insists that she only forgot her part when there was something uncongenial in the words, when some speck of grit had got into the marvellous machine of her genius. When the part was congenial, when she was Shakespeare's Portia, Desdemona, Ophelia, every word, every comma was consumed. Even her eyelashes acted. Her body lost its weight. Her son, a mere boy, could lift her in his arms. 'I am not myself,' she said. 'Something comes upon me. . . . I am always-in-the-air, light and bodiless.' We, who can only remember her as Lady Cicely on the little stage at the Court Theatre, only remember what, compared with her Ophelia or her Portia, was a picture postcard compared with the great Velasquez in the gallery.

It is the fate of actors to leave only picture postcards behind them. Every night when the curtain goes down the beautiful coloured canvas is rubbed out. What

remains is at best only a wavering, insubstantial phantom
—a verbal life on the lips of the living. Ellen Terry was
well aware of it. She tried herself, overcome by the
greatness of Irving as Hamlet and indignant at the
caricatures of his detractors, to describe what she remembered. It was in vain. She dropped her pen in despair.
'Oh God, that I were a writer!' she cried. 'Surely a
writer could not string words together about Henry
Irving's Hamlet and say *nothing, nothing*.' It never struck
her, humble as she was, and obsessed by her lack of
book learning, that she was, among other things, a writer.
It never occurred to her when she wrote her autobiography, or scribbled page after page to Bernard Shaw
late at night, dead tired after a rehearsal, that she was
'writing'. The words in her beautiful rapid hand bubbled
off her pen. With dashes and notes of exclamation she
tried to give them the very tone and stress of the spoken
word. It is true, she could not build a house with words,
one room opening out of another, and a staircase connecting the whole. But whatever she took up became
in her warm, sensitive grasp a tool. If it was a rolling-pin,
she made perfect pastry. If it was a carving knife, perfect
slices fell from the leg of mutton. If it were a pen, words
peeled off, some broken, some suspended in mid-air, but
all far more expressive than the tappings of the professional typewriter.

With her pen, then, at odds and ends of time she has
painted a self-portrait. It is not an Academy portrait,
glazed, framed, complete. It is rather a bundle of loose
leaves upon each of which she has dashed off a sketch for
a portrait—here a nose, here an arm, here a foot, and
there a mere scribble in the margin. The sketches done in
different moods, from different angles, sometimes contra-
dict each other. The nose cannot belong to the eyes; the

arm is out of all proportion to the foot. It is difficult to assemble them. And there are blank pages, too. Some very important features are left out. There was a self she did not know, a gap she could not fill. Did she not take Walt Whitman's words for a motto? 'Why, even I myself, I often think, know little or nothing of my real life. Only a few hints—a few diffused faint clues and indirections . . . I seek . . . to trace out here.'

Nevertheless, the first sketch is definite enough. It is the sketch of her childhood. She was born to the stage. The stage was her cradle, her nursery. When other little girls were being taught sums and pot-hooks she was being cuffed and buffeted into the practice of her profession. Her ears were boxed, her muscles suppled. All day she was hard at work on the boards. Late at night when other children were safe in bed she was stumbling along the dark streets wrapped in her father's cloak. And the dark street with its curtained windows was nothing but a sham to that little professional actress, and the rough and tumble life on the boards was her home, her reality. 'It's all such sham there', she wrote—meaning by 'there' what she called 'life in houses'—'sham—cold—hard—pretending. It's not sham here in our theatre—here all is real, warm and kind—we live a lovely spiritual life here.'

That is the first sketch. But turn to the next page. The child born to the stage has become a wife. She is married at sixteen to an elderly famous painter. The theatre has gone; its lights are out and in its place is a quiet studio in a garden. In its place is a world full of pictures and 'gentle artistic people with quiet voices and elegant manners'. She sits mum in her corner while the famous elderly people talk over her head in quiet voices. She is content to wash her husband's brushes; to sit to him; to play her simple tunes on the piano to him while he paints. In the evening she wanders over the Downs with the great poet, Tennyson. 'I was in Heaven,' she wrote. 'I never had one single pang of regret for the theatre.' If only it could have lasted! But somehow—here a blank page intervenes—she was an incongruous element in that quiet studio. She was too young, too vigorous, too vital, perhaps. At any rate, the marriage was a failure.

And so, skipping a page or two, we come to the next sketch. She is a mother now. Two adorable children claim all her devotion. She is living in the depths of the country, in the heart of domesticity. She is up at six. She scrubs, she cooks, she sews. She teaches the children. She harnesses the pony. She fetches the milk. And again she is perfectly happy. To live with children in a cottage, driving her little cart about the lanes, going to church on Sunday in blue and white cotton—that is the ideal life! She asks no more than that it shall go on like that for ever and ever. But one day the wheel comes off the pony cart. Huntsmen in pink leap over the hedge. One of them dismounts and offers help. He looks at the girl in a blue frock and exclaims: 'Good God! It's Nelly!' She looks at the huntsman in pink and cries, 'Charles Reade!' And so, all in a jiffy, back she goes to the stage, and to forty pounds a week. For—that is the reason she gives—the bailiffs are in the house. She must make money.

At this point a very blank page confronts us. There is a gulf which we can only cross at a venture. Two sketches face each other; Ellen Terry in blue cotton among the hens; Ellen Terry robed and crowned as Lady Macbeth on the stage of the Lyceum. The two sketches are contradictory yet they are both of the same woman. She hates the stage; yet she adores it. She worships her children; yet she forsakes them. She would like to live for ever among pigs and ducks in the open air; yet she spends the rest of her life among actors and actresses in the limelight. Her own attempt to explain the discrepancy is hardly convincing. 'I have always been more woman than artist,' she says. Irving put the theatre first. 'He had none of what I may call my bourgeois qualities —the love of being in love, the love of a home, the dislike of solitude.' She tries to persuade us that she was an ordinary woman enough; a better hand at pastry than most; an adept at keeping house; with an eye for colour, a taste for furniture, and a positive passion for washing children's heads. If she went back to the stage it was because—well, what else could she do when the bailiffs were in the house?

This is the little sketch that she offers us to fill in the gap between the two Ellen Terrys—Ellen the mother, and Ellen the actress. But here we remember her warning: 'Why, even I myself know little or nothing of my real life.' There was something in her that she did not understand; something that came surging up from the depths and swept her away in its clutches. The voice she heard in the lane was not the voice of Charles Reade; nor was it the voice of the bailiffs. It was the voice of her genius; the urgent call of something that she could not define, could not suppress, and must obey. So she left her children and followed the voice back to the stage, back to the Lyceum, back to a long life of incessant toil, anguish, and glory.

But, having gazed at the full-length portrait of Ellen Terry as Sargent painted her, robed and crowned as Lady Macbeth, turn to the next page. It is done from another angle. Pen in hand, she is seated at her desk. A volume of Shakespeare lies before her. It is open at *Cymbeline*, and she is making careful notes in the

margin. The part of Imogen presents great problems. She
is, she says, 'on the rack' about her interpretation. Perhaps Bernard Shaw can throw light upon the question? A
letter from the brilliant young critic of the *Saturday
Review* lies beside Shakespeare. She has never met him,
but for years they have written to each other, intimately,
ardently, disputatiously, some of the best letters in the
language. He says the most outrageous things. He com-
pares dear Henry to an ogre, and Ellen to a captive
chained in his cage. But Ellen Terry is quite capable of
holding her own against Bernard Shaw. She scolds him,
laughs at him, fondles him, and contradicts him. She
has a curious sympathy for the advanced views that
Henry Irving abominated. But what suggestions has the
brilliant critic to make about Imogen? None apparently
that she has not already thought for herself. She is as
close and critical a student of Shakespeare as he is. She
has studied every line, weighed the meaning of each
word, experimented with every gesture. Each of those
golden moments when she becomes bodyless, not herself, is the result of months of minute and careful study.
'Art,' she quotes, 'needs that which we can give her, I
assure you.' In fact this mutable woman, all instinct,
sympathy, and sensation, is as painstaking a student and
as careful of the dignity of her art as Flaubert himself.

But once more the expression on that serious face
changes. She works like a slave—none harder. But she is
quick to tell Mr. Shaw that she does not work with her
brain only. She is not in the least clever. Indeed, she is
happy she tells him, '*not to be clever*'. She stresses the
point with a jab of her pen. 'You clever people', as she
calls him and his friends, miss so much, mar so much.
As for education, she never had a day's schooling in her
life. As far as she can see, but the problem baffles her,

the main spring of her art is imagination. Visit mad-houses, if you like; take notes; observe; study endlessly. But first, imagine. And so she takes her part away from the books out into the woods. Rambling down grassy rides, she lives her part until she is it. If a word jars or grates, she must re-think it, re-write it. Then when every phrase is her own, and every gesture spontaneous, out she comes on to the stage and is Imogen, Ophelia, Desdemona.

But is she, even when the great moments are on her, a great actress? She doubts it. 'I cared more for love and life,' she says. Her face, too, has been no help to her. She cannot sustain emotion. Certainly she is not a great tragic actress. Now and again, perhaps, she has acted some comic part to perfection. But even while she analyses herself, as one artist to another, the sun slants upon an old kitchen chair. 'Thank the Lord for my eyes!' she exclaims. What a world of joy her eyes have brought her! Gazing at the old 'rush-bottomed, sturdy-legged, and wavy-backed' chair, the stage is gone, the limelights are out, the famous actress is forgotten.

Which, then, of all these women is the real Ellen Terry? How are we to put the scattered sketches to-gether? Is she mother, wife, cook, critic, actress, or should she have been, after all, a painter? Each part seems the right part until she throws it aside and plays another. Something of Ellen Terry it seems overflowed every part and remained unacted. Shakespeare could not fit her; nor Ibsen; nor Shaw. The stage could not hold her; nor the nursery. But there is, after all, a greater dramatist than Shakespeare, Ibsen, or Shaw. There is Nature. Hers is so vast a stage, and so innumerable a company of actors, that for the most part she fobs them off with a tag or two. They come on and they go off without breaking the ranks. But now and again Nature creates a new part, an original part. The actors who act that part always defy our attempts to name them. They will not act the stock parts—they forget the words, they improvise others of their own. But when they come on the stage falls like a pack of cards and the limelights are extinguished. That was Ellen Terry's fate—to act a new part. And thus while other actors are remembered because they were Hamlet, Phèdre, or Cleopatra, Ellen Terry is remembered because she was Ellen Terry.

VIRGINIA WOOLF: from *The Moment and Other Essays* (1947).

7

Sons and Daughters Long Ago

In these present days of educational advance and changing school methods, it is interesting and instructive to look back for comparison to the ' common schooling' of our ancestors. Grammar Schools then and now are far asunder in the scope of the education provided, for they were then what their name implied, grammar schools, though as G. M. Trevelyan points out (writing of the eighteenth century), there were also schools (or academies) at which a coming ' man of the world' might acquire a variety of accomplishments, some of which would now be considered beyond the limits of formal education.

G. M. TREVELYAN

THE EXPENDITURE required of a country gentleman, rich or poor, was in one respect very small. It was not then considered obligatory that his sons should be sent at great cost to exclusively patrician schools. At the nearest local grammar school, the squire's children sat beside those sons of yeomen and shopkeepers who had been selected for a clerical career; otherwise the young gentlemen were taught at home by a neighbouring parson, or in wealthier families by the private chaplain. Where a tutor was specially employed, he was often a Huguenot refugee, for the land was full of educated men of this type, welcomed by careful parents for their French, and

40

doubly welcome in Whig families for their sufferings and their principles. Eton, Winchester and Westminster were indeed patronized by many, but not by most, of the aristocracy. And even at Westminster there could be found at the end of Anne's reign 'houses at which boys pay but £20 a year for boarding, and the schooling but five or six guineas'. Harrow, founded under Elizabeth to meet local and plebeian needs, began to rise into the rank of the fashionable schools in the reign of George I.

It followed that, whereas a gentleman of moderate means in our day often thinks himself obliged to spend a sixth part of his income on the schooling of one boy, he could in those days be satisfied to spend a hundredth. Thus squire Molesworth, at a time when he was drawing a rental of just under £2,000, paid £20 a year for each of his sons—including board, instruction, clothes and all charges. His heavy parental liabilities only began when the two lads left school, and the younger went into the army. Then indeed 'Dick must be furnished with a hundred pounds or he cannot stir a step. He has both horses, clothes and equipage to buy.' As 'he was not in the list of officers slain in the late glorious battle of Blenheim', which would have been a sad economy, nor yet 'in any of the desperate attacks on Lille', Dick continued for many years to be an increasing source of expenditure and pride to his Yorkshire home. The elder, Jack, had chosen diplomacy, a no less costly method of serving the State. In 1710 the father writes: 'I verily believe these two sons of ours have spent between them £10,000 within the last seven or eight years; they and the daughters are all money-bound. It is well they have a good father's house to tarry in.' Five years later Dick's zeal for his regiment caused him to 'lay out £600 above what was allowed him, so well he loves the service'.

Smaller squires paid equally little for their son's schooling, and then prenticed them to cheaper trades than the army or diplomatic service. In the plays of Congreve and Farquhar the younger son of the manor may still expect to be 'bound prentice', perhaps 'to a felt-maker in Shrewsbury'; and Steele declares that 'younger brothers are generally condemned to shops, colleges and inns of court'. On these terms the gentry could afford to have large families, and although a great proportion of their children died young, they kept England supplied with a constant stream of high-spirited young men, who led her along the forward path at home and overseas. For the younger sons were willing, as the cadets of the continental nobility were not, to mingle in the common avocations of mankind and not to stand upon their gentry. The fact that the younger son went out to make his fortune in the army or at the bar, in industry or in commerce, was one of the general causes favouring the Whigs and their alliance with those interests, as against the desire of the High Tories to keep the landed gentry an exclusive as well as a dominant class. Dominant it remained for another century, but only on condition of opening its doors wide to newcomers, and fostering in a hundred different ways close alliance with interests other than agriculture, in scenes far remote from the manor-house and the village church. The country gentlemen ruled Eighteenth Century England, but they ruled it largely in the interest of commerce and empire.

The common schooling of the upper and middle class was already being criticized for its rigidly classical curriculum. It was even declared by some that 'a girl which is educated at home with her mother is wiser at twelve than a boy of sixteen' who knows only Latin. Yet the second classical language was so ill-taught at school and college that the excellent Latinists of Christ Church had not enough Greek to be aware that Bentley had proved them dunces over the *Letters of Phalaris*. It was only in the nineteenth century that the typical English scholar was equally at home with Aristophanes and with Horace.

Even so, Greek scholarship in the England of Bentley had not fallen as low as in the rest of Europe. In the Germany of that day not only was classical Greek no longer studied, but the names and stories of the mythology and history of Hellas were unknown. But they were familiar to educated people in England, if not through Greek then through Latin and English authors. Every man of fashion in the reign of George I had at least to pretend an acquaintance with Pope's rendering of Homer. Milton was now rising to a place only a little lower than Shakespeare in the hierarchy of English literary reputations, and the use that he made of classical ideas and mythology set an example to the poets of this later age, though few were scholars of his calibre. In architecture and its ornaments, the 'Gothic' had disappeared, and had been replaced by ideas suggested directly or indirectly by the temples and statues of the ancient world.

But it would be a mistake to suppose that nothing was anywhere taught but classics; there was considerable variety in the type of school patronized by gentlemen. Thus Robert Pitt, father of a mighty son, writes in 1704 to his own scarcely less formidable father, Governor Pitt of Madras:

My two brothers are at Mr. Meure's Academy, near Soho Square, esteemed the best in England. They learn Latin, French and accounts, fencing, dancing and drawing. I think of settling them in Holland for their better education next summer: and should my wife's father-in-law, Lt. Gen. Stewart, accompany the Duke of Marlborough, of placing them under his care to see a campaign.

Among the critics of our educational methods were the wise Locke and the good-natured Steele, who both urged that perpetual flogging was not the best method of imparting knowledge and maintaining discipline. Upper-class education was admitted on all hands to need reform, yet nothing was done to reform it. Swift, for all his hatred of the Scots, agreed for once with Burnet that the lairds gave their sons more sound book-learning than the wealthier and idler English.

Yet the eighteenth century, in spite of its educational defects, produced a larger proportion of remarkable and original English men from among those who passed through its schools than our highly educated and over-regulated age is able to do. And in spite of cruel flogging by 'those licensed tyrants the schoolmasters', and cruel bullying by the unlicensed tyranny of ill-disciplined schoolfellows, there was also much happiness in boy-hood, that still had leisure and still spent it in the free range of the countryside. Nor was severity universal: a young lord, newly arrived at Eton, writes home, 'I think Eaton a very easy scholl. I am shure one cannot offend without they be meare rakes indeed.'

Women's education was sadly to seek. Among the lower classes it was perhaps not much worse than men's, but the daughters of the well-to-do had admittedly less education than their brothers. It was before the days of 'ladies' academies', and though there were 'boarding

schools' for girls, they were few and indifferent. Most
ladies learnt from their mothers to read, write, sew and
manage the household. We hear of no fair Grecians, like
Lady Jane Grey and Queen Elizabeth in days of old. But
a few ladies could read the Italian poets and were therefore held in some awe by their swains. And at least two
women could meet Swift on terms of something like
intellectual equality. Yet it was he who lamented 'that
not one gentleman's daughter in a thousand should be
brought to read her own natural tongue, or be judge of
the easiest books that are written in it'. The want of
education in the sex was discussed as an admitted fact,
one side defending it as necessary in order to keep wives
in due subjection, while the other side, led by the chief
literary men of the day, ascribed the frivolity and the
gambling habits of ladies of fashion to an upbringing
which debarred them from more serious interests.

Nevertheless, country-house letters of the period show
us wives and daughters writing as intelligent advisers
of their menfolk. Such correspondents were something
better than brainless playthings or household drudges. A
whole class of the literature of the day, from the *Spectator* downwards, was written as much for ladies as for
their fathers and brothers. And it was observed that the
ladies took a part, often too eager, in the Whig and Tory
feuds that divided town and country. As to rural pas-
times, the prototype of Diana Vernon in *Rob Roy* is to be
found in Melinda of Farquhar's play, who tells her
friend, 'I can gallop all the morning after the hunting
horn and all the evening after a fiddle. In short I can do
everything with my father but drink and shoot flying.'

In the upper and middle classes, husbands were often
found for girls on the principle of frank barter. 'As to
Cloky,' writes her father, squire Molesworth, 'we shall

C

not have money enough to dispose of her here,' so she must be sent to Ireland to seek there a husband at a cheaper rate. Another squire, named Guise, who is in search of a wife for himself, writes, 'Lady Diana sent a very venerable person to view my estates, and was well satisfied with the report and I think did sincerely desire I might have her daughter.' But the daughter had other views, so Guise found consolation elsewhere:

Being on the Bench at the Quarter Session, a Justice of the Peace took me aside and asked me whether I would marry a woman worth twenty-thousand pounds. The lady I had seen but never spoke to, and upon the whole readily accepted his offer.

A Cornet of Horse writes with equal frankness:

Not expecting anything this campaign I had taken thoughts another way, to try my fortune under Venus, and accordingly about a fortnight ago was (by some friends) proposed to a lady of a very good fortune: but how I shall speed (farther than a favourable interview already) I can't tell.

Since almost everyone regarded it as a grave misfortune to remain single, women did not account it a universal grievance that their hands should often be disposed of by others. They were no doubt usually consulted as to their destiny, much or little according to character and circumstance. Swift, in writing 'to a very young lady on her marriage', speaks of 'the person your father and mother have chosen for your husband', and almost immediately adds, 'yours was a match of prudence and common good liking, without any mixture of

the ridiculous passion' of romantic love. And this description would probably have covered a vast proportion
of the 'arranged' marriages of the day. But since the
'ridiculous passion' often asserted itself, runaway
matches were common enough, as in the case of Lady
Mary Wortley Montagu. And even without that desperate expedient, an ever-increasing proportion of ordinary marriages were the outcome of mutual affection.

G. M. TREVELYAN: from *English Social History* (1942).

8

A People Slow to Anger

Future generations, when reading the history of our time, will perhaps view the German air-raids on England in 1940 and the following years in much the same perspective as we see the Spanish Armada. But the threat of 1588 may not even have reached the ears of a considerable number of the people of England at that time. Their descendants in the 1940s, however, whether in remote villages or in the great cities, were all aware from moment to moment of the threat of destruction and the likelihood of invasion. Richard Hillary was one of the many young men who fought in the skies and suffered grievous injuries during the prolonged ordeal which has become compressed into a brief phrase as the Battle of Britain. His book is one of the finest memorials of personal experience in the Second World War, and the passage from it printed here reflects the period in its personal and in its community aspects.

RICHARD HILLARY

I LAY in that hospital and watched summer turn to winter. Through my window I watched the leaves of my solitary tree gradually turn brown, and then, shaken by an ever-freshening wind, fall one by one. I watched the sun change from a great ball of fire to a watery glimmer, watched the rain beating on the glass and the small broken clouds drifting a few hundred feet above,

48

and in that time I had ample opportunity for thinking.

I thought of the men I had known, of the men who were living and the men who were dead; and I came to this conclusion. It was to the Carburys and the Berrys of this war that Britain must look, to the tough practical men who had come up the hard way, who were not fighting this war for any philosophical principles or economic ideals; who, unlike the average Oxford undergraduate, were not flying for æsthetic reasons, but because of an instinctive knowledge that this was the job for which they were most suited. These were the men who had blasted and would continue to blast the Luftwaffe out of the sky while their more intellectual comrades would, alas, in the main be killed. They might answer, if asked why they fought, 'To smash Hitler!' But instinctively, inarticulately, they too were fighting for the things that Peter had died to preserve.

Was there perhaps a new race of Englishmen arising out of this war, a race of men bred by the war, a harmonious synthesis of the governing class and the great rest of England; that synthesis of disparate backgrounds and upbringings to be seen at its most obvious best in R.A.F. squadrons? While they were now possessed of no other thought than to win the war, yet having won it, would they this time refuse to step aside and remain indifferent to the peace-time fate of the country, once again leave government to the old governing class? I thought it possible. Indeed, the process might be said to have already begun. They now had as their representative Churchill, a man of initiative, determination, and no Party. But they would not always have him; and what then? Would they see to it that there arose from their fusion representatives, not of the old gang, deciding at Lady Cufuffle's that Henry should have the Foreign

Office and George the Ministry of Food, nor figureheads
for an angry but ineffectual Labour Party, but true representatives of the new England that should emerge from
this struggle? And if they did, what then? Could they
unite on a policy of humanity and sense to arrive at the
settlement of problems which six thousand years of
civilization had failed to solve? And even though they
should fail, was there an obligation for the more thinking of them to try to contribute, at whatever personal
cost 'their little drop', however small, to the betterment
of mankind? Was there that obligation, was that the
goal towards which all those should strive who were left,
strengthened and confirmed by those who had died? Or
was it still possible for men to lead the egocentric life, to
work out their own salvation without concern for the
rest; could they simply look to themselves—or, more
important, could I? I still thought so.

The day came when I was allowed out of the hospital
for a few hours. Sue got me dressed, and with a pair of
dark glasses, cotton-wool under my eyes, and my right
arm in a sling, I looked fairly presentable. I walked out
through the swing-doors and took a deep breath.

London in the morning was still the best place in the
world. The smell of wet streets, of sawdust in the
butchers' shops, of tar melted on the blocks, was exhilarating. Peter had been right: I loved the capital. The wind
on the heath might call for a time, but the facile glitter
of the city was the stronger. Self-esteem, I suppose, is one
cause; for in the city, work of man, one is somebody, feet
on the pavement, suit on the body, anybody's equal and
nobody's fool; but in the country, work of God, one is
nothing, less than the earth, the birds, and the trees;
one is discordant—a blot.

I walked slowly through Ravenscourt Park and looked

into many faces. Life was good, but if I hoped to find some reflection of my feeling, I was disappointed. One or two looked at me with pity, and for a moment I was angry; but when I gazed again at their faces, closed in as on some dread secret, their owners hurrying along, unseeing, unfeeling, eager to get to their jobs, unaware of the life within them, I was sorry for them. I felt a desire to stop and shake them and say: 'You fools, it's you who should be pitied and not I; for this day I am alive while you are dead.'

* * *

While the bombs were dropping on London (and they were dropping every night in my time in the hospital), and while half London was enjoying itself, the other half was not asleep. It was striving to make London as normal a city by night as it had become by day. Anti-aircraft crews, studded around fields, parks, and streets, were momentarily silhouetted against the sky by the sudden flash of their guns. The Auxiliary Fire Service, spread out in a network of squads through the capital, was standing by, ready at a moment's notice to deal with the inevitable fires; air-raid wardens, tireless in their care of shelters and work of rescue, patrolled their areas watchfully. One heavy night I poked my nose out of the Dorchester, which was rocking gently, to find a cab calmly coasting down Park Lane. I hailed it and was driven back to the hospital. The driver turned to me: 'Thank God, sir,' he said, 'Jerry's wasting 'is time trying to break our morale, when 'e might be doing real damage on some small town.'

With the break of day London shook herself and went back to work. Women with husbands in Government jobs were no longer to be seen at noon draped along the bars of the West End as their first appointment of the day. They were up and at work with determined efficiency in administrative posts of the Red Cross, the women's voluntary services, and the prisoners-of-war organizations. The Home Guards and air-raid wardens of the previous night would return home, take a bath, and go off to their respective offices. The soldier was back with his regiment, the airman with his squadron; the charming frivolous creatures with whom they had dined were themselves in uniform, effective in their jobs of driving, typing, or nursing.

That, I discovered, was a little of what London was doing. But what was London feeling? Perhaps a not irrelevant example was an experience of Sheep Gilroy's when flying with the Squadron. He was sitting in his bath when a 'flap' was called. Pulling on a few clothes and not bothering to put on his tunic, he dashed out to his plane and took off. A few minutes later he was hit by an incendiary bullet and the machine caught fire. He baled out, quite badly burned, and landed by a parachute in one of the poorer districts of London. With no identifying tunic, he was at once set upon by two hundred silent and coldly angry women, armed with knives and rolling-pins. For him no doubt it was a harrowing experience, until he finally established his nationality by producing all the most lurid words in his vocabulary; but as an omen for the day when the cream of Hitler's Aryan youth should attempt to land in Britain it was most interesting.

All this went on at a time when night after night the East End was taking a terrible beating, and it was rumoured that the people were ominously quiet. Could their morale be cracking? The answer was provided in a story that was going the rounds. A young man went down to see a chaplain whom he knew in the East End. He noticed not only that the damage was considerable but that the people were saying practically nothing at all. 'How are they taking it?' he asked nervously. The chaplain shook his head. 'I'm afraid,' he said, 'that my people have fallen from grace: they are beginning to feel a little bitter towards the Germans.'

The understatement in that remark was impressive because it was typical. The war was practically never discussed except as a joke. The casual observer might easily have drawn one of two conclusions: either that London was spent of all feeling, or that it was a city waiting like a blind man, unseeing, uncaring, for the end. Either conclusion would have been wide of the mark. Londoners are slow to anger. They had shown for long enough that they could take it; now they were waiting on the time when it would be their turn to dish it out, when their cold rage would need more than a Panzer division to stamp it out.

RICHARD HILLARY: from *The Last Enemy* (1942).

C*

9

The Making of an Artist

Many novels have been written about geniuses. Sometimes the 'genius' is a poet, sometimes a painter, but it is only very rarely that a novelist succeeds in convincing his readers that the character really is a genius, for the author needs to do much more than simply tell us: we must be made to feel in our bones, as it were, that the character could and did write great poems or paint great pictures. When a novelist dares to give specimens of the poems, any evidence of genius is invariably lacking; and no novelist attempts to give specimens of his genius's paintings. The success of Joyce Cary depended largely upon his ability to think and imagine himself into the personalities of the many different characters he created, whether they were Europeans or Africans, and whether men or women. Consequently his artist, Gully Jimson, in The Horse's Mouth *is a convincing creation, and we have little or no difficulty in accepting him as a genius—a rip-roaring scoundrel of a genius, but burstingly alive and capable of anything from great paintings downwards. The whole novel must of course be read to get Gully Jimson in his entirety, though something of his vital character can be seen through the extract given here. We see him passing from clerk to artist, and as an artist passing through stages of development in which he is influenced by various other painters and art movements before he at length discovers his own individual and original style—the style towards which he is still groping at the end of this passage.*

JOYCE CARY

. . . ONE DAY when I was sitting in our London office on Bankside, I dropped a blot on an envelope; and having nothing to do just then, I pushed it about with my pen to try and make it look more like a face. And the next thing was I was drawing figures in red and black, on the same envelope. And from that moment I was done for. Everyone was very sympathetic. The boss sent for me at the end of the month and said, 'I'm sorry, Jimson, but I've had another complaint about your work. I warned you last week that this was your last chance. But I don't want to sack you. You might never get another job, and what is going to happen then to your poor young wife and her baby. Look here, Jimson, I like you, everyone likes you. You can trust me, I hope. Tell me what's gone wrong. Never mind what it is. I'm not going to be stupid about it. Is it debts? You haven't been gambling, I suppose? Is your petty cash all right? Take a couple of days off and think it over.'

But of course I couldn't think of anything except how to get my figures right. I started as a Classic. About 1800 was my period. And I was having a hell of a time with my anatomy and the laws of perspective.

> *Her fingers numbered every nerve*
> *Just as a miser counts his gold.*

I spent my holiday at a life class, and when I went back to the firm, I didn't last two days. Of course, I was a bad case. I had a bad infection, galloping art. I was at it about twelve hours a day and I had a picture in the old Water Colour Society that year. Very classical. Early Turner. Almost Sandby.

My wife was nearly starving, and we had pawned most of the furniture, but what did I care. Well, of course, I worried a bit. But I felt like an old master. So I was, very old. I was at about the period when my poor old father was knocked out. I'd gone through a lot to get my experience, my technique, and I was going to paint like that all my life. It was the only way to paint. I knew all the rules. I could turn you off a picture, all correct, in an afternoon. Not that it was what you call a work of imagination. It was just a piece of stuff. Like a nice sausage. Lovely forms. But I wasn't looking any more than a sausage machine. I was the old school, the old Classic, the old church.

> *An aged shadow soon he fades*
> *Wandering round an earthly cot*
> *Full filled all with gems and gold*
> *Which he by industry has got.*

I even sold some pictures, nice water-colours of London churches. But one day I happened to see a Manet. Because some chaps were laughing at it. And it gave me the shock of my life. Like a flash of lightning. It skinned my eyes for me and when I came out I was a different man. And I saw the world again, the world of colour. By Gee and Jay, I said, I was dead, and I didn't know it.

> *From the fire on the hearth*
> *A little female babe did spring.*

I felt her jump. But, of course, the old classic put up a fight. It was the Church against Darwin, the old Lords against the Radicals. And I was the battleground. I had a bad time of it that year. I couldn't paint at all. I botched my nice architectural water-colours with impressionist smudges. And I made such a mess of my impressionist landscapes that I couldn't bear to look at them myself. Of course, I lost all my kind patrons. The first time, but not the last. But that didn't upset me. What gave me the horrors was that I couldn't paint. I was so wretched that I hardly noticed when we were sold up and my wife went off, or even when my mother died. It was a good thing she did die, or she would have had to go to the workhouse. And really, I suppose she died of a broken heart at seeing her youngest go down the drain.

Of course, I was a bit upset about it. I thought my heart was broken. But even at the funeral I couldn't tell whether I was in agony about my poor mother's death, or about my awful pictures. For I didn't know what to do with myself. My old stuff made me sick. In the living world that I'd suddenly discovered, it looked like a rotten corpse that somebody had forgotten to bury. But the new world wouldn't come to my hand. I couldn't catch it, that lovely vibrating light, that floating tissue of colour. Not local colour but aerial colour, a sensation of the mind; that maiden vision.

> *And she was all of solid fire*
> *And gems and gold, that none his hand*
> *Dare stretch to touch her baby form*
> *Or wrap her in her swaddling band*
> *But she comes to the man she loves*
> *If young or old, or rich or poor,*
> *They soon drive out the aged host*
> *A beggar at another's door.*

I got her after about four years. At least I got rid of

every bit of the grand style, the old church. I came to the pure sensation without a thought in my head. Just a harp in the wind. And a lot of my stuff was good. Purest go-as-you-please.

And I sold it too. I made more money then than I ever did again. People like Impressionism. Still do, because it hasn't any idea in it. Because it doesn't ask anything from them—because it's just a nice sensation, a little song. Good for the drawing-room. Tea-cakes.

But I got tired of sugar. I grew up.

And when they showed me a room full of my own confections, I felt quite sick. Like grandpa brought to a nursery tea. As for icing any more éclairs, I couldn't bring myself to it. I gradually stopped painting and took to arguing instead. Arguing and reading and drinking; politics, philosophy and pub-crawling; all the things chaps do who can't do anything else. Who've run up against the buffers. And I got in such a low state that I was frightened of the dark. Yes, as every night approached, I fairly trembled. I knew what it would be like. A vacuum sucking one's skull into a black glass bottle; all in silence. I used to go out and get drunk, to keep some kind of illumination going in my dome.

> *He wanders weeping far away*
> *Until some other take him in*
> *Oft blind and age bent, sore distrest*
> *Until he can a maiden win.*

And then I began to make a few little pencil sketches, studies, and I took Blake's Job drawings out of somebody's bookshelf and peeped into them and shut them up again. Like a chap who's fallen down the cellar steps and knocked his skull in and opens a window too quick,

on something too big. I did a little modelling and tried
my hand at composition. I found myself wandering
round the marbles at the British Museum and brooding
over the torso of some battered old Venus without any
head, arms or legs, and a kind of smallpox all over the
rest of her. Trying to find out why her lumps seemed so
much more important than any bar-lady with a gold
fringe; or water-lily pool.

> And to allay his freezing eye
> The poor man took her in his arms
> The cottage fades before his sight
> The garden and its lovely charms.

Good-bye impressionism, anarchism, nihilism, Darwin-
ism and the giddy goat, now staggering with rheumatism.
Hail, the new Classic. But you might say it was in the
air about then, at the turn of the century when the
young Liberals were beginning to bend away from
laissez-faire and to look for their Marx, and science took
a mathematical twist, and the old biologists found themselves high and dry among the has-beens, blowing their
own trumpets because no one else would do it for them.
And I studied Blake and Persian carpets and Raphael's
cartoons and took to painting walls.

But I rubbed most of them out again. They looked like
bad imitations of the old master; or made-up, pompous
stuff. They didn't belong to the world I lived in. A new
world with a new normal character.

I had a worse time than the last time. I drank more
than ever. To keep up my self-respect. But it didn't have
the same effect. I was gloomy even in drink. I didn't
seem to be getting anywhere very much. If there was
anywhere to get to.

> *The stars, sun, moon all shrink away,*
> *A desert vast without a bound,*
> *And nothing left to eat or drink*
> *And a dark desert all around.*

And, of course, no one would buy anything. They didn't know what I was driving at. I probably didn't know myself.

JOYCE CARY: from *The Horse's Mouth* (1944).

10

A Penny for Thoughts

L. P. Hartley's The Shrimp and the Anemone *is the first of three linked novels, the second and the third called* The Sixth Heaven *and* Eustace and Hilda. *The first shows Eustace and his sister in childhood, and in the episode chosen here the sensitive little boy is troubled by the memory of a grown-up's remark which his imagination mistakenly interprets as foreshadowing a personal tragedy.*

L. P. HARTLEY

'I DON'T think we'll do any lessons this morning,' said Miss Cherrington. 'Eustace is looking a bit tired. Why don't you both go down and play on the sands? It's only ten o'clock so you'll have all the morning for it. You won't get many more days like this.'

Armed with their spades they started off across the ragged stretch of chalky green that intervened between Cambo and the cliffs. On their left the sun shone brightly with a promise of more than September warmth. Its loving touch lay on everything they looked at, but Eustace walked in silence, dragging his spade. 'You won't get many more days like this.' Making for a gap in the broken fence they passed the threatening brown bulk of Mr. Johnson's school. A hum of voices came from it, the boys were lining up for physical exercises in the play-

ground. Almost for the first time Eustace felt a twinge
of envy mingle with the mistrust in which he habitually
held them. Soon, stretching away to the right, came the
familiar vista, the First Shelter, the Second Shelter, the
rise in the ground that hid all but the red roof of the
Third Shelter, and then the mysterious round white
summit of the lighthouse. Even at this distance you
could see the sun striking the great rainbow-coloured
lantern within, a sight that seldom failed to move
Eustace. But it did not move him to-day.

They stopped from habit among the penny-in-the-slot
machines at the head of the concrete staircase which
zigzagged its way majestically below, and looked down
at the beach to see whether the rocks that formed the
bastions of their pond had been appropriated by others.
As they gazed, their faces, even Eustace's, took on the
intent forbidding look of a gamekeeper on the watch for
poachers. No, the rocks were free—it was too early for
marauders—and the beach was nearly deserted.

' A penny for your thoughts,' said Hilda.

Eustace started.

' If you give me the penny now, may I tell you my
thoughts later on? '

Hilda considered.

' But you may be thinking something else then.'

' No, I shall still be thinking the same thing.'

' Very well, then.' Hilda produced a purse from the
pocket halfway down her dress and gave him a penny.

' But why do you want it now? '

Eustace looked rather shamefaced.

' I wanted to see how strong I was.'

He advanced cautiously upon the Try-your-grip
machine. Flanked on one side by a bold-faced gipsy
offering to tell your fortune, and on the other by an

apparatus for giving you an electric shock, the Try-your-grip machine responded to Eustace's diffident inspection with a secret, surly expression. Dark green and battered, it had a disreputable air as indeed had all its neighbours, and Eustace vaguely felt that he was in bad company.

'I shouldn't try if I were you,' said Hilda, coming up behind him.

'Why not?'

'Oh, you never know what they might do. Besides, it's wasting money.'

Eustace thought she was right, but he had gone too far to retreat with self-respect. He had issued a challenge and the machine, withdrawn and sullen as it was, must have heard. Destiny, which had its eye on Eustace, must have heard too. 'Moderate strength rings the bell: great strength returns the penny.' He pondered. After all, one never could be sure. Supposing the bell rang; supposing the penny were returned: wouldn't that prove something, wouldn't he feel different afterwards? He looked round. The green feathers of the tamarisk hedge were waving restlessly; he had liked them once but there was no comfort in them now, no comfort in the bow-windows, the beetling walls, the turrets and pinnacles of Palmerston Parade looking down on him: no comfort in the day.

He slipped the penny in the slot. The machine was cold and repellent to his touch; he screwed his face up and tried to give it a look as hostile as its own. Then he pressed his palm against the brass bar and curled his finger-tips, which would only just reach, round the inner handle, and pulled. The handle bit cruelly into his soft flesh; the indicator, vibrating wildly, travelled as far across the dial as the figure 10, and stopped, still flickering. Eustace saw that he must get it to 130 for the penny to be returned. Scarlet in the face he redoubled his efforts. The indicator began to lose ground. In desperation he was bringing up his left hand as a reinforcement when he heard Hilda's voice.

'That's against the rules! You're cheating!'

Crestfallen and ashamed, Eustace relaxed his grip. The needle flashed back to zero and the machine, radiating malevolence from all its hard dull surfaces, with a contemptuous click gathered the penny into its secret maw. Breathing gustily Eustace stared back at it, like a boxer who has received a disabling blow but must not take his eyes off his enemy.

'I told you not to try,' said Hilda. 'You'll only strain yourself.' She added more kindly: 'Those machines are just there for show. I expect they're all rusted up inside, really.'

'Do you think Daddy could get the penny back?' asked Eustace.

'He couldn't have at your age. Now you must tell me what you were thinking of. I know you've forgotten.'

'I'll tell you when we get down on the beach,' said Eustace evasively.

They began the descent. September winds had blown the sand up to the topmost steps; they felt gritty to the tread. In the corners where the staircase turned, paper bags whirled and eddied; quite large pieces of orange-peel sprang to life, pirouetted and dropped down dead. Around, below, above, gulls wheeled and screamed, borne aloft on the airs that came racing from the sea. All this pother plucked at the nerves and whipped up the blood, but Eustace plodded stolidly in Hilda's wake, secretly examining his reddened palm and wondering how he would be able to hold the spade. If he was as weak as the machine said, he would soon have to stop digging any-how.

'Let's make the pond larger this time,' said Hilda when they reached the familiar scene of irrigation. 'We're earlier than we generally are, we may not get a chance like this again.'

'Much larger?' asked Eustace.

'Well, we could take in this rock here,' said Hilda, walking with long strides to a distant boulder. 'Then the wall would go like this'—and cutting with her spade a line through the sand she sketched an ambitious exten-sion of their traditional ground plan. 'It will look won-derful from the cliff,' she added persuasively. 'Like a real lake.'

'Don't you think it's more than we can manage?' asked Eustace, still smarting from his defeat at the hands of the automatic machine.

'You can't tell till you try,' Hilda said, and immedi-ately set to work on the retaining wall. Eustace walked slowly to his post at the far end of the pond. Their cus-tom was to begin at opposite ends and meet in the middle, but Eustace seldom reached the halfway mark. Now that mark, thanks to Hilda's grandiose scheme, was at least two yards further off than it used to be. Con-sciousness of this increased his bodily and mental lan-guor. For him the pond had ceased to be a symbol. Of old, each time it rose from the sands and spread its silver surface to the sky it proclaimed that the Cherrington children had measured their strength against the uni-verse, and won. They had imposed an order; they had left a mark; they had added a meaning to life. That was why the last moment, when the completion of the work was only distant by a few spadefuls, was so tense and exciting. In those moments the glory of living gathered itself into a wave and flowed over them. The experience was ecstatic and timeless, it opened a window upon eternity, and whilst it lasted, and again when they surveyed their handiwork from the cliff-top, they felt themselves to be immortal.

But what assurance of immortality could there be for Eustace now, when at any moment the clock would strike, the sounds in the house would cease, the call would come and he would pass through the open front door to find the chariot standing outside. Sometimes it was just the landau with Mr. Craddock on the box, staring ahead; sometimes it was a hearse; sometimes it was a vehicle of indefinite design, edged with light much brighter than the day, and seeming scarcely to rest upon the ground. The vision never carried him beyond that point, but it brought with it an indescribable impression of finality, it was a black curtain stretched across every avenue of thought, absorbing whatever energies of mind and spirit he had left. Why go on digging? Why do anything? But no; even in this featureless chaos something remained to be done.

He straightened himself, and shook his head vigorously.

'What's the matter?' said Hilda. 'Is a fly bothering you?'

'No,' said Eustace, 'it was some thoughts I had.'

'Well, you won't get rid of them like that, and your hat will come off. Oh, and that reminds me! You promised to tell me what your thoughts were, and you haven't. I knew you'd forget.'

'No, I haven't forgotten,' said Eustace.

'Well, come on. I'm waiting.'

An overpowering reluctance, like a spasm in the throat, seized Eustace, almost robbing him of speech.

'Just give me a little longer.'

'Very well, then, I'll give you five minutes from now.'
Digging her chin into her chest she looked at the watch
which hung suspended there. 'That'll be five minutes past
eleven.'

They worked on in silence, Eustace searching franti-
cally for a formula for what he had to say and finding
none. So acute was his sense of the passing minutes that
he began to feel himself ticking like a clock. Twice he
saw Hilda surreptitiously glancing at her watch.

'Time's up,' she said at last.

Eustace gazed at her blankly.

'Well?'

'Do you really want to know?' Eustace temporized,
shuffling with his feet.

'I don't suppose it's anything important, but as I've
paid for it I might as well have it.'

'It is important in a way, to me at any rate. But I
don't think you'll like to hear what I'm going to say, any
more than I shall like telling you. At least I hope you
won't.'

Hilda frowned. 'What *is* all this about?'

The rapids were close at hand now and he could hear
the roar of the cataract. He plunged.

'You see, I want to make my will.'

If Eustace had counted on making an effect, he ought
to have been gratified. Hilda opened her eyes and stared
at him. She opened her mouth, too, but no words came.

'You didn't know about me then? I didn't think you
did.'

'Know what?' said Hilda at length.

'That I was going away.'

Hilda's heart turned over, but bewilderment was still
uppermost in her mind.

'I thought they hadn't told you. It was so as not to worry you, I expect.'

'But who told *you*?' asked Hilda, making crosses in the sand with her spade.

'Mr. Craddock told me first, the evening we drove back from Frontisham. He said I was going away and he would be sorry to lose me. And then I asked Minney, and she told me not to pay any attention to what Mr. Craddock said because he was an old cabman. But she didn't say it wasn't true, and I could see she knew it was. You know how you can sometimes tell with grown-up people.'

Understandingly but unwillingly Hilda nodded.

'And then I asked Daddy.'

'What did he say?'

'He said something about not taking offences before you come to them, which I didn't quite understand, and not meeting trouble halfway. He was angry with Mr. Craddock too, I could see that. He said he was a silly old gossip. He said it wouldn't be as bad as I thought, and that everyone had to go through it sooner or later, and I shouldn't mind much when the time came, and I wasn't to think about it, because that only made it worse.'

'They never said anything to me,' said Hilda.

'Well, I had to tell you because, you see, I wanted to give you my things before I go away.'

Hilda said nothing to this, but she sat down rather suddenly on a rock, with back bent and knees spread out, in the attitude Eustace knew so well.

'I've been thinking about it,' he went on with an effort, 'because, you see, unless I leave a will you might not get my things at all—they might go into Chancery. But I haven't many that would do for someone who

isn't a boy.' (Eustace was unwilling to call Hilda a girl, it
would sound like a kind of taunt.) 'My clothes wouldn't
be any use, except my combinations, and they're too
small. I should like you to have my handkerchiefs,
though. They would be washed by that time, of course.'

'There's your red silk scarf,' said Hilda, with the
stirring of self-interest that no beneficiary, however
tender-hearted, can quite succeed in stifling.

'I was just coming to that. And my woolly gloves too.
You've often worn them and they've stretched a bit.
When you had the scarf on and the gloves, and one of
my handkerchiefs, it would look almost as though I was
still walking about.'

'No one could ever mistake me for you if that's what
you mean,' said Hilda.

'It wasn't quite what I meant,' said Eustace, but a
doubt crossed his mind as to what he really did mean,
and he went on:

'My hairbrushes wouldn't be any good because they
haven't got handles, and besides you have some. Perhaps Daddy could use them when his wear out. Then
there's my sponge and toothbrush and flannel. Some poor
boy might like them when they've been well dried.'
Raised interrogatively, Eustace's voice trailed away when
the suggestion met with no response.

'I doubt it,' said Hilda practically, 'but of course we
could try.'

'There isn't much more,' said Eustace. 'I should like
Minney to have the watch that Miss Fothergill gave me.
Of course it's rather large for a lady, but it goes very
well because I've never been allowed to take it out of my
room, and hers doesn't; and you have yours, the one that
belonged to Mother.'

'I've never seen a lady wear a watch that size,' said

Hilda. 'But she could tuck it in her belt where it wouldn't show, though of course it would leave a bulge.'

A shadow passed over Eustace's face.

'Well, perhaps she could use it as a clock. Then I thought I'd give all my toys to Barbara, except Jumbo, who you take to bed. She uses them already, I know, so it wouldn't seem like a present, but she might like to know that they were hers by law.'

'I don't think she minds about that,' said Hilda. 'She takes anything she can get hold of.'

'Yes, she's different from us, isn't she?' said Eustace. 'She doesn't seem to care whether something is right or wrong. It will be a great handicap to her, won't it, in after life.'

'Not if she doesn't mind about it,' Hilda said.

'I've nearly done now, and then we can go on with the pond. I haven't anything to leave to Daddy and Aunt Sarah, so I thought I'd take two of those sheets of writing-paper from the drawing-room table, which we only use to thank for presents, and write 'Love from Eustace' on them. I think I should print the messages in different coloured inks, and then put them in envelopes addressed to Mr. Cherrington and Miss Cherrington, and drop them in the letter-box when the time came, and they might think they had come by post, and it would be a surprise.'

'Yes,' said Hilda, 'that's a good idea.'

'And all the rest I should leave to you, Hilda. That is, my money in the money-box, and my books, and my guide-book, and my knife, and my pencils, and the ball of string, and the indiarubber rings, and the pink rosette that I wore at the election, and the picture postcard of Zena Dare, and the General View of Mt. Pelée before the earthquake.'

'You won't want to be parted from that,' said Hilda. 'I should take that with you.'

'I don't think I should be allowed to,' said Eustace. 'You see . . .' marvelling at Hilda's obtuseness, he left the sentence unfinished. 'I won't leave the things lying about, I'll put them all in the drawer with the pencil-box —the one with marguerites on the lid—so you'll know where to find them.'

'I always know better than you do, really,' said Hilda.

Eustace let this pass.

'The only thing I'm not sure about is how to get my money out of the Post Office. There's quite a lot there, thirty-three pounds. Do you think if I went and asked for it they'd give it me? They ought to, because it belongs to me, but I don't think they would. Daddy once told me that banks use your money for themselves. I shall have to ask Daddy and I don't want to do that.'

'Why not?'

'Because I don't want to talk about it to anyone but you. And I only told you because I thought you didn't know what was going to happen. But I shall write everything down and put it in an envelope under your pillow, so that's where you'll find it when the time comes.'

'When will that be?' said Hilda.

'I don't quite know yet.'

L. P. HARTLEY: from *The Shrimp and the Anemone* (1944).

11

Bobbie's English Class

A scientist, a scholar, a man of action, and a distinguished author: F. D. Ommanney is all these. As a man of action he has had such arduous and thrilling experiences as he described excitingly in South Latitude. *The section of his autobiography reproduced here indicates that a love of books and reading is no unsuitable preparation for such a life, while it also gives a fine portrait of a schoolmaster who made poetry suddenly come alive in the mind and imagination of a boy who shared the rest of the class's dislike and contempt when Bobbie, the master, made an astonishing and distressing Saturday morning announcement.*

F. D. OMMANNEY

... AFTER THE exams were over, all the masters, who had charge of our souls, evidently thought they had done their best or worst, and rested from their labours like the Almighty after the Creation. They suddenly lost interest in our souls. After all they were not very important. So, on the last few days of the term, they came into class with an exhausted air as though they had fought a long and fruitless battle. 'Well,' they would say, 'we won't do any grammar' (or maths or geometry or whatever it was they had been trying to instil into us) 'this morning. You can read if you want to.' We all knew this was going to happen and had come prepared. We had

magazines or detective stories or novels stuffed into our
pockets or beneath our coats or between the leaves of our
exercise books. On the word these appeared like magic.
Even the noisiest class became strangely quiet on the
last few days of the term.

I read greedily with a concentration I never brought to
any other occupation. When reading I drifted off into
that shadowy dream world where I seemed to spend so
much of my time. I frequently floated off into it also
when I was supposed to be filling my imaginary tanks,
playing cricket or listening to the Headmaster's sermons.
The familiar inhabitants of this other world accompanied
me on my walks on Sunday afternoons. They spoke to
me when I was trying to listen to Bland's discourses about
biology. Perhaps it was because I lived so much in my
imagination that my favourite reading in those days were
highly imaginative novels like the early romances of
H. G. Wells, Jules Verne and Rider Haggard. Especially
Rider Haggard. I developed an extraordinary passion for
that prolific writer and I think that during the years I
was at school I must have read almost every book he produced. Some of the better-known ones, such as *King
Solomon's Mines* and *She*, I read three or four times over.
Allan Quatermain was my hero—Heaven knows why,
for if I had ever met him I am sure I should have been
bored to death. However, I do not think my choice of a
favourite author was a bad one. He led me into scenes
of colour and splendour whose brightness still glows in
my memory. But some time ago I tried to read *She* again
and could have wept with disappointment when I found
I could not do it. Allan Quatermain and Sir Henry Cur-
tis and Captain Good, R.N., even old Umslopogaas himself, had lost their glamour. As soon as I found the spell
was broken I put *She* away. I could not endure that these

splendid figures of my youth should fade. I knew that they themselves must be exactly the same as they were thirty years ago since the printed word does not change. It was the shades of the prison house. It was I who had changed.

But there was one master at least whose care for our youthful souls did not apparently cease when the exams were over. Into his gentle hands my ripening intellect passed in my first term. He was one of the few schoolmasters to whom my memory turns now with affection and respect. He had a gentle manner and a sorrowful voice which he never raised. He maintained order in his class without ever, so far as I can remember, resorting to that ruthless wielding of the stick that so many of his colleagues found necessary. He was very tall and thin and wore a pair of pince-nez that perched precariously on the end of his long nose. Down this nose he would gaze at a miscreant with one pale sad eye and one glass one which was exactly the same colour as its fellow but fixed, expressionless and unwinking. Sometimes he would be seen to place his handkerchief to this eye and keep it there for some seconds. It was said that, when he did this, mysterious manœuvres with the glass eye took place behind the cover of the handkerchief. He was thought to be removing it and turning it round so that when he took the handkerchief away again the glass eye was the other way up. No one was ever able to detect any difference afterwards, but whenever he put his handkerchief to his eye the whole class might have been seen to look up furtively from its books with sudden rapt attention. Bobbie had an air of perpetual sorrow for the sins and follies of small boys and seemed always about to burst into tears on their account. 'Next boy', he would say in class, letting his asymmetrical regard travel down the rows in front of him, 'Next. And the next boy. Well, next then.' And so more and more tearfully down to the boy who sat ignominiously at the bottom—not infrequently myself. 'Well, then. Tell them, top,' he would appeal sweeping his single eye back up the class again. And, when the top boy failed him also, all the grief and despair in the world were in his voice, as though he had been utterly and finally let down. 'Oh, my dear boy. How often have I told you—the verb at the end of the sentence.' The boys imitated him ceaselessly, laughed at him behind his back, respected him and loved him. It was said that he had been a magnificent athlete in his youth, a champion runner, fives player and a rugger blue. No one had ever seen him show the slightest sign of athletic activity and he displayed only a mild fatherly interest in inter-house matches and sports. But when a man in late middle age earns the love of the young he must bear, like a cross, a reputation for youthful prowess. When asked about it he only smiled and shook his head. They said he lost his eye when playing rugger for Cambridge but no one really knew the truth about it. Bobbie left the school for an honourable retirement at the end of my last term. When the taxi that took him and his wife to the station turned out of the school gate the boys pursued it down the drive and down the hill past the chapel, climbing on to the running boards and shouting 'Good-bye, sir! Good-bye and good luck! Come back soon! Good old Bobbie!' Inside Bobbie held his handkerchief to both his eyes. He was really weeping. Perhaps for the sins and follies of an old man who loved boys.

It was the last period of the last Saturday morning of my first summer term—an hour usually devoted to Bobbie's English class. Most of the class were bored to death by the study of the treasures of their own language. Indeed who would not be, for it was made uninteresting enough? We paraphrased great chunks of Shakespeare, very often passages that I find difficult even now, such as Richard the Second's soliloquy in his cell or Hamlet's broodings over the skull of Yorick. We analysed the ponderous sentences of Gibbon. We wrestled with the Anglo-German of Thomas Carlyle. We learnt slabs of Milton parrot fashion. The result was that English Literature—with a capital L—became a sweat and a bore. Any Friday evening during the term boys might have been seen pacing up and down the quadrangle with measured tread, as though taking part in an imaginary funeral procession, their heads bent and their eyes fixed on grubby dog-eared books. Their lips moved as though in prayer. Occasionally they raised their eyes to heaven while their lips continued to move in some mysterious incantation. What strange act of devotion, what mystic preparation was this? What indeed? They were preparing for Bobbie's English class next day. For the following morning one or two of them, chosen at random by the high priest, would be called upon to rise from his seat and haltingly repeat:

> Once more, O ye laurels, and once more,
> Ye myrtles brown, with ivy never sere,—um—
> I come to pluck your berries harsh and crude,
> And—er—with forced fingers rude
> Shatter your—shatter your—

And while he stumbled on, those around him waited like hungry wolves for a hesitant pause. 'Sir! Oh, sir! Please, sir!' they hissed with raised hands at the first sign of uncertainty. The classroom sounded like a cage full of snakes.

'Well, then, tell him, next boy—next—next.'

'Please, sir—"Leaves", sir, "Shatter your leaves before the mellowing year."'

And he would begin with shame to take a lower place.

This too was my introduction to the Elysian Fields of poetry and like all the rest I regarded them as a desert waste. Many years of this sort of thing at academies for young gentlemen had produced a state of mind in young gentlemen exceedingly hostile to poetry and literature and everything that went with them. Poetry was effeminate balderdash. Anyone with a taste for poetry was automatically regarded with deep suspicion. He was suspected of being a cissy. Anybody who could string words together himself was obviously beyond the pale. Hence the persecution that descended on me as a result of my flight of fancy about spring. 'He'll be writing bloody poetry next,' they said. I myself learnt to regard poetry as something of a bore and I could see no charm in the difficult slabs of Milton and Shakespeare I was forced to swallow and spew up again in class.

So we felt nothing but relief on that last Saturday morning when the English period came round and we knew we should not be called upon, for once, to stand up and give a ponderous and meaningless recitation. Forestalling events, we came into class with our favourite story-books in our pockets, with detective magazines inside our exercise books. I had my latest Rider Haggard. I was in the middle of *Nada the Lily* and itched to hear the tramp of T'Chaka's impis once again.

Imagine, then, our bored consternation when Bobbie, gazing sorrowfully at us for a moment over the top of his glasses, smiled gently and said:

'There'll be no lesson to-day. Put your books on one side. I'm going to read some poetry to you.'

D

Poetry! And on the last Saturday morning of the term! Could there be a greater refinement of cruelty than that? No words could express our contempt and dislike for Bobbie in that moment. We gasped and stared blankly at one another. This was too much.

In a quiet, even, sorrowful voice Bobbie began to read Matthew Arnold's *Sohrab and Rustum*. Before he had gone very far I had forgotten *Nada the Lily*. I was listening to a new and strange music. The classroom with its ink-stained desks and its blackboard covered with yesterday's vulgar fractions faded from before my eyes. The listening boys, some attentive and some bored, took on the shape of tents pitched upon a great waste of sand under the blazing sun. All the distance that stretched before my mind's eye was filled with a host of dark-skinned strangely accoutred warriors, watching and silent. In a square cleared in their midst the lovely youth lay gasping on the ground,

> Like some rich hyacinth which by the scythe
> Of an unskilled gardener has been cut,
> Mowing the garden grass-plots near its bed,
> And lies, a fragrant tower of purple bloom,
> On the mown, dying grass.

His blood flowed out from his white side and clotted on the sand—a dark question mark draining out his life. Over him his father, huge and dark and bearded, who had just cut down his own son in mortal combat, knelt weeping. His sword and shield were cast away. He held the boy's drooping head upon his arm. Silently and in sorrow the warriors turned away in twos and threes and went back to their tents. The sun went down and their camp fires came out and glowed upon the plain. They left the father in the growing darkness weeping for his son. Soon the host of Heaven shone passionless upon the dead boy and the strong man undone by grief.

> But the majestic river floated on,
> Out of the mist and hum of that low land,
> Into the frosty starlight, and there moved,
> Rejoicing, through the hushed Chorasmian waste,
> Under the solitary moon: . . . till at last
> The longed-for dash of waves is heard, and wide
> His luminous home of waters opens, bright
> And tranquil, from whose floor the new-bathed stars
> Emerge, and shine upon the Aral Sea.

He ceased. The night desert and the stars faded from my sight. The tents once more took the form of boys sitting, black-coated and slumped in attitudes of boredom or resignation, at their stained desks. The white dead boy and the old warrior vanished. But there, on the cardboard cover of *Nada the Lily*, were the tears I had shed for them, hiding my face with my hands. There was silence for a few minutes. Only a blind cord tapped against the window. Nothing seemed to move but the sunlight through the leaves of a plane-tree outside.

F. D. OMMANNEY: from *The House in the Park* (1944).

12

Picnics and Bedtimes

The Sitwells—Edith, Osbert, and Sacheverell—spent their early years mainly in their family's ancestral home in Yorkshire, a house called Renishaw, near Scarborough. All of them have since become prominent in literature as poets and prose writers. Their father, Sir George Sitwell (1860-1943), was a somewhat eccentric baronet, of whom a wonderfully fascinating account is given by his son Osbert, the present baronet, in the autobiographical volumes which began with the book from which these early memories are drawn. Life as it was lived by and for the young Sitwells in the beginning years of the twentieth century now seems as remote as a long-past age, and the recollections of picnics and bedtimes and all else in their childhood happily preserved by Sir Osbert are a part of the domestic history of England.

SIR OSBERT SITWELL

How DELICIOUS were those long picnics on the lake, in the wide, flat-bottomed boat, blue-painted, that yet rots somewhere in the disused stables; those long, hot, calm, drowsy, sun-spangled afternoons of childhood spent on that mirror-flat, cool surface, the slow movement and the sound of the rowlocks as Davis listlessly plied the oar, the hours in which we drifted, yet never wasted our time, for if Edith and I leant over the thick blue wall of the boat, we could watch the fish flickering in their chequered mail through trailing avenues of weeds. And sometimes my father would appear and carry me off for a swift darting journey in a canoe, while his spaniel flopped and splashed after us in the water, or, after shaking himself in the sun on the bank, until his dangling ears flapped wildly and a smell of hot wool ascended from his steaming body, then tried, if we were near enough, to jump upon our prow, and, missing it, fell into his other element again.

Edith and Davis would be watching us from the boat, now moored by the island under the light shadow of a grove of young trees. At four-thirty a footman would come down with a hamper, and we would begin collecting dry wood to make a fire upon which to boil the kettle. The twigs crackled and burst, and the kettle began soon to hiss. Presently my mother and her friends would join us, and their grown-up laughter—laughter at things hidden and beyond our sight—would sound among the tea-cups. But my mother, with her own children and with others', but especially with her sons, was like a child herself, absorbed in their interests. Her friends, however, were thinking of themselves and how they looked; their air was patronizing in its unnecessary and false kindness (this stricture, of course, in no way applies to the several we loved, and who treated us as equals). Soon my mother would light a cigarette to keep the midges away. (In those times, women who smoked usually did so to be daring, but she smoked for pleasure.) But time was passing, and soon we would climb the steep sun-baked hill to the house, entering the garden, sweeter than ever in these hours of dwindling light.

In the lamp-room, under the heavy fumes of paraffin, the sightless Stephen Pare—with his vast and hollow

eyes, that now I understand resembled the gaping eyes
of an antique mask of tragedy—was already lighting the
wicks, which, by an unhappy irony, were to make clear
for everyone else the exterior world, to him so dim, and
indicate the shape and corners of chair and table, blurred
to him and fading. Indeed he was the only person to gain
no benefit from the process; he could not read at all,
even, and he felt his way by instinct through the lofty,
darkening rooms. But never, during the many years I
knew him, did he make a mistake; he placed things down
more softly than would any man who could see. Many of
the rooms were now beginning to glow with a light
forgotten today, for we belong to the last generation of
children brought up by candlelight, and the smell of
snuffed wax lay heavy on our nostrils as we went to sleep.
There was, however, though it was already time for bed,
still a grateful hour or two before we must go to sleep,
for I hated darkness here, was frightened in this large
rambling old house, haunted and haunting, and counted
every moment until my mother came upstairs after
dinner to bid me a second good-night—a custom strictly
forbidden by my father—bringing with her the comfort
of her warm and, to me, loving presence, and the
scent of the gardenias and tuberoses she was wearing,
and usually—which was also prohibited—a peach, straw-
berry water-ice, or some delicacy of that sort. She would
bend above me, standing close to me, talking to me as
to one of her own age, telling me how her cousins, who
were staying with us, had behaved at dinner, of how
Henry, still a footman, had suddenly laughed at something that was said, and of how difficult my father was
being, with all his new ideas—probably he would alter
them all again, tomorrow. . . . But though I was so
frightened of the night, there was never a moment when

I would not rather have been here than elsewhere. I loved the impalpable essence—what later one learns to call the 'atmosphere'—of the house, a strange prevalence, laden with the dying memories of three centuries; pervading the mind like a scent fairly detected, the smell of wood-smoke, for example, that seems to colour a whole room with its fragrance though a year has passed.

My mother, who looked so beautiful in her light-coloured evening dresses, pale pink or yellow, would say good-night, and unless already I was in an almost trance-like condition of fatigue, I would struggle to prevent her going. With her, as she walked out of the door, she took the last remainder of all the light that the day had held. The lingering breath of strong scent she affected, and of the warmth of a physical presence that, as with other members of her family, was Italian in its radiance and, at first sight, apparent simplicity, only made the night still darker than it had been before she arrived. There was nothing now except darkness, out of which substance ghosts are spun and torn. Through the door, however, left open on purpose, I could, if I removed the sheet from over my ears, hear the monotonous, grating tone of Davis's voice as she talked to the nursery-maid in the day nursery. It was a dull sound, but I loved it, because it supported me on its safe wings, even the smell of cheese and beer which accompanied it—for they were having their supper—though at other moments it made me feel sick, now seemed pleasant to me, exhaling a human warmth and animal coarseness. A piece of garlic hung outside the window, says the folklore of South-East Europe, secures a sleeper against vampires, and, equally, I can testify that the scent of bread and cheese can dispose of ghosts for children. I would listen to the voices,

and then, the next thing I knew, it was morning and
the blinds were being drawn up in our room level with
the highest tree-tops.

SIR OSBERT SITWELL: from *Left Hand Right Hand*
(1945).

13

Pet Marjory

*Precocious children are not as a rule considered one of
the lovable sections of humanity, and there can be no
certainty that we should have found Marjory Fleming
other than a tiresome child. In print, however, she is
altogether delightful, and there is no one like her elsewhere in literature. Probably there has never been anyone like her in life either. There is enough in Sir Desmond MacCarthy's essay to enable any reader to form
an opinion of her. Both as a letter writer and as a versi-
fier Marjory had a way all her own, even in her grammar
and rhyming. If she had lived longer and learned more
maybe she would have been forgotten long ago.*

SIR DESMOND MacCARTHY

CHILDREN ARE a subject on which I can speak with some
authority as I have been a child myself. Later on, I had
three children of my own—nice ones—and when a parent
I discovered what was the most charming thing about
children—they're so easy to make happy, so quickly
pleased. Thus in their company the adult enjoys, on
exceptionally easy terms, the sensation of being himself
or herself the best of company. With children, one's
small jokes, perhaps hardly good enough for general
circulation, have an instant and tremendous success.
What's more, they can be repeated with equal success.
And—joy!—so can one's stories! No need to watch a

D*

child's eyes for that glassy look. You can maunder on about what you did and saw either yesterday or twenty years ago, it will be received with the same flattering attention. And then how pleasant it is to be treated as a mine of undisputed, if inaccurate, information.

In a garden at evening you can explain: 'Look, look at the moon', without inspiring a nervous dread in your companion that you are about to turn poetical.

Yes, the enormous advantage of children's society is that we can be natural in their company.

Again, what a business it is giving a present to a contemporary. Would my friend like this or prefer that? And even if he would prefer that, isn't it the sort of thing he would rather choose for himself? Oh those questions! But almost any object will delight a child— a box, a bright clean tin, a bottle of red ink, a nice tight white roll of cord—I've had a success with old brass door knobs—and of course anything that bangs, squeaks or toots will do. And compare in the two cases the reception: with your friend, the moment of transfer is often one to be got through as quickly as possible. And it's almost shamefaced if the object happens to be expensive. 'I'm sure', says he, 'It's most awfully good of you. . . .' 'Oh I only thought. . . .' 'But you really oughtn't to have—hrrm, hrrm. Indeed I'm. . . .' 'Yes, yes,' the donor nervously interrupts, 'only I knew you'd . . .' and then hastily, 'Oh! aren't you going away next week?' Ouff! the relief! The transaction's over, and you're both back on the familiar footing. If the recipient is a woman, perhaps she'll say, 'It really *is* sweet of you. Now I *must* give you your tea'—and that's that!

Now recall what it's like giving a present to a child! One of two things happen, either whoop! a radiant creature is in your arms, or it stands solemnly taking stock of the object and, later, while you're thinking of other things, lo! a small silent figure stands at your elbow still holding the object, suggesting perhaps a shade of reproach, as much as to say, 'You've forgotten the little box.'

Oh, there's no doubt to whom, children or grown-ups, it is most *rewarding* to give a present. I don't wonder that children are popular, though of course we know (especially since the psychologists have been analysing them) that like ourselves they are festering with wickedness. But that doesn't matter a bean. They're lovable and make us happy, so much so that if you see a small white arm lying on the road after a blitz, a rage, not merely against your country's enemies, but the idiocy of mankind, boils and bubbles in your breast.

There is only one child in the English *Dictionary of National Biography*, Marjory Fleming, who died in her ninth year in 1811.

About fifty years later a journalist called Farnie (like her, a native of Kirkcaldy, in Scotland) published extracts from her journal. He called his pamphlet *Pet Marjory: the story of a child fifty years ago.* I've never read it, but I am prepared to trust her more recent editor, Mr. Esdaile, that everything readable in it is Marjory's own. 'She seems', he says, 'to have been visited by a premonition of her first biographer when she observed in her journal that 'a great many authors have expressed themselves too sentimentally'.

It was Farnie who invented the name 'Pet Marjory', for she was known to her family as Madie, Madgie, or Muffy. But it was Dr. John Brown, the author of *Rab and his Friends*, who made her famous. John Brown has been reprinted in Everyman's Library. He made Marjory live again, quoting her freely and now and then altering her text. The late Mr. Frank Sidgwick, another of Marjory's editors, has told us that in her famous poems on 'The Turkeys' and on 'The Charming Pug', Brown sometimes improved her rough lines. Marjory's most famous couplet is about the turkey who lost her three chicks:

> But she was more than usual calm;
> She did not give a single dam.

But these trifles are only grave in the eyes of scholars whose appreciation takes the form of treating a child's text with excessive reverence. After all, it is really thanks to Dr. Brown alone that we are acquainted with this brilliant child.

He was an artist in his sentimental way, and he saw what a delightful subject she would make if only there were another sympathetic figure in the picture. Walter Scott knew her, and nothing suited his canvas better than to portray Marjory as Scott's 'pet'. Scott was related to the Keiths, who were related to Marjory's mother. But both Esdaile and Sidgwick, Marjory's recent editors, have thrown doubt on the pretty embroideries which John Brown wove round the child and the novelist. His readers will remember how his account of Marjory Fleming begins.

We are watching Walter Scott, who has just taken up *Waverley* again, walking from the Parliament House in Edinburgh back to his home, and then sitting down in his large green morocco elbow-chair, in front of his writing apparatus. Next Brown imagines him discovering that he is in no mood for writing, and exclaiming: 'I can make nothing of *Waverley* today; I'll awa' to Marjory.' So Scott makes his way through a snowfall to

the house of his friend Mrs. Keith, with his dog Maida at
his heels. He takes the child home, wrapped in his plaid,
and the two remain together for 'three or more hours,
making the house ring with their laughter'. First, Scott
has to say his lessons, repeating nursery rhymes till
Marjory is satisfied that he is word-perfect; then 'he
would read ballads to her in his own glorious way, the
two getting wild with excitement over 'Gill Morrice' or
the 'Baron of Smailholm'; and he would take her on
his knee and make her repeat Constance's speeches in
King John till he swayed to and fro, sobbing his fill'.
Dr. Brown asks us to imagine 'the little creature drawing herself up to the height of her great argument':

> I will instruct my sorrows to be proud
> For grief is proud, and makes his owner stoop, . . .
> Here I and sorrows sit.

'Scott used to say', Brown adds, 'that he was amazed at
her power over him, saying to Mrs. Keith, "She's the
most extraordinary creature I ever met with, and her
repeating of Shakespeare overpowers me as nothing else
does."'

Of course there is writing-up in all this; it's the product
of imaginative expansion. And yet for my part I shall
continue to see this engaging child where I first found
her—on Walter Scott's knee—although Marjory only
mentions Scott once, and then only as the author of her
favourite ballad 'Helvellyn', while he never mentions
her at all in any of his letters.

Now here is a letter from Marjory herself to her elder
sister.

My dear Isa, I now sit down on my bottom to answer
all your kind and beloved letters which you was so

good as to write to me. This is the first time I ever wrote a letter in my life. There are a great many Girls in the Square and they cry just like a pig when we are under the painful necessity of putting it to Death. Miss Potune a Lady of my acquaintance praises me dreadfully. I repeat something out of Dean Swift and she said I was fit for the stage and you may think I was primed up with majestic Pride, but upon my word I felt myself turn a little birsay. Birsay is a word which is a word that William composed, which is—as you may suppose —a little enraged. This horrid fat simpleton says that my aunt is beautiful which is entirely impossible for that is not her nature.

And now listen to her poem on her monkey:

Sonnet

O lovely O most charming pug
Thy gracefull air & heavenly mug
The beauties of his mind do shine
And every bit is shaped so fine
Your very tail is most devine
Your teeth is whiter then the snow
Yor are a great buck & a bow
Your eyes are of so fine a shape
More like a christians then an ape
His cheeks is like the roses blume
Your hair is like the ravens plume
His noses cast is of the roman
He is a very pretty weomen
I could not get a ryhme for roman
And was oblidged to call it weoman

Both her latest editors quote a passage from one of Stevenson's letters, 'Marjory Fleming was possibly—no, I take back possibly—she was one of the noblest works of God'. That is an outburst excusable in a letter, but to quote it solemnly seems to me a mistake. If it were possible to make me hate children some ecstatic child-worshippers would do it; if it were possible to make Marjory Fleming dull it could be done by treating her as 'a classic'.

Marjory was a child-genius, and a natural one. Alas, they can also be manufactured. I trust no self-indulgent parent . . . will take the hint of how to do it from what I am about to say, for the process is not good for children; a child can be made, temporarily, into a genius in two ways: either by making it precociously self-conscious at an early age; or by retarding later its natural development. The first method works when the child has excellent faculties and a sensitive, sympathetic temperament. By playing on this it can be made to say or even write many pretty, quaint, unexpected things, which when quoted are likely to rouse wondering envy in other parents. But even if the child is slow and stolid, much the same results can be obtained at a later stage by forcing it to continue living in a dream-world when it is naturally becoming interested in humdrum realities.

Marjory Fleming was not subject to such treatment. She lived at a time when it was still considered the duty of children to grow up as quickly as possible, and she was born with a little battery of quick wits. She had a temper which she often found occasion to deplore, though now it even helps to make her attractive to us. She was a darling, but don't let us make too much fuss over her.

SIR DESMOND MACCARTHY: 'Pet Marjory' (1945), from *Memories.*

14

'Old Slowcoach'

In the next section of this book (pp. 98-105) the writer suggests that happiness depends largely upon creation, i.e. upon making things. Some people—engineers for example—are still fortunate in being able to find such happiness in their daily work, but machines now manufacture most things that men formerly found satisfaction and joy in making with their own hands. When we admire stone carvings in cathedrals and other churches built in the Middle Ages, we cannot help but marvel that it was by the slow labour of patient and loving hands that all that beauty was created. Happily in the new English cathedrals—Guildford, Coventry, and Liverpool—there has still been scope for craftsmen and craftswomen in the carvings and the stained glass and tapestries, yet it is nevertheless a sad fact that many fine workmen must have shared the experience of Thomas Hearne, nicknamed 'Old Slowcoach', in finding that their skill and devotion could not withstand the new demand for speed and cheapness.

FLORA THOMPSON

THOMAS HEARNE was a native of Restharrow, a stonemason, who, after spending his active years working for a firm of builders in a distant part of the county, had in his old age drifted back to the home of his childhood. Hearne had in his day been a first-class workman with experience, skill, and that something beyond skill which is a compound of taste and imagination. His firm had valued his services. When there had been a difficult or a delicate job to be done, it had been given to Hearne as a matter of course. Specimens of his workmanship stood, and some must still be standing, all over that country-side, in the renovated stonework of restored churches, the arches of bridges, stone piers at entrance gates, and on the façades of mansions. He had in his day instructed two generations of apprentices.

But by the eighteen-eighties Hearne's day was over. Physically he was past his prime, though still hale and hearty and capable of a full day's work at his bench in the shop, or of walking, toolbag on shoulder, three or four miles or more to an outside job. But times and ideas had changed and his fastidious, painstaking methods were out of date. Speed had become more important than craftsmanship and the artistry which aimed at nothing less than perfection was little esteemed. The more important jobs were being given to younger men, smart fellows who knew all the latest dodges for saving time and materials. Young workmen, apprentices but yesterday, would take upon themselves to instruct him in his craft. It had been all very well in his day, they told him, to go in for all this undercutting and finishing, but who was going to wait or to pay for it now? and the kindly disposed would bring their mallets and chisels over to Hearne's bench and show him what they called the tricks of the trade.

But Hearne had no use for tricks. He preferred to work as he had been taught to work, leisurely and lovingly, striving always to approach as nearly as possible to his own vision of perfection. For a few more years he con-tinued to use the bench which for more than a quarter of a century had been known as 'Hearne's', working steadily at such jobs as were given him, consulted by others less often than formerly and respected less, but never abating his own self-respect. In his home village he was liked and respected as a man with a good trade in his hands, who had a good wife and a pleasant, cheerful cottage, and there were some there who envied him those blessings, for it was a poor agricultural neighbourhood.

This state of things might have lasted until his working life had ended in the natural way had not his old employer, the head of the firm, died and his son, a young man with modern ideas and a determination to increase his business, come into possession. The firm was reorganized, the latest and cheapest methods were instituted, and in the new scheme there was no place for Hearne as leading mason. He was called into the office and told that a younger and smarter man was to have his bench in the shop. The young builder was about to add that he had no idea of cutting adrift an old servant like Hearne, that as long as he was able to work there would still be a job in the yard for him, an old man's job with an old man's wages, but, before he could speak further, Hearne took him up sharply. 'Is anything wrong with my work?' he demanded. His young employer hummed and hawed, for he had no wish to hurt Hearne's feelings. 'Well, since you ask me,' he said, 'I'll say that you're a bit too finicking. You put in too much time on a job to justify your wage in these competitive times.'

'But look at my work!' cried Hearne. 'Look at that east window tracery in Tisley Church, and the new keystone I let into the Norman arch at Bradbury, and that bridge over the Ouse at Biddingfold; masterpieces all

of 'em, though I says it as shouldn't. Other jobs, too.
You've only got to take a walk in the cool of the evening
and use your eyes and wherever you go in any direction
you'll find summat worth seein' with my mark 'pon it,'
and this he said, not pleadingly, but rather by way of a
challenge, and as he spoke he stretched out his arms as
though to call the whole neighbourhood as witness.

The young builder was in a difficult position. 'I know
all that,' he said. 'I'm not denying you've been a good
mason, a first-rate man in your day. But those were the
days of my father and grandfather and those times have
gone, the world's on the move, and the truth of the
matter, though I'm sorry to say it, is that you do your
work too well. You take too much time over it, and that
doesn't pay in these days. We've been out of pocket by
you for years.'

Hearne's fine dark eyes flamed and his long, thin old
figure shook with rage. 'Too much time over it!' he
shouted. 'Too much time! And how d'ee think good
work's allus been done? By hurrying? By scamping? By
begrudging a stroke here or a moment there? Look at
the churches round here. Bloxham for length, Adder-
bury for strength, and Kings Sutton for beauty! Think
they grew out o' th' ground like mushrooms? Or were
flung together by slick youngsters such as yourn? Let
me tell yer, young feller-me-lad, I learnt my craft from
them as made a craft o't, not a come day go day means
o' puttin' a bit o' bread in their mouths, and I ain't
goin' to alter my ways and disgrace my upbringin' for
nobody. I'll make up my time-sheet and you can put
one o' your slick youngsters at my bench, for I've done
with th' firm. And this I'll say before I've done with you
for ever: th' work of my hands'll be standin' to bear
witness for me when you and your like be frizzlin' in the

spot old Nick keeps specially hotted for bad workmen! '

Old Hearne neither starved nor entered the workhouse. For some years longer he made a poor livelihood by replacing roof tiles, building pigsties, setting grates, repairing walls, sweeping chimneys, or any other odd job which could be regarded, however remotely, as included in his own trade. When his wife died he left the village near the town where he had worked and returned to his native Restharrow, where he still owned the cottage in which he had been born, and there carried on his humble occupation of jobbing mason. On chimney-sweeping days he was grimy, but, at other times, he went about his work in the immemorial garb of his craft, corduroy trousers scrubbed white, or whitish, white apron girded up round the waist for walking, billy-cock hat and nondescript coat powdered with stone and mortar dust. He had become, as they said, as thin as a rake, and his fine dark eyes, into which the fire of fanaticism was creeping, had become so sunken that his forehead looked like that of a skull. By the time Charity first remembered him, he had become queer in his ways. Harvesters going to the fields at daybreak would meet him far from home, wild-eyed and wild-haired and dew-soaked. When asked where he had been he would whisper confidentially that he had been out all night, guarding some church or other building, but who had set him to guard them or what they were to be guarded against he would not say. Otherwise he talked more freely than he had been used to do and with many a 'he sez' and 'sez I' he would relate the story of his last interview with his former employer to anyone he could buttonhole. Everybody in the parish had heard the story, though few with sympathy, for it seemed to most of his listeners but an instance of a man throwing away a good job in a fit of temper, and, to save themselves from a third or fourth recital, when they saw Hearne in the distance they would turn aside to avoid a meeting. The more kindly spoke of him as 'poor old Tom Hearne', the less kindly as 'that tiresome old fool', and the children would tease him by calling after him, 'Tom! you're slow! You're too slow for a funeral! Old Slowcoach! Old Slowcoach!'

FLORA THOMPSON: from *Still Glides the Stream* (1948).

15

Happiness

Freya Stark is one of the most travelled and most intrepid of modern Englishwomen. Her journeyings in Arabia provided her with material for several fine travel books, and her autobiographical volumes are among the best of their kind. Long experience has convinced her, she declares in the present essay, that happiness comes from loving and making.

FREYA STARK

MY FATHER lived in a small wooden house in western Canada, where he carved himself out a fruit orchard from the hillside and the forest. He had chosen it with one of the most beautiful views in the world, an open valley and a river winding, with mountains beyond, and the Kootenay lake just visible in the north; and built himself a wide window, to look out on three sides. This window, and six Chippendale chairs which he had rescued in a farmer's sale, and a few of his sketches on the walls, were all the luxury of the place. I spent two winters with him, and once brought him a pot of primulas while the snow still lay heavy all around; but he soon took an occasion to say casually that he was not fond of forced plants: they took away something for him of the first rapture of the spring. His loves were very deep and gentle; they seemed not to be centred in islands of

98

possession, like most human loves, but to be diffused among people and animals and plants, and even the shapes of things he saw; for he was a most sensitive artist. He lived among flowers and was first in his valley to send for bulbs from Holland and to fill his orchard with daffodils under the flowering trees. He was a good rider and a great walker and fond of the woodsmen and the hunters, and those who spend half the year away from their fellow men visiting traps in the mountain forests.

Four years before his death, when he was seventy-two, a stroke took away from him the open-air life he loved; and though by the strength of his will he managed, step by step, with the passing months, to walk a mile or so with a stick to lean on, most of his time came to be spent in the window that looked out on his view. Here, he told me, the changing clouds and light of the river would fill his mind with pleasantness for hours at a time and lead his thoughts into endless variation: and I believe this to be true, and that he was happy, for not only did he never complain, but his whole atmosphere was one of serenity and peaceful interest in all things as they came. And later, when I have thought of happiness and what it may be, I have always seen his gentle old head in the window, with the hillside full of tame pheasants and pigeons, and the valley and the mountains beyond, and have felt that the secret must have something in it of those older worlds which were as real to him as ours.

There is, of course, an animal contentment—the simple joy of running or sleeping or lying in the sun—whose deep and satisfying streams creep into our veins from ages far remoter than man. This is perhaps the oldest happiness. Love is almost as old, and older in this world than we are; there seems to me no reason to call the finer feelings instinct, and to think of them as different in kind from ours when they belong to creatures other than ourselves. A few years before the war, the municipality of Venice awarded a medal and a daily saucer of milk to a cat who lived in amity with a neighbour on the edge of the same canal. They had their litters of kittens at the same time, and no doubt shared adventures and gossip until the neighbour slipped one day and was drowned. Her friend dived and tried unsuccessfully to save her; she then adopted the orphan family and suckled it with her own; and the municipality of Venice recognized and rewarded her.

I once spent two months taming a small lizard rescued from Beduin Arabs of the south, till he ate from my hand and knew me. If he was frightened he would swell himself out to the shape of a miniature balloon and shrink again at the touch and safety of my hand. He had small bright triangular black eyes, and would hold his head on one side and look out of them with a Pan-like wisdom, gay and remote from ours, and—for me alone when I stroked him—these eyes turned suddenly round in their sockets; this is a strange but, according to books, natural way for lizards to express affection. The small reptile body had to die unless the sun's rays warmed a blood that runs differently from ours; yet human qualities of curiosity and courage were strangely vivid within it. He crouched, as still and small and flat as he could make himself, under the shadow of a bird overhead, or of an aeroplane which he obviously held to belong to the same species; but he was ready to pick up his meal where he left it as soon as the shadow had passed, and to run round the garden nibbling at plants he had never known before. As I watched him I found it pleasant to see these human things—courage, fear, affection, anger—tracing back to a pedigree so immensely more ancient than ours.

Who can say in what remoteness of time, in what difference of earthly shape, love first came to us as a stranger in the jungle? We, in our human family, know him through dependence in childhood, through possession in youth, through sorrow and loss in their season. In childhood we are happy to receive; it is the first opening of love. In youth we take and give, dedicate and possess —rapture and anguish are mingled, until parenthood brings a dedication that, to be happy, must ask for no return. All these are new horizons of content, which the lust of holding, the enemy of love, slowly contaminates. Loss, sorrow and separation come, sickness and death; possession, that tormented us, is nothing in our hands; it vanishes. Love's elusive enchantment, his ubiquitous presence, again become apparent; and in age we may reach a haven that asking for nothing knows how to enjoy. Perhaps the whole of life is a learning how to accept—to become as children and wiser, with hands outstretched and open, grasping nothing?

However this may be, we see that the happiness of every age is in this creature love, incomplete or growing according to its place. In the desert of the world he is the angel who guards our sleep in Time; whose ladder is planted on the early forms of things and stretches through us far beyond our vision, with rich and dangerous rungs. Almost alone of all earthly gifts, the gift of loving is shared with God.

Embracing the familiar, it looks to the unknown and gazes like a child in its new world, with one hand ever for safety on the breast of earth its mother; and every revelation comes through some material door. A tendril of curl or curve of eyelash can unfold the universe: for the palpable world is our window, and there is no end to the perspective of ordinary things; the scenes of our life constantly open upon regions to which themselves scarcely belong. Sometimes, in some stillness, the secret is all about us, never held but almost to be perceived. In such moments the individual ceases to be conscious of himself; he has dissolved the familiar, he is part of what he looks at, a part of Happiness: for an instant he has stepped into that ocean of which we are the scattered pools and these moments are never forgotten. They make our lives like journeys through the plain whose vaporous summer hides the mountain ranges; until one day, through some bite of autumn in the air the mist dissolves, and reality appears unexpected; the hills shine on the horizon, luminous and lightly shadowed like crumpled almond blossom transparent to the sun: the hidden summits are discovered, and ever afterwards we know that they are there.

I remember one such time on Mount Carmel, when in the sunset the sea was dove-grey, with a rosy light like the neck of a dove. From my stony height it looked burnished with innumerable ridges, but flat and wide so that Beato Angelico could have made angels walk there with hems lightly lifted, into the dying furnace of the sun. The sky was green jade, very pale; and there were clouds grey and white, the colour of ashes, and a slim moon, translucent as the wax of candles burning, and spanned as a thin eyebrow, or tartar bow. All these things were subdued, except the evening star; and that shone, not gold, but like an alloy of brass and silver and with its pale light stood in the van of the shadows of dusk.

The door is opened by beauty or pain, delight or sorrow, into a universe whose processes are not complete —a divine workshop where one can live in the active partnership of God.

Creativeness, too, we share with the divine in our degree: and because of this partnership which exists only in loving or creating, I believe that these two energies alone can give us happiness.

The power to create does not appear to have grown like love, slowly out of the building of earth; it is our Promethean gift. The delight of it is felt in its simple stages, by the child with his toy boat on the stream, by the mechanic over his screw, or the painter at his easel. The wraith of this happiness still hovers on flint edges chipped evenly round the honey-coloured flakes men worked into axe or spear-head shapes in caves. I have seen a woman in an Indian village painting round-bellied jars baked in a fire of dung, crouching with her skirts circular on the bare hard threshing floor, where the chaff dances in the dry wind and sun. With one hand she held the jar, spanning its neck and pivoting it slowly on itself, while with the other, with grasses dipped in a mess of earth or ashes brown and white, she traced easy patterns that mankind has treasured throughout its prehistoric migrations.

I think the chain of continued creation makes the charm of old inhabited places and the melancholy of those fallen to ruin, which seem to testify to the waste of this best divinity in man. It is certainly the charm of Italy, where the whole landscape has been altered and indeed almost fashioned by the chisel or the plough. There is a grey keep crowning the little hill on which our town is settled; it looks like a windowless ark riding the last wave-crest of the small volcanic range which holds us; and its foundations are said to have been built, long before the Romans, by the Euganeans who left their name to another small volcanic range across the plain. Then the Romans must have made some *castrum* here, when they established us as a centre of government, and built baths beneath what is now the parish church, and a theatre in what is now my garden. In the Middle Ages the keep grew to its present shape, with thin battlements against the sky, and a wedge of walls down the steep grass slopes to embrace the town; into which the Renaissance built painted houses with Venetian Gothic windows and columns cut in stone. All this we have adapted to our use and live happily on the tangle, looking out, to the plain or to the other hill slopes far and near, at other small towns and hamlets freshly blossoming out of their ancient past. We look and realize that no other animal, except in a small way a beaver or an ant, has actually changed the appearance of the world as man is constantly doing.

Why should there be a quarrel between his past and future, between the tradition of his forgotten creativeness and his invention as it comes? The substance of both is the same: it is as if one footstep quarrelled with another on a slope where each climbs his own measure of the way.

But while there is pleasure in looking back over accomplishment, the word *happiness* must surely be reserved for that which actually allows us to share in the transformation. No mere knowledge, not even the acquisition of new knowledge, can give this firm delight. In it the amateur is joyful, the craftsman content, and the artist free of the weight of age. It is the secret of the pleasure women sometimes find in embroidery and men in gardens. Something is made, some combination of thoughts, materials, colours, which was not there before: imperfect as love, it shares with love the only divinity we have; it is our partnership in Creation.

FREYA STARK: 'Happiness', from *Perseus in the Wind* (1948).

16

A Cavalier Lady

The love letters written during the years 1652-54 by Dorothy Osborne to Sir William Temple, the diplomat and essayist whom she married in 1655 after a long engagement, are among the masterpieces of English literature, though they were not published until 1888 and she had no thought at all that they ever would be published. Written in the Commonwealth period, they have a double interest and attraction, for they introduce us to the atmosphere and feeling of that troubled time and also bring us into close touch with an enchanting young woman whose love for her husband-to-be was combined with unshakable personal dignity, and whose letters touch upon domestic subjects such as quince marmalade as well as upon affairs of greater moment.

LORD DAVID CECIL

DOROTHY SAW a certain amount of the neighbours: for, though the disturbances of the time had diminished the social life of the country gentry, it had not upset the structure of society so much as to stop it altogether. On occasions of official festivity, like Christmas, people still climbed into their coaches to jolt over the cart-tracks they called roads, in order to consume a heavy dinner together. Married couples and recent arrivals to the district still paid and received visits of ceremony. County society was no more brilliant than it is now; certainly not

106

so brilliant as to lure Dorothy from her shell. For the most part she found these entertainments a burden. Still, they had their compensations. It was delightful to get the chance to look at beautiful Lady Grey de Ruthin for example; or to talk over the news with charming, intelligent Lady Diana Rich. Though Dorothy preferred living out of the great world, she was always interested to hear about it. Now, especially, when she was buried down at Chicksands, she drank up every item of information. Sometimes the news was political. With ironical amusement Dorothy heard of the difficulties overtaking the revolutionary government. Cromwell's expulsion of the Parliament, for example; what would Mr. Pym have said, she wondered, had he lived to see this consequence of the victory of the so-called party of freedom. No doubt such speculations were treasonable she commented sarcastically; she had better check them. She was also entertained that people should be so shocked at General Monk marrying a seamstress. Surely she was no more unsuitable to her position than the rest of the Parliamentary ladies. For the most part, however, Dorothy kept off politics. They reminded her too painfully of what she longed to forget. For the dark cloud of death and defeat still brooded, ominous and unbroken over the landscape of the private scene. If one raised one's eyes there it was, casting a shadow over the spirit. Nearly every family of her acquaintance had its tragedy. Lady Diana Rich's father had been executed; so had Lady Anne Wentworth's. Dorothy heard that Mr. Waller, the poet, was writing a romance about the recent war. 'If he does not mingle it with a great deal of pleasing fiction it cannot be very diverting, sure,' she said, 'the subject is so sad.'

There was nothing sad about social news, however. Dorothy enjoyed this thoroughly. The scandals and the vagaries of the Caroline aristocracy dance their way through her pages, blending strangely with the melancholy of her reflections on life and the sweetness of her words of love. Fancy Lady Isabella Thynne marrying a man 'no better than a beast, only because he had a great estate'; or Miss de Mayerne falling in love with 'a buffle-headed French Marquis' and kissing him publicly in the Park too; or Lord Leicester quarrelling with his wife after forty years of tranquil marriage, and dismissing all the servants just to spite her; or the fantastic Lady Newcastle publishing a book of verses! 'They say 'tis ten times more extravagant than her dress', said Dorothy; and, when she had read it, 'I am satisfied there are many soberer people in Bedlam.'

News and visitors, however, were only an occasional interruption in her sequestered existence. Indeed, though they might entertain her for a moment, they only ruffled the surface of her attention. During the long hours she spent alone she thought little about them; and these were the hours she valued most. Throughout the cold spring months, she escaped from company whenever she could to muse with a book over the fire; or, when the days warmed and lengthened, to wander in the countryside. Summer weather quickened her feelings to a peculiar intensity. Living as they did far closer to the primitive earth than we do, the Carolines were far more affected by its moods. How untiringly and with what an unfailingly responsive zest do their poets harp on the changes of the seasons; green Spring, Summer with its July flowers, the rich fecundity of Autumn. The cold dark Winter months, spent in those unheated houses, chilled and darkened the hearts of their inhabitants. At the turn of the year, when the buds broke and the birds began to sing and build, their spirits too bloomed and

carolled in sympathy. Dorothy has left us a record of a
typical summer day at Chicksands. She rose early, and
after seeing to the household, stepped out into the garden
to taste the morning freshness. When it grew too hot—
they seem to have been strangely sensitive to heat in
those days—she went to pay a visit to Sir Peter lying
always immobile in his bedroom before settling down to
array herself in all the elaboration of Caroline full dress.
Next came dinner, conducted—even if she were alone or
with a single guest—with formal ceremony in the great
dining-room. The afternoon was spent in retirement,
reading or sewing. Then, when the fierceness of the day's
heat had begun to abate, she went out once more. ' About
six or seven o'clock I walk out into a common that lies
hard by the house, where a great many young wenches
keep sheep and cows and sit in the shade singing ballads.
I go to them and compare their voices and beauties to
some ancient shepherdesses that I have read of, and find
a vast difference there. But, trust me, I think these are as
innocent as those could be. I talk to them and find they
want nothing to make them the happiest people in the
world but the knowledge that they are so. Most commonly, when we are in the midst of our discourse, one
looks about her and spies a cow going into the corn, and
away they all run as if they had wings at their heels. I
that am not so nimble stay behind, and, when I see
them driving home their cattle, I think 'tis time for me
to retire too.' Supper followed; and after supper back
into the open air where, amid the fading twilight, sweet
with the vagrant scents of a country evening, she would
stroll in the garden or sit by the banks of the stream,
dreaming—of Temple and love undying and hope
deferred—while time slipped by unnoticed, till suddenly she looked up and it was night and she must steal

E

back into the silence of the sleeping house, and, candle in hand, climb the shadowy staircase to bed.

The current of her meditations was coloured by her reading. Dorothy read enormously, anything she could lay hands on, poetry, travels, devotional works, romances. Romances were what she liked best. It seems odd that it should have been so; for the romances of that age are, to our eyes, very tedious affairs; incredible, interminable tales, couched in a style of stilted rhetoric about Amestris and Aglatides, Artibis and Cleobuline, kings and princesses of preposterous beauty and virtue, who strut their way, volume after volume, through a monotonous labyrinth of improbable intrigue, conventional sentiment, and far-fetched punctilios of honour. Dorothy, however, discussed their characters as seriously as we should discuss that of Anna Karenina, cried over their troubles, and was so enthralled by their adventures that she would sit up reading, night after night, long after she should have been in bed. Like the rest of her contemporaries, she was accustomed to rhetoric, and found no difficulty in believing the improbable. Besides, the subject of these romances was love. And love was to Dorothy the most interesting subject in the world.

How should it have been otherwise! In the radiant warmth of her re-union with Temple, the flower of her passion had opened wide, so that it now diffused its invisible perfume over her every mood and thought. 'My very dreams are yours', she cries to him. Wherever she was and whatever she was doing—gazing at the shepherdesses, topicking with cousin Molle, drowsily watching by her father's bedside in the silence of the night—the figure of Temple floated before her mental eye, obscuring the outside world. She grew more abstracted than ever. One evening, seated by the fire in company with her brother and a friend of his, lost in her own thoughts, she found her attention suddenly seized by their conversation. They were talking about flying. Ah! If she could cover the distance between herself and Temple with such an airy swiftness! To their amused surprise Dorothy suddenly broke silence, demanding excitedly if flying was really going to be possible. Nor did love only increase her absentmindedness. The arrival of the post, for instance, agitated her so violently as to make her for the time being quite unlike her usual controlled self. She would shout to the maid, calling her in the dim dawn to tear open the curtains in order that she might see if any of the letters that had come to her were from Temple; she would drop her hand in the middle of a game of cards because she heard a courier from London riding by; and she would stand in the mud and straw of the stable exasperatedly upbraiding the groom for daring to unharness his horse before opening the letter bag. When they did come, Temple's letters never seemed long enough for her. 'If you do not send me long letters, then you are the cruellest person that can be. If you love me you will, and, if you do not, I shall never love myself.'

Interest in her own love-story led her to speculate on the subject of love in general. In this she was the child of her age. It is hardly to be supposed that the Carolines felt the passion of love more intensely than we do; but certainly they thought about it much more. Four-fifths of their poetry is love-poetry; and their prose too is largely devoted to celebrating its glories, analysing its nature and cataloguing its varieties. The fact that they were an aristocratic society accounts partly for this preoccupation. Alas, it is only people untroubled by the necessity of making a living who have the leisure and energy to study their sentiments with this elaborate refinement. But in the Carolines, natural tendency was encouraged by their ideal mode of thought. If love was a worthy passion, then it had to be fitted into their general philosophical scheme, and its relation to the principle of virtue must be discovered and defined. Further, believing in form as they did, they were interested to decide the correct mode for love's expression. How should a lover speak and dress and behave himself in the presence of his mistress, they asked themselves. With what appropriate graces should he adorn the utterance of his heart? At once a faith and a fine art, love was to them a necessary element of the good life, and as such required intensive study.

Yet their view of it was not the same as that of latter-day amorists. Nowhere does their peculiar blend of realism and romance appear more conspicuously. In some ways it was a highly romantic view. Did they not see in the affinity of two noble spirits a symbol and revelation of the divine harmony of the universe, and in the lover's desire for the beloved an expression of the desire of the soul for perfection? But they did not think in the Byronic fashion that love had a right to override every other consideration in order to achieve its fulfilment. On the contrary, the very fact that they considered it a necessary element of the good life meant that it must not be permitted to clash with its other elements. At every turn passion must take account of the obligations of religion, of man's duty to society and his family. Dorothy's conviction of the value of convention made her especially conscious of these obligations. For although love meant so much to her, she thought it should be kept on a tight rein. Unbridled passion was always wrong, above all in women. A woman must be sure her love was requited before she yielded to it, much less confess it to the man of her choice. Even then she should make sure that it was a rational passion, founded on esteem for his character. Apart from anything else, what she had seen of the world had taught Dorothy that unless it was so founded, it would soon evaporate. 'When there is no reason to uphold a passion', she notes, 'it will sink of itself.'

'But', she goes on, 'when there is, it may last eternally.' If all the conditions were satisfied, if it was grounded on regard and ruled by principle, then Dorothy conceived of love with all the enthusiastic elevation of her age. True love was the expression of a complete and unique harmony between two minds and hearts. An equal harmony too; for though, for form's sake, lovers might speak of one another as mistress and servant, in relation to their love they were free and equal partners.

LORD DAVID CECIL: from 'Dorthy Osborne' in *Two Quiet Lives* (1948).

17

An English Cricketer

There are more good books about cricket than about any other English sport. Fishing has its masterpiece in Izaak Walton's The Compleat Angler (1653), and there is a scattering of readable books about boxing and horse-racing and hunting. Let us hope that masterpieces will one day be written about football. Among contemporary writers Neville Cardus on cricket has been outstanding, but his best pieces on this topic were done before 1940. John Arlott's cricket broadcasts were for some years a compensation for any inability to play or watch the game. Here he portrays in character and action one of cricket's modern masters. Compton not only made big scores, he also made them in a graceful and joyous style.

JOHN ARLOTT

THE YEAR 1947 saw Denis Compton break Hobbs's record for the number of centuries scored in an English season and Tom Hayward's record for a season's aggregate. Yet, and this is the most important thing about Denis Compton, he broke those records without ever, for a moment, adopting the customary manner of the record-breaker. This method, as we have seen it of recent years in almost every sport, is the stolid, machine-like, quantitative triumph of soullessness, attained by complete elimination of risk and beauty in execution. It is a sign of grace that Denis Compton broke two great records without

114

sign of such method. He went through the warm summer of 1947 playing cricket gaily, and it happened that in doing so he made so many runs that two records were broken. Never, in either of his innings which finally broke the records, was any trace to be observed of Compton doing any other than playing just as Denis Compton always plays.

And how does Denis Compton play? He simply *plays*—like a boy striking at a rubber ball with a paling from a fence—for fun. He plays happily. Oh yes, many of his strokes cause the academically minded cricket critics to turn in horror—only to be won back at once by the air of charm which Compton lends to every game he plays. His bat may be a foot from his left leg when he plays forward through the covers. He will start to go down the wicket before the ball is bowled, and then, when it cannot be driven and he is, apparently, high and dry two yards down the pitch, he will ruefully change his shot and, with the handle of the bat sticking into his navel, take a casual poke at the ball to send it scuttling between cover and third man for four runs. Rarely has a man made runs so negligently, never has a man made so many runs without seeming to take thought for the safety of his method.

Analysis of Compton's method shows, as Alan Melville's field-placing underlined, that he plays very little between widish mid-off and widish mid-on. This gap apart, he will play the ball almost anywhere in the field with an advantage—due to an almost inhuman capacity for knowing, as he plays the ball, just where the field is. It has been observed of some great badminton players that they can take their eye off the fastest shuttle for a split second as it comes to them, or, colloquially, look out of the corner of the eye, to see, or feel, exactly where the opposition is stationed. This gift Compton possesses to an amazing degree: his strokes seem, time and again, to pass between the fielders with uncanny accuracy. He has a perfect eye and his sense of the behaviour of a ball is born in him, so that timing is to him like breathing. He must, being partly unconscious of the rarity of his own gifts, and never having known the lack of them, sometimes wonder why people make so much fuss about batting.

There is the enviable, delightful paradox: Compton obtains all the results of care and study by methods which seem negligent. He hits through the covers as hard as the greatest batsmen, yet with off-handed strokes: he shrugs the ball off his leg stump to long leg, he late cuts like a boy playing touch-last, and he seems to have more time than there is to play his hook wide of the fieldsman —yet to play that shot as a makeshift because he cannot be bothered to remember any other stroke. To watch Compton is to see the ball travelling all over the ground with bowlers and fieldsmen almost hopeless. Characteristically, he is happiest of all with the most difficult of all balls to play—the ball that leaves the bat off the pitch; Compton hits it away on the offside and will even raise a foot in a negligent kick along the line of the departed ball.

It may be that, when his magnificent eye dims a little, when his fitness diminishes with age, he will be unable to play as he does now. It may be that, when that happens, his brain will not be sufficiently utilitarian to eliminate his more risky shots. If that day comes, then we may find some of his contemporaries better batsmen in their dog-days than Compton. Then we shall know that this glorious phase of Compton was only possible in one summer, the sun's summer of a century and the summer of a man's life. And that will help to adjust perspective: then facts will confirm our impression that we have seen, in this year of 1947, a rare fire of batsmanship that can never burn again because it was unique—the 'rose that once has blown'. It cannot go on. Never again, surely, shall we watch even Denis Compton make all the runs in the world in a few weeks, yet, so far from tiring of watching him, wish that he might go on for ever. To close the eyes is to see again that easy, happy figure at the wicket, pushing an unruly forelock out of the eyes and then, as it falls down again, playing, off the wrong foot, a stroke which passes deep point like a bullet. Never again will cold, hard figures be smashed so light-heartedly, never again will the boyish delight in hitting a ball with a piece of wood flower directly into charm and gaiety and all the wealth of achievement.

Compton is not merely a batsman, he is a cricketer, a natural cricketer who almost makes the spectators believe that there was never a genuine natural cricketer before. He fields with a dash, anticipation, and negligent assurance of hand that is the despair of all who have laboured long for less return of grace and effect.

He rarely bowls; yet he was trusted with England's slow left-arm bowling, and once he almost succeeded, once failed. Then he took bowling seriously for almost a week: as a long-scoring batsman, he did not need to bowl at all, but now batting, deep-fielding and all, he appeared bowling the 'Chinaman' and the Fleetwood-Smith googly with an accomplishment which would have been commendable after a season of practice. His bowling will obviously be better when he pauses to think and take breath between deliveries rather than trot back, turn, run up, and bowl, letting the weight of the ball swing the arm over, in a rapid, unbroken flow of action.

E*

But are there any rules to be quoted in respect of the cricket of Denis Compton? I doubt it: if he were not so gaily, chucklingly friendly with us we might regard his batting as a kind of fairy story—and, in the end, when a younger generation, who never saw him, ridicules our stories of him behind our backs, then we shall know that it *was* all a fairy story—that it was a dream that passed across English cricket in a summer of amazing sun and lit the farthest corner of every field in the land.

JOHN ARLOTT: from *Gone to the Cricket* (1948).

18

Producing a Play

Everyone knows that Bernard Shaw was a great play-
wright and a great critic of drama and music, but fewer
know that he was also great as a producer and rehearser
of his own plays. He knew what he wanted, knew how it
was to be done, and knew how to show others how to do
it. He might infuriate the actors with his demands if
things were going awry, but there were few who did not
trust and respect him, for he trusted and respected them
also, if they knew their business. Shaw continued to write
plays and much else throughout the period covered by
this anthology, but all his best creative work was done
before 1940. The present essay on play-production has
not been reprinted among his collected works, but its
preservation here makes a good deal of valuable practical
experience available to those concerned with school or
other amateur dramatic performances.

BERNARD SHAW

THE PRODUCER, having considered the play, and decided
to undertake the job of producing it, has no further
concern with its literary merits or its doctrine (if any).

In selecting the cast no regard should be given to
whether the actors understand the play or not (players
are not walking encyclopedias); but their ages and personalities should be suitable, and their voices should not
be alike. The four principals should be soprano, alto,

tenor, and bass. Vocal contrast is of the greatest importance, and is indispensable for broadcasting.

The play should be read to the company, preferably
by the author if he or she is a competent dramatic
reader: if not, by the best available substitute. If none is
available, no reading is better than a bad one.

To the first rehearsals the producer must come with
the stage business thoroughly studied, and every entry,
movement, rising and sitting, disposal of hat and umbrella, etc., is settled ready for instant dictation; so that
each player will be in the most effective position to
deliver his lines and not have to address an intimate
speech to a player at the other side of the stage, nor to
follow such a player without a line or movement to transfer the attention of the audience accordingly. The exits
must be carefully arranged so that the players leave the
stage immediately on their last word, and not hold up
the play until they have walked to the door. If the
producer arrives at the first rehearsal without this blue-
print, and proceeds to waste the players' time improvising
at their expense, he will never gain their confidence;
and they will be perfectly justified in going home
after telling him not to call them again until they can
devote all the rehearsals to their proper function of
acting.

To appreciate the necessity for this laborious planning
one has only to imagine a trial-at-law in a room without
bench, bar, or jury box, or a service in a cathedral without altar, choir, or pews: in short, without an appointed
place for anybody. This is what the stage is until the
producer has made a complete plan, called a prompt
copy. Properly such a plan is the business of the author;
for stage directions are as integral to a play as spoken
dialogue. But the author may be dead. Or in view of the

fact that writing dialogue (of *Hamlet,* for instance) is a pleasurable act of creation, whereas deciding whether the Ghost shall enter from the right or the left is pure drudgery, the author may leave the drudgery to the producer. He mostly does.

It is not necessary to use a model stage for this job. All that is necessary is a chessboard with its chessmen, and a boy's box of assorted bricks. With these all scenes and furniture can be indicated and all movements made. Unless this is done some movements, especially exits, are likely to be forgotten by even the most experienced producer.

The players should be instructed not to study their parts at this stage, and to rehearse, book in hand, without any exercise of memory.

When the movements are thoroughly rehearsed and mastered, the producer should ask the players whether they are comfortable for them all, and if not, what is wrong.

All being satisfactorily arranged, books are discarded, and rehearsals called 'perfect': that is, with the parts memorized. The producer now leaves the stage and sits in the front of the house with an electric torch and a notebook; and from that moment he should watch the stage as a cat watches a mouse, but never utter a word nor interrupt a scene during its repetition no matter how completely the play goes to pieces, as it must at first when the players are trying to remember their parts and cues so desperately that they are incapable of acting. Nothing betrays the inexperienced producer more than dismay at this collapse, with outbursts of reproach and attempts to get everything right at every rehearsal. The old hand knows that he must let the players memorize their words before they can act their parts.

At the end of each act, the producer returns to the stage to explain or demonstrate such of his notes as may be judicious at the moment. But no fault should be mentioned or corrected unless and until its constant repetition shows that the player will not correct it in his or her own way as the play is gradually learnt. When all the players are letter perfect their memorizing will be so mechanical that if one of them makes a slip by repeating an early cue later on, the rest will pick it up again and repeat what they have just been through, proving that the memorizing phase is over. The producer can now return to the stage and interrupt as often as may be necessary.

The danger is that as the players can now utter their words without thinking they will catch one another's speed and tone, betraying to the audience that they are only gabbling off a prearranged list of words, each knowing what the other will say next and fielding their cues like cricketers. The producer must accordingly take care that every speech contrasts as strongly as possible in speed, tone, manner, and pitch with the one which provokes it, as if coming unexpected as a shock, surprise, stimulant, offence, amusement, or what not. It is for the author to make this possible; for in it lies the difference between dramatic dialogue and epic narrative. A play by a great poet, in which every speech is a literary masterpiece, may fail hopelessly on the stage because the splendid speeches are merely strung together without provoking one another, whereas a trumpery farce may win an uproarious success by its retortive backchat.

The final phase of production is that of 'dress rehearsal' with costumes, scenery, and make-up all complete as for public performance, instead of everyday dress and a bare stage with the doors marked with a couple of chairs. It is now the producer's turn to be more upset by the change than the actors. Everything seems to have become wrong and incredible. However, the producer soon learns to be prepared for this, even if he never quite gets over the first shock of it. He is now back on the stage, going through the passages that need finishing, and generally doing what he likes. A bad last rehearsal need not alarm him: in fact he should connive at its failure lest the players should be too confident of success 'on the night' and not do their utter best.

The time needed for the production of a full-length play on this method is roughly a week for the stage movements, book in hand, with the producer on the stage; a fortnight for the memorizing, with the producer off the stage silent, watching, and taking notes; and a week for the dress, with the producer on the stage again, directing and interrupting *ad lib*.

Rehearsals should be most strictly private. No journalist or lay visitor of any kind should be present. When for some reason it may be necessary to allow strangers to witness a rehearsal, no instruction nor correction should be addressed in their presence to a player; and the consent of every player should be obtained before the permission is granted. To emphasize the fact that what the visitors are witnessing is only a rehearsal, a pre-arranged instruction should be addressed to a stage carpenter, never to a player.

During the memorizing phase a muffed passage must never be repeated on the spot, even if the players desire it. The producer's word must be, 'No: you will not be able to repeat it on the night; and you must not make a habit of a mistake. Go right on.' A producer who says, 'We must go over and over this again until we get it right' is not producing: he is schoolmastering, which is the worst thing he can do. Repetitions on the spot do not improve: they deteriorate every time.

Never find fault until you know the remedy; and never discuss a passage with a player: shew how the passage should be done as a suggestion, not an order; and exaggerate your demonstration sufficiently to prevent the player giving a mere imitation of it. A performance in which the players are all mimicking the producer, instead of following his suggestions in their own different ways, is a bad performance. Above all, do not, instead of demonstrating a passage, say, 'This scene is essentially pathetic' (or comic as the case may be). If you do, the player will come to the next rehearsal bathed in tears from the first word to the last, or clowning for all he is worth all the time.

The notes taken by the producer as he silently watches the players are a test of his competence. If, for example, he writes, 'Shew influence of Kierkegaard on Ibsen in this scene,' or 'The Edipus complex must be very apparent here. Discuss with the Queen,' the sooner he is packed out of the theatre and replaced the better. If they run, 'Ears too red,' 'Further up to make room for X,' 'Pleecemin,' 'Reel and Ideel,' 'Mariar Ann,' 'He, not Ee,' 'Contrast,' 'Change speed: Andante,' 'Shoe sole arches not blacked,' 'Unladylike: keep knees together,' 'More dialogue to give them time to get off,' 'This comes too suddenly,' '? Cut this???' and the like, then the producer knows his job and his place.

When a play is by Shakespeare such notes will crop up as 'The green one red,' 'Tibbeeyernottibeethatiz,' 'Become to Dunsinane,' 'Babbled,' 'Lo here I lenthee thishar pointed sword,' meaning that the playing should say, 'Making the green, one red,' 'To be? Or NOT to be? that is the question,' 'Though Birnam Wood BE come to

Dunsinane'; that Malone's silly 'A babbled o' green fields' should be discarded for his original, 'His nose was as sharp as a pen on a table of green frieze'; and that consecutive consonants must be articulated, as in 'lend thee' and 'sharp pointed'. Othello must not change chaste stars into chaste tars.

The duration of rehearsals is limited by the producer's endurance. Continuous watching with the necessary concentration is much more exhausting than acting, as the players, having only their own parts to deal with, are not continually on the stage, whilst the producer has all the parts to watch without a break. Three hours is the utmost a thoroughly vigilant and capable producer can manage. If he goes on longer he is doing no good.

In arranging hours players with only a few lines to speak should not be kept hanging about all day whilst the principals are rehearsing. Late night rehearsals are most objectionable. Neither players nor producers should work when they ought to be in bed. If such rehearsals are unavoidable the players who are kept too late for their last trains or buses should be paid their taxi fares home.

A play may need to be cut, added to, or otherwise altered, sometimes to improve it as a play, sometimes to overcome some mechanical difficulty on the stage, sometimes by a passage proving too much for an otherwise indispensable player. These are highly-skilled jobs, and should be done by the author, if available, or if not, by a qualified playwright, not by a player, nor by the callboy. Copyright in all such changes passes to the author. A player who reveals the plot or words of an unperformed play to the Press can be sued for breach of confidence at common law or under the Copyright Act.

These rules are founded on experience. They are of no use to a producer who regards players not as fellow-

artists collaborating with him, but as employees on whom
he can impose his own notions of acting and his own
interpretation of the author's meaning. He must let the
players learn the play, and not expect them to know it all
as well as he does at the first rehearsal. He must distinguish between born actors who should be let alone to
find their own way, and spook actors who have to be
coached sentence by sentence and are helpless without
such coaching. There are so many degrees between these
extremes that the tact and judgment of producers in
their very delicate relations with players are sometimes
strained to the utmost; and there is no effective check on
the despotism of the producer except his own conscience,
because only the most ungovernable players dare risk
being blacklisted by an authority so potent in the selection of casts as the producer. This is why docile players
are usually less often unemployed (which means running
into debt) than better rebellious ones.

In stock companies, where the programme changes
from week to week or even from night to night, there can
be no selection of the cast and no time to learn the play.
Players have to 'swallow' their speeches as best they can,
and deliver them, not in the author's characterization, but
in their specialities such as juvenile lead, *ingénue*, walking
gentleman, light comedian, singing chambermaid (*sou-
brette*), heavy old man (*père noble*), old woman, utility,
and so forth. Each plays every part in the same way:
there neither is nor can be any distinction between Pol-
onius and Lafeu, Adam and old Gobbo, Countess Rousil-
lon and Lady Macbeth, Juliet and Ophelia, Aguecheek
and Roderigo. Each male player has one combat (sixes);
and all have one stepdance for the Christmas pantomime.
Obviously the foregoing production method has a very
limited application here; but the preparation beforehand

of the producer's prompt copy—if there be a producer—
is doubly necessary to save time.

Repertory companies which, instead of 'supporting'
touring stars, rely on their own performances of the best
plays they can get, are genuine prentice schools of acting,
because the players are not 'rats of the theatre', in it
only because as children of players they are born to it,
but because they come from the educated laity, and have
made their way into the theatre against all prudent
parental advice, for love of it. Stock players are a
hereditary caste. Though their power of swallowing
words in a few hours and improvising (ponging) and
gagging is amazing, they finally become incapable of
character study, and are never really word-perfect. When
age brings loss of memory they have to be fed by the
prompter word for word, as Italian actors are always as
a matter of course. They are obsessed with stage tradi-
tions and superstitions: to them all religious sages are
Tartuffes or Malvolios, all old husbands cuckolds, all
women either brides or Lady Wishforts, and all plays
either fictitious police news of murders committed by
Heavies (villains), or harlequinades, or an orotund but
senseless variety of stage-work called shakespeare.

Some good players can act sobriety perfectly, though
off the stage they are drunk and incapable. The same is
true of fever temperatures, sciatica, lameness, and even
partial paralysis. This curious fact, apparently unknown
to psychologists, must be taken into account by producers lest they should sack an Edmund Kean or
Frederick Robson (who both drank themselves into
heroic fame and premature death) and retain a Gustavus
Brooke (a great actor when sober, reeling and inarticu-
late when drunk, as he often was). In the logbooks of
Drury Lane, when it was a patent theatre in the eigh-

teenth century, are such entries as 'No performance: Mr. Kemble drunk.'

When a player repeatedly omits some physical feat or movement, the producer must conclude that it is made impossible by some infirmity which the player would rather die than disclose. In such cases the business must be altered.

A producer sometimes has an antiquarian job. He may be called on to produce a play by, say, Euripides or Aristophanes as it was produced in Athens 2356 years ago. Or one of the pious Mysteries as the Church produced them in the Middle Ages. Or an Elizabethan drama on an Elizabethan stage. Or a Restoration or early Victorian play on a stage with proscenium, wings, and flats.

He should know that the Athenian stage was an imposing tribune in the open air on which the actors, in mask, sock, and busken, strutted in conventional hierarchic costumes, and that as scenery and curtains were undreamt of, and changes of place impossible, the action of the play had to pass in the same place on the same day. These conditions are called the Unities. On later stages and on the cinema screen they are negligible superstitions, but their observance still has great dramatic value. On the medieval stage unity of place was got rid of by a wide stage on which half a dozen different places were shown simultaneously. Heaven, the jaws of hell, the throne of the Blessed Virgin, the Garden of Gethsemane, the Mount of Olives, the Court of Pilate, the house of Caiaphas, were all in full view together, with the actors moving from one to the other as the story dictated. The Elizabethan stage, adaptable to inn yards, had no scenery. The stage was surrounded by inn galleries, and had a balcony and an inner stage in the middle with curtains called traverses in which indoor scenes were played.

This inner stage, still in use at Oberammergau and elsewhere for Passion Plays, is important because it enables actors entering from the back at opposite sides to be seen by the audience before they can see one another, thus making possible such scenes as the first in Romeo and Juliet, in which the Montagues and Capulets talk out of sight of one another, and set the spectators wondering what will happen when they meet. The best example, however, is at Oberammergau, where the procession to Calvary starts upstage on the prompt side, and has to turn two corners before it passes out up the opposite avenue. At the first corner it is confronted with a comic character, Simon, going to market with his basket. He is seized by the soldiers, who compel him to help Jesus to carry the heavy cross. But as the fainting Christ in extreme exhaustion drags himself towards the second corner, the Virgin appears descending the avenue, and it is apparent that they must meet and turn the crude fun of the Simon encounter into the deepest tragedy.

It was for the sake of such effects that when the Elizabethan stage was succeeded by the Restoration stage with painted scenery viewed through a proscenium acting as a picture frame, the scenes were pierced to provide avenues through which the actors could be seen before they could see one another. There were also doors in the proscenium through which the principal players could enter, with pages bearing the women's trains, not in historic costumes, but in the full court dress of the period. Old toy theatres preserve this type of stage. Every producer should possess one; for effects are possible on it that are not possible in modern built-in sets. For instance, when there are three wide entrances between the wings on both sides of the stage a crowd can be cleared off it almost instantaneously. The very few who are old enough to have seen Queen Elizabeth and her court apparently sink into the earth and disappear when Ristori, as Marie Stewart, called her 'the Bastard of England', will appreciate how a modern producer is hampered by having to clear the stage through one door.

Modern production includes film production, in which there is no limit to scenic possibilities; and producers may spend millions of pounds profitably instead of a few thousands. The results so far include megalomaniac demoralization, disorganization, and waste of time and money. These evils will cure themselves. Meanwhile the art of the playwright and producer remains basically the same. The playwright has to tell a good story, and the producer to 'get it across'.

This is all that can be learned by a producer from anything but experience and natural vocation. Like all methods it depends for success on the taste and talent with which it is practised.

There is no sex disqualification for producing. Women producers are at no disadvantage in comparison with men. As in marriage and queenship, the grey mare is often the better horse.

BERNARD SHAW: from 'Rules for Play Producers'
in the *Strand Magazine* (July 1949).

19

A Gentleman Pretending

*When Bernard Shaw reached the age of ninety in 1946,
a large number of his eminent friends and admirers col-
laborated to produce a book in his honour entitled* G.B.S.
90: Aspects of Bernard Shaw's Life and Work. *For many
years critics and others who knew little or nothing about
his private life and personality had spread the impression
that he was a hard-hearted and ungenerous man; but
the truth appeared from the personal essays in* G.B.S. 90
*that he was ' one of the kindest and most generous men '
—words written by Professor Gilbert Murray who had
been one of Shaw's multitude of friends for half a century; while another old associate, Dr. W. R. Inge, Dean
of St. Paul's Cathedral, started his essay ' Mr. Shaw, one
of the kindest friends I ever had . . .'. In the essay
printed below, a well-known writer belonging to a
younger generation gives an impression of Bernard Shaw
which is free from any bias that personal friendship
might give. The value of J. B. Priestley's essay is that,
whether his conclusions are right or wrong, he observes
the various aspects of character that Shaw displayed to
the public. He acknowledges Shaw's ' patience and good
humour and courtesy ' and quotes with understanding
the honest remark of Hilaire Belloc (who, as an impas-
sioned Roman Catholic, was no sympathizer with Shaw's
scepticism) that however Bernard Shaw might pretend
otherwise he was a gentleman—in the proper sense of
that word.*

131

J. B. PRIESTLEY[1]

NEARLY FORTY-FIVE years ago, when I began writing a weekly page for the *Bradford Pioneer*, I became acquainted with a group of enthusiastic Shavians, who lived for the Master's next work or pronouncement. When they attended one of his plays, everything in it—costumes, wigs, and all—brought screams of laughter from them. They seemed to me then rather silly people, and I doubt if I would change my mind now. They also gave me a prejudice against their wonderful, inimitable G.B.S. and it took me years to get it out of my system, if ever I completely did. I met him on a good many occasions, not only on committees and at parties but also under his own roof and mine; but though we had the theatre as common ground, I never felt at ease with him: he was too much my senior, nearly forty years; he might be considerate both as host and guest, as indeed he was, but it was clear that I was heavily addicted to all the smaller vices from which he was free; on the other hand, he seemed to me the victim of two vices from which I felt myself to be reasonably free, namely, talking too much and showing off. But of course by this time he was fixed in his role of The Ancient of Days; I never even caught a glimpse of him—though I might easily have done, for he often visited Bradford—in his earlier and greater role as a red-bearded, Jaeger-type Mephistopheles.

It was the greater role because, to my mind, that was when his best work was done. Although he became almost a symbolic figure of old age, it was G.B.S. in early middle-age who wrote the plays that will last

[1] This article on Bernard Shaw appeared in *The New Statesman and Nation* after Shaw's death in 1950 and was reprinted in the volume named at the end.

longest. I am not even excepting *Saint Joan* and *Heart-break House*. For a time I thought the latter his supreme masterpiece, but on the last occasion when I took in that third act, when we were all sitting under a giant bomb, its emotional impact seemed inadequate. This inadequacy has to be faced in Shaw. When I was a boy, ordinary stupid people thought him a self-advertising intellectual clown, who would say anything to attract attention. This view of him was dismissed with contempt even by those, like Chesterton, who sharply disagreed with him. And, of course, it was nonsense. Yet there was in it, as there often is in the judgments of ordinary stupid people, a valuable grain of truth. He held many beliefs but he did not hold them as most of us do. He never appeared to be emotionally committed to them. He could advance or defend them without anger. His warmest admirers tell us that this was because he was almost a saint. The opposite party say it was because he had a great deal of the charlatan in him. What is certain is that his peculiar relation to his beliefs gave him both the strength and the weakness characteristic of him.

He and Wells, whom I knew better than I did Shaw, offered some valuable contrasts. Wells always behaved far worse than Shaw; he was too impatient; he made mischief; he lost his temper and screamed insults and slander. (Belloc once said that Wells was a cad who didn't pretend to be anything but a cad; that Bennett was a cad pretending to be a gentleman; that Shaw was a gentleman pretending to be a cad.) These tantrums threw into relief Shaw's patience and good humour and courtesy; and in any debate between these two, G.B.S. would win easily on points. Yet for my part I was always admiringly and affectionately aware of H.G.'s honesty of mind, his frankness, his raging desire to discover and to announce the truth. To those redeeming qualities it seemed to me that Shaw opposed something personally attractive and polemically formidable, but disingenuous and dubious.

Thus, Shaw might win the argument about Stalin and the Soviet Union, but it was Wells who was nearer the truth, and was not playing any monkey tricks with his own values. Sometimes, both when I read him or heard him in private, I felt that Shaw deliberately switched off his imagination when dealing with certain topics. It is not that he was downright dishonest, but that he refused to follow his debating points into the world of flesh and blood. So he could defend or even admire dictators when he must have known that he could never have endured their authority. He could cheerfully advocate the 'liquidation' of anti-social types, as if they were merely being barred from a summer school. He did not see them as real people, shrieking and bleeding, but as creatures of paper and ink, characters with no entrances in the third act.

I never felt he came through into the world that followed 1914. Often he seemed to have persuaded himself that we were all still in the Edwardian world of debate, where the man who disagreed with you so violently on the public platform would be found, smiling a welcome, at the next week-end house-party. During that long fine afternoon it was fun to listen to a witty Irish Socialist, even if you did not believe a word he said. Later, especially after 1917, it was different. There had arrived the world of passports and visas, secret police and strange disappearances, labour camps and gas chambers. Even in England there were changes. The Socialist was no longer a crank but a menace; it was fortunate for G.B.S. that he now became a grand old man, and escaped most of the new hard abuse and the elaborate smearing.

Again, there is to my mind something dubious, disingenuous, too, reminiscent of those rather fatuous Shavian groups, in much of his handling of our non-intellectual, emotional life. He would pretend to be through with sex, as if it were fretwork or stamp-collecting, when really he had hurriedly by-passed it. This pretence almost ruins some of his plays. Those maternal managing heroines of his ought to have had fourth acts composed for them by Strindberg. As for his assorted kittens, from Cleopatra to Orinthia, they are hygienic toys with never a gland in working order between them. No wonder that his greatest part for an actress is Joan of Arc.

All this seems very damaging, and so it would be if it were not for the fact that most of his plays rest on his strength as well as on his weakness. Because he could hold his beliefs in his own peculiar fashion, keeping them free of negative emotions, he was able to create his own kind of comedy, good enough to put him among the world's great dramatists. This comedy of his has light without heat. The superbly theatrical wit crackles and dazzles and strikes without wounding. Behind the cut-and-thrust of the talk, like some smiling landscape behind a battle scene, is a vast golden good humour. The master quite early of a magnificent debating style, he heightened it and orchestrated it to provide us with this comedy of argument, the Mozartian opera of witty debate. And this is not far-fetched, for it was opera and not other men's plays, the stuff he had denounced as a critic, that offered him models. He told me himself how he nearly always began without any ground-plan of action, hearing and not seeing his characters, trying a duet, then a trio, then perhaps a full ensemble. It is this method, together with an absence of fine shades and atmosphere, that explains why repertory companies in a hurry so often choose a Shaw play. You have only to learn the lines, slam them across, and the piece comes to life.

Treat Chekhov in this hell-for-leather style and you have nothing that the Russian master had in mind. For these two, the best who have written in this century, are complete opposites. And here is an odd thing. It is the dramatically simple, forthright Shaw and not the delicate, evasive Chekhov who is the dangerous influence. No playwright was ever the worse for being influenced by Chekhov. But Shaw's direct influence has been the kiss of death: no survivor is in sight. This is not hard to explain. Chekhov opened out a new dramatic method, whereas the Shaw play is a highly personal *tour de force*, demanding his unique style and temperament. I never felt myself that G.B.S. was really interested in dramatic method, though, of course, he may have tired of the theatre by the time I knew him. He despised the content of the plays he criticized in the *Saturday Review*, but he was not above using some of their oldest tricks. When an act was getting a bit dull he would bring on a gorgeous uniform or some fancy dress; and some of his deliberate clowning, as distinct from the expression of his wit, is just embarrassing.

Saint or charlatan, he was Irish, not English. What would have been fighting words in a Cockney or Lancashire accent seemed delicious banter in that rich, soft brogue. His debating tricks, which were often outrageous, were in the Dublin tradition, and so, of course, was his assumption of a public character part, starring in a cast that had Wilde, George Moore, Yeats, 'A.E.', James

Stephens, all playing character parts. Like Chekhov's Gaev, he was 'a man of the "Eighties"'—with some Edwardian ripening. After that, he was with us but not of us. Like a man in a cautionary fairy tale, he had his wish granted—to live a long time—and it was all different and wrong. He became—and who can blame him? —a very vain old super-V.I.P. I remember once coming across him at the Grand Canyon, and found him peevish, refusing to admire it, or even look at it properly. He was jealous of it. Later still, the crisply assertive style, which he kept almost to the very end, deceived people into imagining that he was still thinking hard when he was often being rather foolish. His wife was no intellectual giant, but it seemed to me that her mind was still open long after his had finally closed.

You might say that he made up his mind too early, which gave him an immense advantage in debate, arming him at all points, but cost him something in wisdom. Bertrand Russell, who had known him a long time, said that G.B.S. was an immensely clever man but not a wise man. He seemed to me to have a sort of natural wisdom in his ordinary dealings with life (he must have given people in private more really good advice than any other man of his time), but to be perverse, obstinate, cranky, wrong-headed, in his positive philosophy. He was, in fact —and came at just the right moment—a great destroyer, head of the Victorian rubbish disposal squad. He hid any doubts he might have about his positive wisdom in quick mocking laughter, just as he hid so much of his face behind a beard, red and white at the proper seasons. But because he was an iconoclast, this does not mean, as many people imagine, that all his work will 'date' itself into obscurity. I suspect that all the 'dating' that can happen has already happened. His best pieces, those

comedies unique in style and spirit, have the vitality that
defies time and all social changes. Their character, their
appeal, may be different—for notice how early plays like
Arms and the Man and *You Never Can Tell*, once
thought to be grimly shocking, now seem to bubble and
sparkle with wit and delicious nonsense—but they will
be alive. And existing still behind the work will be the
memory and the legend of the man, half saint and half
clown, preposterous in his Jaeger outfit and assorted
fads, glorious in his long stride towards some kingdom
worthy of the spirit—the wittiest of all pilgrims, hum-
ming an air by Mozart.

J. B. PRIESTLEY: 'Shaw' (1950),
from *Thoughts in the Wilderness.*

20

Youth Among the Ruins

*The English girl Barbary Deniston and the French boy
Raoul Michel were brought up near each other in
France during the Second World War. After the defeat
of the Germans they come to England to study, but
spend much of their time together on the bombed sites
in the City of London and haunting the ruins of the
buildings and streets around St. Paul's Cathedral. The
novel from which this chapter comes gives a strikingly
accurate impression of the City as it was during several
years after 1945 and until it rose again in a new shape,
with wide roads and lofty modern-style buildings upon
the places where previously there had been only narrow
streets and old warehouses reduced by air-raids to a
wilderness of 'shrubs and bracken and fireweed' where
Nature had taken over from the destructive forces of
Man.*

DAME ROSE MACAULAY

BARBARY AND Raoul picked up two bicycles in an alley
off Cheapside one Sunday, rode them to Gresham Street,
and hid them in one of the deep caves of Haberdashers'
Hall.

'We will put them back in the same street after a few
days,' Barbary said, having been bidden by her father
not to steal.

'Why?' asked Raoul. 'That would be silly. They will

be very useful to us. We were fortunate to find them unguarded and unlocked. We will keep them, and ride about London.'

'They might be recognized,' Barbary doubtfully suggested; but he shrugged his shoulders.

'Little probable, among so many machines, so many people. If they are, we will say that we found them abandoned and took charge of them. It is the truth.'

'Yes,' Barbary agreed. 'So it is.'

They stood together in the tall, tangled jungle of Haberdashers' Hall, knee-deep in shrubs and bracken and fireweed, outside the deep door that led to the cave where the bicycles had been thrust. Round them the bees buzzed and hummed, like merchants chaffering.

'I find it very English, this city,' Raoul said, using the English word. 'A great habitation of merchants, that is what it was.'

The innocent cunning of the merchants bumbled about them in the warm, sleepy afternoon. What careful, crafty affairs had they transacted in the Hall of the Haberdashers, in that of the Goldsmiths and of the Wax-chandlers across the road, at the wholesale umbrella manufacturers whose wrecked foundations crumbled on the corner, in the office of Mr. Perara on the first floor of the shell of flats at Addle Street? Had they pledged each other in good wine at the Coopers' Arms, which only a board now marked? Had they, on Sunday mornings, attended Divine Service at St. Anne's and St. Agnes' among the fig-trees, at St. Alban's, at St. Giles's, at St. Vedast's which had been St. Foster's, and, long ago, at the parish church of St. Olave in Silver Street, 'a small thing,' perished long since? Had they drunk from dairy-maids' pails in Milk Street ('so called of milk sold there'), counted their shillings in Silver Street ('I think of silversmiths dwelling there'), swindled the peers who dwelt in Noble Street, that alley twisting through the wilderness of weeds, bought tables (as Pepys did) from the joiners in Wood Street, and courted in Love Lane ('so called of wantons')? What orgies, what cheepings, what market-shaking deals had been conducted in those jungled alleys and caves behind those broken, gaping, painted doors? What gems, what wines, what barley and what oil, had been stored in those labyrinthine mazes of cellars, where now rats and rabbits scuttered and gnawed? Cellars so solid, on foundations so deep dug, that two great fires and more, storming over them, had yet left their bases set. 'We saw the fire grow . . . in corners and upon steeples, and between churches and houses, as far as we could see up the hill of the city, in a most horrid malicious bloody flame, not like the fine flame of an ordinary fire. . . . The churches, houses, and all on fire and flaming at once; and a horrid noise the flames made, and the cracking of houses at their ruin. . . .'

Still the ghosts of the centuries-old merchant cunning crept and murmured among weeds and broken stones, flitted like bats about dust-heaped, gaping rooms. But their companion ghosts, ghosts of ancient probity, honourable and mercantile and proud and tough, that had lived side by side with cunning in the stone ways, and in the great blocks of warehouses and offices and halls, had deserted and fled without trace, leaving their broken dwellings to the creeping jungle and the crafty shades.

Barbary, sitting presently on the top floor of a high ladder of offices in Addle Street ('the reason of which name I know not, for at this present it is replenished with fair buildings on both sides'), painted on postcards the

F

rambling ruins to the west, where Silver Street ran
through a golden and green and purple wilderness, past
St. Olave's churchyard, past the halls of Parish Clerks
and Coachmakers, past the Coopers' Arms to Noble
Street and tiny Monkwell Street that ran north to Cripple-
gate. She painted rapidly, impressionistically: out of the
flowering jungle, shells of towered churches sprang,
shells of flats soared skyward on twisting stairs, staring
empty-eyed at desolation. She could sell all her postcards
at a shilling each, standing outside the café in Fore
Street, where a few people strolled by and paused to
look. She and Raoul had become known figures to the
few who came and went in those ruined streets; on week
days workmen busy excavating would greet them, and
passing policemen would eye them without malice or
more suspicion than policemen must necessarily entertain
for juvenile loiterers. They would enter the narrow strip
of St. Giles's churchyard and eat their lunch or tea
seated on the flat tomb of Sir William Staines and his
large family. Then they would often climb through a
window into the great roofless church, and there Barbary would pace up the aisle to the east end, kneel in
devotion before the vanished altar, and chant the Dies
Irae. Raoul, finding this a bore, would not always enter
the church; he preferred to climb about the flat terrace
of Somerset Chambers and peer down through the great
round frame of the lost east window.

After they had acquired the bicycles, they would often
go for rides, up and down the steep streets that run from
Cheapside to the river, down Queen Street to the wharfs
—Brooks Wharf, Darkhouse Lane, Queen Hithe Stairs,
Anchor Alley, Southwark Bridge Stairs, and along the
wharfs between All Hallows Lane and London Bridge.
They joined other wharf rats, scrambling among bales

and warehouses, sneaking, when unwatched, on to barges, climbing up and down water-lapped stairs, while the dark and shining river swirled muddily by. Often they went farther afield, pedalling through hideous grey suburbs, or to Regent's Park or Battersea, slipping perilously between the rushing monsters that thundered along the streets, imitating these in ignoring traffic lights, riding fast and furious, crouched low over bent handles. Raoul, being French, could go fastest; neither experienced fear. At times they were thrown, and injured not seriously; once Raoul's wheel was buckled; he left the machine on the kerb and boarded a bus; in three days he had picked up another. They had begun to believe in themselves as pickers up; the professional crook's exhilaration of self-confidence succeeded the amateur's apprehension, which, long since trained out of them in France, had afflicted them when transported to this new field of operations, whose rules they had not learnt.

Sometimes Barbary would bring Raoul back with her to supper. Mrs. Cox did not object to this, so long as they talked English, so that she could keep a line on the conversation; if it was French, she did not know what they were up to. She had a motherly feeling towards the thin, polite, whey-faced French schoolboy who was her one-time mistress's stepson. She refused, however, to admit Barbary's other friends, the low types that she seemed to pick up like fleas when out. No blandishments of these young men, and occasional young women, concealed from her experienced eyes what they were, which was spivs. And spivs she had no intention of admitting into the house.

'Your Pa,' she said firmly to Barbary, 'would *not* wish it. And nor, which is more, would there be the right

number of spoons and forks remaining to the house, once
those sat down to a meal here. No, Miss Barbary, I know
bad characters when I see them, however soft they speak,
and I'll say that those young men are well spoken enough
to me; but inside these doors they do not push. And
you'll be wise not to let them get too familiar with you,
my dear, for no good will come of that, and so your Pa
would tell you.'

Having reflected a little further, while she and Barbary laid the table for supper, she said, aloofly, ' Deserters.
That's what those young men are, if you ask me.
Deserters, that left the army before they should, and
have been on the run ever since. It's they deserters that
commit half the crimes. They are unsafe young men, my
dear, and you shouldn't go with them. By rights, I should
write to your Pa. . . .'

' Oh, no, Coxy, don't bother him. I don't go with them,
really—not much. And if you tell father, he might tell
the police, and set them hunting for them. It wouldn't be
fair. Besides, he wants to be let alone, fishing and shooting. Please, Coxy.'

' Very well, my dear, I won't write for the present. I'm
sure it's not my wish to upset your Pa without need. But
into this house those young men do not come, and neither
will good food go out of it for them. Like others, those
young men can work for their bread. Or so I presume;
and if they cannot, there is good reason why not, and
that reason no credit to them.'

Barbary thought of the discredited young men, the
hunted, the hunters, the hiders, so quick, so furtive, so
fugitive, like lizards poised on a rock, glancing right and
left for enemies, like wild cats in the maquis, glancing
up and down for prey. No, nothing was any credit to
them; they had no credit in the world; all their affairs

went kimkam; but still, elusive, evasive, violent, crafty, they managed to exist.

'And I ask, Miss Barbary, that on no account will you ever *trust* those young men, for of trust they will never be deserving.'

Barbary, experienced in discredited young men, had never thought of trusting any of them. Lend them something, and you never had it back; leave anything about near them, and you did not see it again. If they could derive advantage from betraying you, betray you they would; these were the simple laws of their lives, the simple, easy laws of the bad, who had not to reckon with the complication of scruples, but only with gain and loss, comfort and hardship, safety and risk. Specious and crafty as they were, the young men had no credit, no trust; they were wild cats in the maquis, sneaking into larders and streaking out again, licking the cream from their whiskers as they fled back to their lairs. Sometimes they vanished, and you did not see them again, for good reasons that were, as Mrs. Cox would say, no credit to them. Three days ago two of them had stolen from the jungle-grown cellar in Haberdashers' Hall the bicycles that had been hidden there, and had ridden them away. Next day they had looked innocent, licking the cream from their whiskers, denying knowledge of the theft. Nothing could be done about it, in that jungle world in which justice could not be invoked, in which the only safety—and how incomplete—from betrayal was the universal guilt, in which the hated enemy, pacing ominously heavily, on the jungle margins, integrated its denizens into a wary school-tie solidarity, defensive yet precarious.

'Oh, no, Coxy,' Barbary said, in surprise at the eccentric idea suggested to her. 'I should never trust them. I mean, trust them with *what*? Or to do what? There couldn't be anything. . . .'

No, there was nothing. Not bicycles, not secrets, not money, not help in any emergency, not life; only the simple law of their being, to take what they could and how they could, and to keep, if they could, out of the way of the enemy.

ROSE MACAULAY: from *The World My Wilderness* (1950).

21

Poetry on the Stage

No writer since Dr. Johnson in the eighteenth century has so strongly imposed his literary and critical principles upon his own generation as T. S. Eliot in the present century. It became rare to find any contemporary book of criticism or literary history which failed to quote him. The Waste Land (1922) and his later poems turned English poetry into new channels, and from the time his first play Murder in the Cathedral *appeared in 1935 his theories about poetry on the stage received widespread attention from other writers of verse plays and from actors, some of whom mistakenly carried his views into performances of Shakespeare by speaking blank verse in a prose style. As is shown below, Eliot believes that in poetic drama the poetry should not be 'poetic' but should 'justify itself dramatically' in the characters. The opinions he expresses on this matter have seemed bleak to theatregoers who prefer to hear poetry spoken as poetry in Shakespeare performances, and who hold that Eliot's own verse plays sound much like plays in prose.*

T. S. ELIOT

As I have gradually learned more about the problems of poetic drama, and the conditions which it must fulfil if it is to justify itself, I have made a little clearer to myself, not only my own reasons for wanting to write in this form, but the more general reasons for wanting to see

147

it restored to its place. And I think that if I say something about these problems and conditions, it should make clearer to other people whether and if so why poetic drama has anything potentially to offer the playgoer, that prose drama cannot. For I start with the assumption that if poetry is merely a decoration, an added embellishment, if it merely gives people of literary tastes the pleasure of listening to poetry at the same time that they are witnessing a play, then it is superfluous. It must justify itself dramatically, and not merely be fine poetry shaped into a dramatic form. From this it follows that no play should be written in verse for which prose is *dramatically* adequate. And from this it follows, again, that the audience, its attention held by the dramatic action, its emotions stirred by the situation between the characters, should be too intent upon the play to be wholly conscious of the medium.

Whether we use prose or verse on the stage, they are both but means to an end. The difference, from one point of view, is not so great as we might think. In those prose plays which survive, which are read and produced on the stage by later generations, the prose in which the characters speak is as remote, for the best part, from the vocabulary, syntax and rhythm of our ordinary speech—with its fumbling for words, its constant recourse to approximation, its disorder and its unfinished sentences —as verse is. Like verse, it has been written, and re-written. Our two greatest prose stylists in the drama— apart from Shakespeare and the other Elizabethans who mixed prose and verse in the same play—are, I believe, Congreve and Bernard Shaw. A speech by a character of Congreve or of Shaw has—however clearly the characters may be differentiated—that unmistakable personal rhythm which is the mark of a prose style, and of which only the most accomplished conversationalists—who are for that matter usually monologuists—show any trace in their talk. We have all heard (too often!) of Molière's character who expressed surprise when told that he spoke prose. But it was M. Jourdain who was right, and not his mentor or his creator: he did not speak prose—he only talked. For I mean to draw a triple distinction: between prose, and verse, and our ordinary speech which is mostly below the level of either verse or prose. So if you look at it in this way, it will appear that prose, on the stage, is as artificial as verse: or alternatively, that verse can be as natural as prose.

But while the sensitive member of the audience will appreciate, when he hears fine prose spoken in a play, that this is something better than ordinary conversation, he does not regard it as a wholly different language from that which he himself speaks, for that would interpose a barrier between himself and the imaginary characters on the stage. Too many people, on the other hand, approach a play which they know to be in verse, with the consciousness of the difference. It is unfortunate when they are repelled by verse, but can also be deplorable when they are attracted by it—if that means that they are prepared to enjoy the play and the language of the play as two separate things. The chief effect of style and rhythm in dramatic speech, whether in prose or verse, should be unconscious.

From this it follows that a mixture of prose and verse in the same play is generally to be avoided: each transition makes the auditor aware, with a jolt, of the medium. It is, we may say, justifiable when the author wishes to produce this jolt: when, that is, he wishes to transport the audience violently from one plane of reality to another. I suspect that this kind of transition was easily

F*

acceptable to an Elizabethan audience, to whose ears both prose and verse came naturally; who liked high-falutin and low comedy in the same play; and to whom it seemed perhaps proper that the more humble and rustic characters should speak in a homely language, and that those of more exalted rank should rant in verse. But even in the plays of Shakespeare some of the prose passages seem to be designed for an effect of contrast which, when achieved, is something that can never become old-fashioned. The knocking at the gate in *Macbeth* is an example that comes to everyone's mind; but it has long seemed to me that the alternation of scenes in prose with scenes in verse in *Henry IV* points an ironic contrast between the world of high politics and the world of common life. The audience probably thought they were getting their accustomed chronicle play garnished with amusing scenes of low life; yet the prose scenes of both Part I and Part II provide a sardonic comment upon the bustling ambitions of the chiefs of the parties in the insurrection of the Percys.

Today, however, because of the handicap under which verse drama suffers, I believe that prose should be used very sparingly indeed; that we should aim at a form of verse in which everything can be said that has to be said; and that when we find some situation which is intractable in verse, it is merely that our form of verse is inelastic. And if there prove to be scenes which we cannot put in verse, we must either develop our verse, or avoid having to introduce such scenes. For we have to accustom our audiences to verse to the point at which they will cease to be conscious of it; and to introduce prose dialogue would only be to distract their attention from the play itself to the medium of its expression. But if our verse is to have so wide a range that it can say anything that has to be said, it follows that it will not be 'poetry' all the time. It will only be 'poetry' when the dramatic situation has reached such a point of intensity that poetry becomes the natural utterance, because then it is the only language in which the emotions can be expressed at all.

It is indeed necessary for any long poem, if it is to escape monotony, to be able to say homely things without bathos, as well as to take the highest flights without sounding exaggerated. And it is still more important in a play, especially if it is concerned with contemporary life. The reason for writing even the more pedestrian parts of a verse play in verse instead of prose is, however, not only to avoid calling the audience's attention to the fact that it is at other moments listening to poetry. It is also that the verse rhythm should have its effect upon the hearers, without their being conscious of it. A brief analysis of one scene of Shakespeare's may illustrate this point. The opening scene of *Hamlet*—as well constructed an opening scene as that of any play ever written—has the advantage of being one that everybody knows.

What we do not notice, when we witness this scene in the theatre, is the great variation of style. Nothing is superfluous, and there is no line of poetry which is not justified by its dramatic value. The first twenty-two lines are built of the simplest words in the most homely idiom. Shakespeare had worked for a long time in the theatre, and written a good many plays, before reaching the point at which he could write those twenty-two lines. There is nothing quite so simplified and sure in his previous work. He first developed conversational, colloquial verse in the monologue of the character part—Faulconbridge in *King John*, and later the Nurse in

Romeo and Juliet. It was a much further step to carry it unobtrusively into the dialogue of brief replies. No poet has begun to master dramatic verse until he can write lines which, like these in *Hamlet*, are *transparent*. You are consciously attending, not to the poetry, but to the meaning of the poetry. If you were hearing *Hamlet* for the first time, without knowing anything about the play, I do not think that it would occur to you to ask whether the speakers were speaking in verse or prose. The verse is having a different effect upon us from prose; but at the moment, what we are aware of is the frosty night, the officers keeping watch on the battlements, and the fore-boding of an ominous action. I do not say that there is no place for the situation in which part of one's pleasure will be the enjoyment of hearing beautiful poetry—providing that the author gives it, in that place, dramatic inevitability. And of course, when we have both seen a play several times and read it between performances, we begin to analyse the means by which the author has pro-duced his effects. But in the immediate impact of this scene we are unconscious of the medium of its expression.

From the short, brusque ejaculations at the beginning, suitable to the situation and to the character of the guards—but not expressing more character than is required for their function in the play—the verse glides into a slower movement with the appearance of the courtiers Horatio and Marcellus:

> *Horatio says 'tis but our fantasy, . . .*

and the movement changes again in the appearance of Royalty, the ghost of the King, into the solemn and sonorous

> *What art thou, that usurp'st this time of night, . . .*

(and note, by the way, this anticipation of the plot conveyed by the use of the verb *usurp*); and majesty is suggested in a reference reminding us whose ghost this is:

> *So frown'd he once, when, in an angry parle,*
> *He smote the sledded Polacks on the ice.*

There is an abrupt change to staccato in Horatio's words to the Ghost on its second appearance; this rhythm changes again with the words

> *We do it wrong, being so majestical,*
> *To offer it the show of violence;*
> *For it is, as the air, invulnerable,*
> *And our vain blows malicious mockery.*

The scene reaches a resolution with the words of Marcellus:

> *It faded on the crowing of the cock.*
> *Some say that ever 'gainst that season comes*
> *Wherein our Saviour's birth is celebrated,*
> *The bird of dawning singeth all night long; . . .*

and Horatio's answer:

> *So have I heard and do in part believe it.*
> *But, look, the morn, in russet mantle clad,*
> *Walks o'er the dew of yon high eastern hill;*
> *Break we our watch up; . . .*

This is great poetry, and it is dramatic; but besides being poetic and dramatic, it is something more. There emerges, when we analyse it, a kind of musical design also which reinforces and is one with the dramatic movement. It has checked and accelerated the pulse of our emotion without our knowing it. Note that in these last

words of Marcellus there is a deliberate brief emergence
of the poetic into consciousness. When we hear the
lines

> *But, look, the morn, in russet mantle clad,*
> *Walks o'er the dew of yon high eastern hill*

we are lifted for a moment beyond character, but with
no sense of unfitness of the words coming, and at this
moment, from the lips of Horatio. The transitions in the
scene obey laws of the music of dramatic poetry. Note
that the two lines of Horatio which I have quoted twice
are preceded by a line of the simplest speech which
might be either verse or prose:

> *So have I heard and do in part believe it*

and that he follows them abruptly with a half line which
is hardly more than a stage direction:

> *Break we our watch up.*

It would be interesting to pursue, by a similar analysis,
this problem of the double pattern in great poetic drama
—the pattern which may be examined from the point
of view of stagecraft or from that of the music. But I
think that the examination of this one scene is enough
to show us that verse is not merely a formalization, or an
added decoration, but that it intensifies the drama. It
should indicate also the importance of the unconscious
effect of the verse upon us. And lastly, I do not think that
this effect is felt only by those members of an audience
who ' like poetry ' but also by those who go for the play
alone. By the people who do not like poetry, I mean those
who cannot sit down with a book of poetry and enjoy
reading it: these people also, when they go to a play in

verse, should be affected by the poetry. And these are the audiences whom the writer of such a play ought to keep in mind.

T. S. ELIOT: from *Poetry and Drama* (1950).

22

A View of Marlowe

Christopher Marlowe, Shakespeare's much admired con-
temporary, has always seemed a mystery-man because of
his murder in a Deptford tavern in 1593, when he was
only twenty-nine. In the past it was usual to say that his
death occurred during a drunken brawl, but recent
opinion supports suggestions that Marlowe was a govern-
ment spy and that it was found convenient to remove
him for political reasons. But while such matters are
interesting to our generation, since we live in an age
when secret agents and cloak-and-dagger affairs are al-
most daily material for the newspapers, it is by his plays
that Marlowe has been remembered for nearly three
hundred years. It is mainly through his plays and their
poetry that Kenneth Tynan sees him here.

KENNETH TYNAN

AND NOW, as briefly as may be, for Marlowe.

The right picture to carry in the mind of this first
giant is, I think, that of the heedless, arrogant attic-
dweller of the Latin Quarter of his day: a crazy, para-
doxical creature, eager to parade his bursting personality,
and unable to show its vastness except by pouring it into
a gigantic emperor who should walk upon the heads of
kings. He has all the solitariness, all the pride, all the
wretched contempt for small men of the intellectual
minority-man of any age. It was fitting that, as the

legend is told, Ingram Frezer should have stabbed him in
the way he did. I have a guess-work picture of Frezer:
suspicion is there, crossed with facile scorn; surliness,
emotional conservatism, a brassy leer of resignation and
defiance as he listened to Marlowe's heresies. The
defiance, that is, of one who has seen or heard, for the
very first time, something splendid: something that
aspires, something unfamiliar. It might be a strange
phrase high-flying in the upper air of Marlowe's argument; or a habit of movement, a big shrug, a breadth
of gesture, when the whole man shuddered into ecstatic
communicativeness; when, after all, the corporal equivalent of an idea or a riposte became more valuable than
the straitjacket inertia of usualness; or it might merely
have been a sympathetic mention of Satan or homosexuality. But whatever the provocation was, Ingram
Frezer's face must have puffed and creased into a look
of small hatred: shifting his eyes aimlessly as he nods
and becks and talks, he lets his squint stare glide over
and past Marlowe; then, suddenly (or so I tell it), the
stare swung back, he stopped talking, nudged his friends,
and together with them assumed the peculiar resentful
look I have described and made Marlowe its target. With
a confiding backward tilt of the head, a curl of lip and
a twinkle of mock-commiserating eyes Ingram Frezer
began the combat which had its climax when a long
knife and the fist that held it were pinned down to a
table, and the point looked upwards, and the free hand
of Ingram Frezer gripped and pushed his adversary's
straining head down on to the sharpness of it, and pushed
until it had transfixed first the eye and then the brain of
Christopher Marlowe. They were a boy's eyes, which
had learnt their elderly glint in some lewder Elizabethan
Chelsea; but their charming arrogance offended Frezer;

they must be cut away and extinguished, those enviable
eyes. Frezer I (not impartially) see as a prototype of
Jonson's Tucca, in the *Poetaster*; Tucca, who says:

> Come hither, Callimachus, thy father tells me thou art
> too poetical, boy: thou must not be so, thou must leave
> them, young novice, thou must: they are a sort of poor
> starved rascals that are ever wrapt up in foul linen,
> and can boast of nothing but a lean visage, peering out
> of a seam-rent suit; the very emblems of beggary.
> No, dost hear? Turn lawyer—thou shalt be my
> solicitor. . . .

These men, for whom a wild boar's head is best served
as pork pie, will admit the poet all too readily (if he
should compromise) to their little circle of *idées reçues*, to
batten on their perpetual high-tea of warmed-up plati-
tude: they are amiable, and overwhelmingly sincere. But
sincerity on some levels of intellect is a vice. Marlowe
would not compromise: in fact, he fell too often into
the opposite error, of making it a life's work to *épater les
bourgeois*. The wonder about Flaubert (who loathed the
bourgeoisie as much as they have ever been loathed)
is not that he gave up so many years to writing *Bovary*,
but that he was master of restraint enough to shut himself up in Rouen and neither collaborate with them nor
join the skirmishing around their impregnable flanks.
The poet is often asked to enter the field against the
bourgeois, as Max du Camp asked Flaubert: the right
way is to refuse. The partisans may dub you a poltroon:
pay no attention. The opposite of a man who won't say
boo to a goose is not necessarily a man who spends his
whole waking life saying boo to geese. But to Marlowe
and his generation the *bourgeois* were new: and he
turned his impatience into poetry.

But I perceive this digression has grown dangerously personal.

Tamburlayne embodied all Marlowe's impatience with normality. We note his hero's deliberate ignorance of the rules of war, his shameless flouting of military precedent; his immeasurable cruelty (he has one good, tender-hearted son, Calyphas, whom he murders: but Marlowe subtly turns Calyphas into a coward so that we may accept Tamburlayne's killing him!) What amazing egotism is his! There has never been more abandoned rhetoric than this:

> I, the chiefest lamp of all the earth,
> First rising in the east with mild aspect,
> But fixed now in the meridian line,
> Will send up fire to your turning spheres,
> And cause the sun to borrow light of you . . .
> As when a fiery exhalation,
> Wrapt in the bowels of a freezing cloud
> Fighting for passage, makes the welkin crack
> And casts a flash of lightning to the earth.

Again:

> Behold my sword. What see you at the point?

The first Virgin replies:

> Nothing but fear and fatal steel, my Lord.

He explains:

> Your fearful minds are thick and misty then;
> For there sits death, there sits imperious death.

It gives a catch to the breath, this young flamboyance, this fantastic and tenacious egoism. It is the beginning of heroic flourish in English literature, saved from vulgarity by its total unreality. For a man to beg to be carried to war against the gods is unbelievable in any but a theatrical context. We feel that it *would* be passing brave to have associates called Usumcasane and Theridamas, and to ride in triumph through Persepolis: we never think it probable, or likely. *Tamburlayne* has elegiac beauty, too, of a gentler sort, rising to the great lament over Zenocrate; and Marlowe shows evidence of considerable command over dramatic prose. Witness Zabina's agony on discovering her lord dead:

> O Bajazet, O Turk, O Emperor! Give him his liquor? Not I: bring milk and fire, and my blood I bring him again: tear me in pieces, give me the sword with a ball of wildfire upon it. Down with him, down with him! Go in, my child, away, away. Ah, save that infant, save him, save him: I, even I speak to her: the sun was down. Streamers white, red, black—here, here, here! Fling the meat in his face. Tamburlayne, Tamburlayne, let the soldiers be buried. Hell, death, Tamburlayne. . . . Hell, make ready my coach, my chair, my jewels: I come, I come, I come. . . .

The doctrine of the four elements is strong in *Tamburlayne*. His physician, at the end, tells us that he died from excess of *Calor*. It was only to be expected. Such phoenix heat could not long be held within one frame.

The other plays are lesser in every respect. *Faustus* is a solemn theological excursion which degenerates into a *jeu d'esprit* and only recovers in the last pages, when it is too late: the fault is inherent in the story, which has a beginning but cannot have a real middle part. Marlowe's flair for stagecraft remains: in particular, observe the silence of the devils when they come to claim Faustus

at the end. It would have been easy to have them threatening and taunting him: but they are quiet.

The Jew of Malta is a cynical, misbegotten tragi-
comedy not least in Marlowe's deliberately perversity in
choosing a Jew for his hero, and making him more than
moderately sympathetic. Barabas says:

> It's no sin to deceive a Christian;
> For they themselves hold it a principle,
> Faith is not to be held with heretics.

His slave Ithacus makes a suggestion:

> Good master, let me poison all the monks.

Barabas's answer is ready:

> Thou shalt not need, for now the nuns are dead
> They'll die of grief.

Who could resist an invitation like this one:

> Please you dine with me, sir, and you shall be most
> heartily poisoned?

In *The Jew* Marlowe shows an agile wit, and the sense
of fun which English drama badly needed.

Edward II has its own perversity, too, in the sympathetic treatment of homosexuality.

> My heart is as an anvil unto sorrow,
> Which beats upon it like the Cyclops' hammers,
> And with the noise turns up my giddy brain,
> And makes me frantic for my Gaveston.

The play is dull whenever Edward or Gaveston is not
speaking: the only superiority of *Richard II* lies in the
fact that its barons and caterpillars are not quite lifeless.

But the two plays are poetically of the same mould: Edward in prison is every bit as poignant as (and much less priggish than) Richard. And there is no pair of lines in Shakespeare's play to equal:

> But what are kings, when regiment is gone,
> But perfect shadows in a sunshine day?

Tamburlayne is the yardstick of Marlowe's achievement. The others are 'aglots on his sleeve, pins on his train'. Tamburlayne is *hubris*, but undoomed *hubris*, pacing the earth in broad sunlight with his lion's rage, exulting. There is no hero elsewhere like this: for once the prototype is the perfected form. 'Continence in a king', wrote Puttenham, 'is of greater merit than in a beggar,' and incontinence in a king, Marlowe might have added, is better theatre than in a shepherd. That is one of the valid excuses for heroic tragedy. You can attack it morally, but not theatrically: and it will not do for Jonson, a despot if ever there was one, to dismiss Marlowe as a purveyor of 'scenical strutting and furious vociferation'.

KENNETH TYNAN: from *He That Plays the King* (1950).

23

Revolution the British Way

Historians speak of 'the Bloodless Revolution' of 1688, when James II was driven from the throne and William III and Mary II came from Holland to replace him. That, however, was a revolution at the top, and though it aroused much enthusiasm it had no marked immediate advantages for the majority of the population. In the years following 1945, when the Second World War ended, a much more important revolution took place in Britain —the establishment of the Welfare State, in which millions of ordinary people are better paid, better fed and clothed and housed than at any previous time. Yet the Welfare State has produced difficult problems, a few of which are outlined below after reminders of some of the steps leading to the Welfare State.

A. C. WARD

BY THE end of the nineteenth century the ferment produced by the combined influence of popular education and popular journalism was augmented by the social influence of a mechanical contrivance—the safety bicycle. This machine began the great exodus from the home which the motor cycle and motor car were to make almost universal in the new century. The bicycle was women's great emancipator; by giving them the freedom of both town and country it benefited women far more than the freedom of parliament which they secured later after years of painful struggle.

The militant Women's Suffrage campaign which began in 1905 was swept aside in 1914 by the beginning of the First World War. When the franchise was extended to women after the war, it was rather as an acknowledgment of wartime services than as a triumphant sequel to the suffrage campaign. That the vote should have been denied to women for so long and that women should have regarded the vote as a kind of passport to paradise on earth are in retrospect equally astonishing. The historical significance of the militant suffrage movement seems now to be in the deplorable lesson which others learned from it—namely, that political violence may be as profitably employed by malcontents for evil ends as for good; a lesson whose consequences were not seen in the fullness of horror until the 1930s.

Political violence might well have become endemic in Britain, as it has elsewhere, but for Shaw's efforts to find a substitute in political education. At the time of his settlement in London in 1876 the principles of revolutionary socialism were well to the fore. Karl Marx had been living and writing in London for many years as an exile from Germany, and after the suppression of the Paris Commune in 1871 there had been an influx of French refugees. In 1881 the first English socialist organization—the Democratic Federation—was founded by H. M. Hyndman, a disciple of Marx. Later its name was changed to the Social Democratic Federation, and among its members was William Morris, whose immense prestige as poet and protean master-craftsman was of immense advantage in bringing within the orbit of the Federation many who would otherwise have given a wide berth to all radicals, for 'Radical' was then the current political bogy-word. Morris broke away from the Social Democratic Federation in 1884 to start the Socialist League, but earlier in that year a body that was to have a far longer life, the Fabian Society, had been established. It began to issue a series of political tracts to which Shaw contributed liberally. The fame of the Fabian Tracts was mainly due to his flair for giving enduring literary quality to almost everything he wrote, so that what would otherwise have been speedily forgotten—in company with most propagandist writings—is preserved among his works in the volume called *Essays in Fabian Socialism*, in which much uncommon common sense is vented in good prose. The Fabian Society began and was named several months before Shaw joined it. Its title was explained on the covers of the early Tracts: 'For the right moment you must wait, as Fabius did most patiently when warring against Hannibal, though many censured his delays; but when the time comes you must strike hard, as Fabius did, or your waiting will be in vain, and pointless.' This waiting policy of the Fabians was in contrast to the more restless aggressive policy of the organizations sponsored by Hyndman and Morris, though the phrase 'you must strike hard' was not used simply as a rhetorical metaphor in the early days of the Fabian Society. There were among its members some at least who believed that the unarmed masses could at need— somehow, somewhen, by some inherent justice and right-eousness of their cause—prevail in physical combat with the police and soldiers of a constituted anti-socialist government. This illusion was not dispelled until the day which came to be known, in the easily heroic terminology of peaceable times, as Bloody Sunday. On that day, 13 November 1887, a mass gathering planned to vindicate the right to assemble and make speeches in

Trafalgar Square, London, was dispersed by police and cavalry. The bloodshed was confined to the effects of truncheon blows and accidental tramplings and jostlings of a crowd out of control, but the experience convinced Shaw, who was an uninjured participant, that mob action against a disciplined force would always be purposeless and productive of nothing but damaging defeat for the insurgents. From that time Shaw's Fabianism was no longer a matter of waiting patiently until the time should come to strike hard, but of teaching persistently until capitalism succumbed to the enlightenment spread abroad by political education.

Between Bloody Sunday and the General Strike which came in 1926—a period of forty years—there were periods of considerable industrial distress, with mass unemployment and chronic poverty. But, notwithstanding labour stoppages which from time to time generated ugly displays of mass anger, there was no serious civil disturbance in Britain. By 1950 it could be said that under a Labour Government a bloodless social revolution had been at least in part effected. The fact that this revolution did not progress entirely without weakening or destroying ancient liberties and personal rights which the British had for centuries cherished and defended, and that it could hardly have progressed at all but for the undermining of the old régime by two wars in which bloodshed was worldwide, does not sweep away the claim that the Fabian Society, acting as the nurse and mentor of future Labour-party statesmen, safeguarded Britain from the excesses of revolutionary violence experienced in other lands.

English Liberalism, from which Radicalism and Socialism derived, and afterwards diverged under the impact of continental zealotry, was closely associated in basic principle with Nonconformity. The Nonconformists or Dissenters—whether organized as Quakers, Congregationalists, Wesleyan Methodists, Baptists, or lumped together in undifferentiating common speech as Puritans—opposing what they believed to be the spurious authoritarianism of the sacerdotal Christian communities, were led also to oppose the privileged social classes. As the parson was often the crony of the squire or the dependant of the lord of the manor, dissent from the established social and political order was consistent with dissent from the Established Church. But dissent in both kinds also remained consistent with Christian conviction and piety: i.e. with the puritanism of the dissenting chapels. By the middle of the nineteenth century there was a well-defined religious and political division, with Church and upper-class Conservatism on the one side, Chapel and working-class Liberalism on the other.

Not until Marxist materialism took root in Britain did an unbridgeable gulf yawn between politics and religion. In the later part of the century Liberal intellectuals gave much earnest consideration to high principled ethical substitutes for Christianity, which was challenged as unacceptable to human reason. Rationalism, agnosticism, atheism were embraced with bleak determination by relatively small numbers, some of whom endeavoured to propagate in speech and writing one or other of those ' reasonable ' creeds, and in a few instances the blasphemy laws were invoked against them. But a religion based upon ethics and ratiocination is not less exacting than religions requiring faith in a supernatural agency; indeed, a religion which demands an unremitting standard of personal conduct and yet offers no rewarding after-life cannot hope to displace Christianity and its promise of heaven. The rationalist movement was not without permanent effect, however. It helped to shake the Christian structure, even though it failed to build any edifice of its own. The stored authority and prestige of the Churches and Chapels of the various Christian denominations kept orthodox belief well in the van of national life, until the First World War removed millions of young people from the home influences that had been the mainstay of Christianity, and faced them with wholesale agony and death which appeared to very many as inconsistent with the Christian idea of God. To the slowly developing scepticism of the pre-war period was now added a vast mushroom growth of cynicism. The harvest was, in some directions, complete indifference to every aspect of religion; but in one quarter at least, from the 1920s onward, a positive anti-religious campaign developed. Communism, centering on Moscow as Catholicism centred on Rome, identified religion with Capitalist oppression and exploitation and adopted the slogan 'Religion is the opium of the masses', inviting the retort 'Politics is the poison of the people'.

The implication that the masses would shed irrational beliefs if they abandoned the orthodox faith was not borne out by experience. Political creeds wholly irrational in character and requiring an absolute irrational obedience from their adherents became new religions, while multitudes of the non-political turned to spiritualism, to astrology, and to substitute religions of various kinds. A generation which had received more schooling than any preceding generation in the history of the world relapsed into credulity and superstition which had hitherto been stigmatized as penalties of heathen ignorance. Reason was again dethroned and the old school of social reformers who put their trust in 'equality of opportunity', 'full employment', and other devices for the Welfare State became conscious that a material Utopia cannot endure in a spiritual vacuum, and that on every social level the enjoyment of individual rights is inseparable from the recognition of individual responsibilities and duties: that men are in truth and in fact members one of another.

A. C. WARD: from *Bernard Shaw* (1951).

24

Creation and Criticism

*Though there need be no enmity, there will always be
disagreement between creators and their critics. Christopher Fry's verse play* The Lady's Not For Burning
*was very enthusiastically received in 1949, for its poetry
seemed like a magnificently gleaming fountain of words,
and for a while it was hoped by many that Fry would
become for his generation what Christopher Marlowe
had been for the sixteenth-century Elizabethans—the
forerunner of a new great age of poetic drama. He was
not welcomed, however, by austere critics under the spell
of T. S. Eliot's theories (see pp. 147-55 above), and it may
be a matter for much literary discussion in the future
whether Fry was turned aside from his true course by
mistaken criticism.*

CHRISTOPHER FRY

SOMETIMES WHEN I am trying to work I think of the
picture of myself which emerges from the press-cuttings,
and it seems, in a way, very splendid. I see a man reeling
intoxicated with words; they flow in a golden—or perhaps pinchbeck—stream from his mouth: they start out
at his ears; they burst like rockets and jumping crackers
and catherine-wheels round his head; they spring in
wanton sport at his feet and trip him; but trip him or not,
he loves them: let them all come, go where they may;
let them strangle sense, flood the stage, break the dams

of form: facility shall have its day. His typewriter continues to chatter long after it has been put back in its case. Words will grow out of him, like fingernails, for some time after his death.

Then, having looked at this picture and marvelled, I turn back to my typewriter. Like an ancient Red Indian chief, I sit for some hours in silence. At last I am ready to speak, and say ' How ', or perhaps some slightly longer word. My two fingers withdraw from the typewriter and the night wears dumbly on towards dawn.

The Lady's Not For Burning, the play which first gave rise to the bacchic figure vomiting his careless words, was five or six months finding its shape before writing began, and eight months in writing. I don't mean that slowness in writing is a virtue: it is an incapacity; but it's hard to relate it to verbal intoxication; it feels more like a slow death by ground glass.

What do I think I'm doing, then, so painfully creating a false impression? Why so many words? Why so many apparent interruptions of the relevant action of the play? There is no doubt that, looked at from many points of view, these are most reasonable questions to ask; and I can only try to explain what was in my mind.

So many words, for instance. We know this criticism doesn't precisely mean what it says. There are the same number of words as in any other play; you have only to count them. It means, I think, that I don't use the same words often enough; or else, or as well, that the words are an ornament on the meaning and not the meaning itself. That is certainly something—perhaps often—true in the comedies, though almost as often I have meant the ornament to be, dramatically or comedically, an essential part of the meaning; and in my more sanguine moments I think the words are as exact to my purpose as I could make them at the time of writing.

And then the question of relevance. The question is, relevance to what? The relevance of one kind of play is not necessarily the relevance of another: I tried to say so in *The Lady* in the line: '*That same laughter, madam, is an irrelevance that almost amounts to revelation*', and I think what I am most anxious to do here is to ask that criticism should look more deeply into the nature of a play, and to pursue the reason for its nature, rather than to try to force it into a category to which it doesn't belong. If a criticism is to be understood and profited by, writer and critic must start with the same premiss.

Comedy is not a drama with the addition of laughs. It is a world of its own, and when we leave it again, it can have given to the world of action we rejoin something of a new cast. It is a world of its own, but not a world all of one kind—it may be of situation; or the sunny, tension-less world of *As You Like It* where, for all Jacques' talk of time, there is all the time in the world; or a world of wit, such as *The Way of the World*, where plot is an infernal nuisance, so huddled together to be out of the way of the true comedy that it took me hours to work it out before I produced it at Oxford; and after a few days of rehearsal I could no longer explain it to any member of the cast who thought perhaps he should know what the story was about.

As comedy is not a drama with laughs, so a verse play is not a prose play which happens to be written in verse. It has its own nature. In a talk on *Poetry and the Theatre* I tried saying something more about this, in these words: 'The dramatist must view the world of his play, and the people of that world, with great precision: the poet-dramatist with the greatest poetic precision. The whole structure depends upon it, what scene follows another, what character goes and what character enters, where description or landscape becomes part of the action, or where it needs a bare exchange. The poetry and the construction are inseparate. Who understands the poetry understands the construction, who understands the construction understands the poetry, for the poetry is the action, and the action—even apart from the words—is the figure of the poetry. . . .'—I do not mean that my own plays live up to this definition; but this is the ground upon which, now and in the future, I must meet the critics.

If this all seems to be turning into a defence of Fry, it is not at all what I mean by it. For every point I raise there are half a dozen more which, in the circumstances, I don't intend to refer to, preferring to withhold, as far as possible, the stick which you could beat me with. But it is a fairly general experience of writers, producers, actors, to find themselves being judged from some altogether other part of the forest, where the critic has dug himself in as though for a siege; and I can best show the kind of misunderstanding I mean by instances from my own experience.

There are many orders of such misunderstanding. There is the criticism which seems wantonly to misrepresent, so that it can make a point; as when, for instance, a well-known critic (not in this country), to prove that I sometimes wrote pretentious nonsense, quoted a line which was not in the play at all!

Or there is the kind of criticism which seems anxious to pick a hole at all costs: such as that which soundly berated an artificial comedy for having no lines in it as simple and highly charged as those in *King Lear*. Or

G

this: in *Venus Observed* the Duke ends a speech with, 'And I, as unlaborious as a laburnum tree, hang in caresses of gold', and the critic then comments, 'An inaccurate observation, since a laburnum is only apparently "unlaborious"'. I see what he means: like the only apparently untoiling and unspinning lilies of the field. These are small matters, but they show the larger fault: that sometimes a critic will rather cavil at the surface than give judgment in depth.

A few paragraphs ago I mentioned the word 'pretentious'. I will state my belief that it is not a critical word. It usually means that, in the critic's opinion, a man's reach has exceeded his grasp, and what hope is there for the theatre without such temeritous reaching? There may be times when we lay ourselves open to it by an insincerity, but even so, it is a dangerously facile word, and too easily covers up a critic's impatience.

A critic rightly expects that those he criticizes should go as far as their powers will take them in whatever art they practise: they should be honest, devoted, sensitive, laborious to perfect what they do, never content to rest on what they have done, but ever restless to increase the scope of what is still to follow. Are they not to expect as much from their critics? But, round and about those who know the gravity of their work, are others whose ability is to make rapid decisions about everything and everybody; and the less they are inclined to consider the greater is their air of omniscience.

They do not belong, evidently, to a recent race of beings. John Gay, in the *Rehearsal at Goatham*, says, 'They can scarce be called critics who must hear and read a thing before they will venture to declare their opinion. Anybody can do that.' And, though I have no doubt that they now in fact attend what they criticize, it is equally sure that they do not take in what they criticize or would even know how to set about it; and, to make up for this apparently unimportant deficiency, their power of scorn is tremendous.

I could give you examples of the games they play, but it is better to move on to something of a more interesting sort; and I must ask your forbearance while once more, and for the last time, I bring my own work in as an example. In this instance it concerns critic and playwright, but, in its kind, it might equally be true of critic and actor, or critic and producer—an example of their not being in accord, and yet the critic serving as that outward eye which can be of such value. Sometimes when we say the critic is wrong, we might do well to ask what, in ourselves, led him to be wrong.

There is a climax in my play *The Firstborn* which several critics whose opinion I respect found to be insufficiently prepared. It was the moment when Moses suddenly understands that the last plague of Egypt, the Death of the Firstborn, means the death of his nephew-by-adoption, Rameses. The critics felt, very reasonably, that the affection between Moses and Rameses had been so barely touched on that three-quarters of the impact of Moses' realization was lost.

Now I had not imagined any such personal affection on the part of Moses. In the play he meets Rameses for a bare five minutes: is touched by his hero-worship: recognizes the boy's sincerity and humanity, and that is all. What I hoped I had shown, and hadn't, was that to Moses the boy represented Moses' own boyhood when he was Prince of Egypt, represented also that love for Egypt which Moses couldn't shake off even while he was fighting her. There are certainly speeches to that effect, and Moses, in the moment of realization, cries, 'Egypt,

Egypt! He was meant for Egypt! '; but the speeches were not enough: I had, in this instance, led the critic to be wrong; and since the writing of *The Firstborn* I have been learning too reluctantly that neither audiences nor critics are clairvoyant.

I hope to mend my ways. We are all, I think, anxious to mend our ways, once we can see clearly where and how they should be mended. But we cannot trust the critic to tell us unless he *also* knows moments of prayer and fasting and self-distrust; unless he judges, not by a jaunty reflex-action, but by drawing into himself what he judges before giving judgment; unless we can be sure that he gets no pleasure from wounding, or belittles others to give himself the appearance of size; and that he has always before him, like a fearful warning, those evasions, dishonesties and tricks protective of self-esteem, which are the badges of the little critic who knows what he likes but will never know anything more. I made a character in a play describe justice as the crossing of mind with mind; and I believe this to be true of just and creative criticism.

CHRISTOPHER FRY: from *An Experience of Critics* (1952).

25

The Complete Man

After his marriage to Princess Elizabeth and following her accession to the throne as Queen Elizabeth II in 1952, Prince Philip's many interests and his sympathetic understanding of present-day problems were reflected in the speeches he made on public occasions. The speech quoted here is characteristic of his clear vision and of his ability to combine courtesy and plain speaking.

PRINCE PHILIP, DUKE OF EDINBURGH

In the Middle Ages it was the Church and the universities which were primarily responsible for knitting together the nations of Europe in a common culture. This amounted to a system of thought and behaviour, conditioned by a reverence for the classics and restrained by religion and social custom. Two world wars and the advent of science have completely upset those conditions and removed those restraints. So far we have neither returned to them nor put anything in their place. The responsibility of the universities is therefore much greater today if they are to minister to the specialized needs of modern society *and* to regain their position as the spiritual and moral reservoirs of Europe and the world.

One of the marks of the Middle Ages was the free movement of scholars from university to university across the face of Europe. Since then the world has grown much smaller and that mobility ought in our day to cover the whole world. Teachers in the arts must surely benefit from a wide personal knowledge of the places where those arts flourished most nobly, and the science teacher must surely draw inspiration from working in the universities which were responsible for some of the greatest strides in science. Perhaps even more important, the movement of teachers and students alike between universities must surely help to break down the narrow nationalism which grows up with isolation. A proper respect for the achievements of others may not be easy in this competitive world, but it is after all the first step towards a broad mind.

European culture, thought, and ideas have drifted all over the world, and although they have received some hard knocks in recent years there are many far-away places where people still believe that Europe has something good to offer. We shall have nothing to offer unless our behaviour, our ideals, and our achievements gain universal respect. We can only have something to offer if the universities have clearly before them what they are aiming to do.

With the inevitable growth of specialization I see the universities facing two great dangers. First, it is very easy to get so involved in the technical details of education that the object of education is lost. And secondly, in an effort to condition a university to the needs of its students and to the needs of the State it may lose its power to make or mould those students into reasonable and responsible men, capable of thinking for themselves and capable of expressing the result of their thoughts to others.

A university must do more than merely provide a high-class professional apprenticeship. It does not matter in the least what a student's specialized line happens to be; the fact that he is a specialist cannot excuse him from his responsibilities as a man. Students must emerge as complete human beings capable of taking their proper place in society as a credit to their universities both for their professional knowledge and as men. There is no conflict between the disciplines here. Nobody can be termed a complete man who has no knowledge of what science has to teach, and, equally, human obligations cannot be escaped on the grounds of being a specialized scientist or technologist.

By human obligations I mean the ability to behave in a reasonable way, to observe restraint so that restraints do not have to be imposed, to be able to think clearly and objectively so that false doctrines cannot gain ground. I believe that it also means the ability to see through nonsense, political, economic, scientific, and so on, and the feeling that it is a duty to resist it. This in no way conflicts with the amount of specialized knowledge, whether scientific, classical, or anything else, which the student can absorb and turn to good account for himself and the community at large.

The universities have a special responsibility to send people of that sort out into the world, because by their influence and example in the community at large they can extend the work of the universities to every corner of the world.

However, to produce the complete man with that balanced sense of obligation and understanding we need to know much more about man himself. Our knowledge of science, the classics, or medicine is beautifully documented, indexed, and ordered. We may not know everything about the subject, but what is known is neatly bound. I imagine that is why we sometimes call this an age of reason, but we forget that—in the midst of all that reasonable knowledge—man himself remains as unreasonable, irrational, and unpredictable as ever.

Everything around us has been found to have laws and order, and there are some who faintly resent the fact that man refuses to be ordered in the same way. But we must take care not to treat man, with his immense variety of prejudices and emotions, as just another statistical unit. There is the conflict; and it is perhaps inclined to become most noticeable in scientists who deal with ordered things and thoughts in their professional lives, but when the problems are human ones it is not altogether surprising that their ideal solutions are not universally accepted. The reverse is, of course, also true. If you spend your life making compromises it is hard to understand why that is not possible in science.

I would like to repeat that the conflict is not between disciplines, between humanism and science. The conflict lies between man and the world he has made for himself. Man has succeeded in changing many things but he has not changed much himself.

It is just because we have got such a grip on nature and such a store of knowledge for its own sake that we must remember the central character, man, and his possibilities, limitations, and the depths he can sink to if he relaxes his self-control.

PRINCE PHILIP, DUKE OF EDINBURGH:
from *Selected Speeches* (1955).

26

The King's Money-Spinner

*Money was certainly the root of evil for King Charles I.
Though he quarrelled with Parliament about a number
of things, none of those would have been likely to cost
him his life if the desperate need for money to conduct
his wars abroad and in Scotland had not led him to defy
and dissolve Parliament and thus bring to a final break-
ing-point the conflict between the theory of the divine
right of kings and the principle of constitutional rule
which subordinates the monarch to the will of his people
expressed through the parliamentary system. The following sketch of the man whose numerous financial
schemes failed to save the nation from civil war and
the king from subsequent execution, shows that the levy-
ing of Ship Money was only one of his many unwise
impositions.*

C. V. WEDGWOOD

THE KING'S financial advisers, like those of his father
before him, were indefatigable in their efforts to find new
sources of income. Two principal methods were employed: the revival of obsolete medieval practices, and
the exploitation of the expanding world of industry and
trade. In both of these the King's principal adviser for
several years was the ingenious old lawyer, William
Noy. An anagram of his name—'I moyl in law'—fitly
described his activities: his moylings unearthed a num-

ber of interesting possibilities, for many of which the King found immediate use.

In feudal England every landowner of a certain standing had been required to do a knight's service for the King in war, or to compound in money if he could not. This practice, to the acute annoyance of the gentry, was now revived and all those who came within the prescribed income limit were required to receive—or, as they put it, to 'endure'—knighthood, paying the necessary fee to exempt them from military service. Those who refused the unwanted title were still liable for the fee.

More profitable still was Noy's revival of the old Forest Laws. When the King had in very truth depended on the game that he killed in the hunting season to feed himself and his retinue, it had been an offence to enclose or encroach on the great stretches of royal forest, which were scattered over the kingdom. Gradually, as the King's need for game grew less urgent, much of what had once been royal forest had been brought under tillage or pasture and had passed into private hands. This made it possible for the King suddenly to institute an inquiry into enclosures of forests within the last fifty years. Those who had offended were fined large sums—or at least they were condemned to pay large sums, although the King often subsequently reduced the fines. The reduction rarely consoled the victim for the inconvenience, interference and fright to which he had been subjected.

Noy's next revival was the Elizabethan tax of Ship Money, a contribution levied on seaports and coastal regions for the building and maintenance of the navy. The sums were fixed by the King's council, collected by the justices of the peace and sheriffs, and paid direct to the treasurer for the navy. This was in many ways the best managed and most economical of the King's plans, for relatively little of the money leaked away in the expense of collection and the tax went direct to the purpose for which it was intended.

Noy's masterpiece was his evasion of the legislation against monopoly. Queen Elizabeth had made the happy discovery that the Crown could raise money by granting the sole right of trade in certain commodities, or the sole right of manufacture, to some rich and favoured person. The abuse of such monopolies and the source of extra-Parliamentary revenue that they gave the Crown, had caused the House of Commons to attack them, and the Parliament of 1624 had finally made them, one and all, illegal.

William Noy found a legal way out of the difficulty. In future, monopolies were granted only to those who had found and wished to develop some new form of manufacture: in order that invention and valuable new processes might be given every encouragement, it was only fair that such people should enjoy special favour and protection. The word *monopoly* was replaced by *patent*. The King granted patents to the *projectors* who wanted sole rights of manufacturing beaver hats or copper pins because they had a specially efficient method which stood in need of protection from competition until it should be established. Some patents were justly given for interesting experiments; the majority were given on the most trivial pretexts. Monopolies, expelled by Parliament, came back fourfold in this transparent disguise. A further ingenious plan was to grant, not the sole right of manufacture, but the sole right of transport of some particular kind of goods. Occasionally the complications went even further, and the King would sell to one projector rights of manufacture and transport, and to another the right to grant, for a consideration, licences to individuals to infringe the privileges of the first projector.

Besides patents, and licences to evade patents, the King also made money out of the so-called incorporations. For a sum of money, he was willing to incorporate new companies of craftsmen—the leather-workers, for instance, the beaver-hat makers and others—granting them the right to organize their own industry. The inspiration for patents and incorporations was chiefly financial, but there was an element of policy behind these expedients. The granting of patents could be used to bring certain industries very closely under the supervision of the Crown, thus creating a primitive nationalization of manufacture. The incorporations arose from a genuine economic grievance and did something to alleviate it. Many of the older companies had ceased to be corporations of craftsmen and become corporations of merchants: they merely *sold* the goods which were made by others. Already the social revolution had turned its quarter-circle; craftsmen were being driven down, by the united pressure of these companies of merchants, into the position of mere suppliers, whence it might be a short step to being hired labourers. The independent craftsmen therefore strove to band themselves together into companies which could negotiate on equal terms with the tradesmen who bought and marketed their wares. Charles's grants of incorporation were a reasonable attempt to improve the conditions of the craftsmen, to stem or alter the course of economic and social changes, and to create a firm attachment between the Crown and the artisan, against possible exploitation from entrenched companies of middlemen.

Charles's policy provided the ground-plan of a politico-economic programme which foreshadows that of Colbert in France fifty years later and which, had it been firmly pursued, might have established the Crown in the affections of the artisan population and set England on the road to an enlightened *étatisme*.

But long-term and constructive economic plans were in pawn to the King's immediate needs. The exaction of fines, not the protection of the poor man's rights from the wealthy encroacher, was the first consideration in applying the forest laws. The somewhat wider laws originally intended to prevent depopulation, and enforced against those who enclosed common and waste land, were used with the same financial purpose and social inconsistency. The King himself enclosed common land and encouraged enclosure when it seemed profitable to do so; he supported the great drainage and enclosure schemes for the fens, and he turned over to tenant farmers a part of the once common land on the royal estates near Berkhampstead.

In the same way, the money that flowed into the treasury, and not the intrinsic merit of patents or of commercial schemes, governed the grants to projectors, and if there was money to be made out of the struggle between a new incorporation and an ancient company, as there often was, the King was prepared to let the quarrel fester, with a concession now to one side, now to another. Four patentees shared the right to trade wholesale in tobacco in the county of Durham; one, the most powerful, took proceedings against the retailers, mostly alehouse keepers, who were buying from the others. Small men were harried, accused and persecuted about twopenny screws of tobacco, and, whoever was to blame, the affair did not make the King popular in Durham.

The King's ingenious bullying of the London Vintners' Company had aroused some ill-feeling in the City. He had demanded from them payment of £4 on every tun of wine. When they refused, the Star Chamber issued a decree forbidding Vintners to cook and serve meat to customers. As most of the Vintners had long practised this auxiliary trade the prohibition hit them hard. They paid £6,000 to the King in the belief that he would proceed no further with the decree. Soon however prosecutions began again and the Vintners learnt that these would be stopped only if they agreed to pay 1d. to the King on every quart of wine sold. Some of them were for resisting and letting the matter go before the Star Chamber, but the Master of the Company, Alderman Abell, was rather a man of business than a man of principle. He saved the Company from further trouble by negotiating a deal through the King's Master of the Horse, the Marquis of Hamilton. The Company would pay £30,000 a year (£4,000 of it to Hamilton) for the privilege of serving meals as well as selling wine.

The King, inspired by a salt shortage early in his reign, had considered making salt into a royal monopoly, as it was in France, thus taxing at the source a prime necessity of life and securing a steady income. The need for immediate funds caused him to grant not one, but two patents for the production of salt. The two patentees naturally came into collision; with the Crown behind them, they also collided with the people of Yarmouth when they tried to set up salt pans on what was time-honoured common land, and they annoyed fishermen and fish merchants throughout the country by interfering with the production and distribution of that absolutely essential commodity, saltfish. Not content with the working of the rival patents, Charles next revived an old tax on salt in order to farm it for a substantial sum; the monopolists claimed exemption and Charles prosecuted them in the interests of the tax farmer; but the tax farmer complained that, as everyone now used Scottish salt, he had lost on the transaction. The Scots added a contradictory note, by claiming that the English monopoly had ruined their trade. Not all the complaints can have been true, but this much at least was true: that the Crown was very little richer and a great deal less liked for the whole business.

More absurd and quite as irritating as the salt business was the trouble over soap. In 1631 the King granted to a group of projectors, several of whom were Roman Catholics, the exclusive right to make soap of vegetable oil for fourteen years. They agreed to pay the King £4 a ton and to make five thousand tons a year at 3d. a pound; they were permitted, in view of the supposed superiority of their soap, to examine all other manufactured soap and impound or destroy any that they thought below standard. At a test held in private in London, their soap was certified better than that of the London soapmakers. It did not fare so well at Bristol where a tavern maid and a laundress lathered away in public at some soiled linen napkins with the projectors' soap and with soap made by the Bristol soap-makers; they demonstrated that the Bristol soap washed whiter and more economically than the projectors' soap. In spite of this the King ordered the closing down of seven out of Bristol's eleven soap-boiling workshops.

In London the struggle went on with unabated venom. The King's projectors prevailed on the King to prohibit the use of fish oil in soap altogether; on the strength of this they seized the stock of the London soap-makers and prosecuted them in the Star Chamber, following this up by an offer to buy them out of business. The London soap-makers refused the bait and some of them were imprisoned. Murmurs were now rising on all sides. While fishing companies were affected by the prohibition on whale oil, the people in general declared that the projectors' soap was bad. The projectors mobilized the Queen's ladies to write testimonials to the excellence of their soap but laundresses and—more important—cloth-workers throughout the country continued to condemn it. In response the King prohibited the private making of soap altogether and gave the projectors the right to enter and search any private house. All in vain. By the summer of 1634 illicit soap was being sold at a shilling the pound or six times its original price, so low was the general opinion of the projectors' soap. At this point the projectors gave up their plan of using only vegetable oil and took to using the fish oil, which they had made illegal for everyone else. In a final effort to drive their rivals out of business the King put a tax of £4 a ton on Bristol soap. The Bristol soap-boilers refused to pay, and fourteen of them followed the London soap-makers to prison. The farce could not continue much longer and in 1637 the King wound up the project and bought in the projectors' rights for £40,000 of which he made the London soap-makers contribute half. He then allowed the London men to go back to their interrupted manufacture on payment of a tax of £8 a ton to the Crown.

The intermittent bullying and imprisonment angered and injured a minority. It was, in the long run, the constant prying interference arising from the King's financial projects which alienated the majority, an interference so marked that quite innocent strangers who asked questions would suddenly find themselves the object of insulting hostility, because they had been taken for government spies.

The salt trouble and the soap trouble had irritated the Scots as much as the English. The poorer nation felt and feared the effect of the King's financial tamperings more than the richer one. England had already a well-established position in the economy of Europe. Scotland was struggling for a place and what was in England an irritation might in Scotland be a disaster. Salt was, after plaiding, the principal export of Scotland, and although the King's planned salt monopoly had in truth done little, if any, damage, it had caused grave anxiety while it lasted. The soap business was more serious, because by restricting the use of whale oil for soap the King had injured the Arctic fishery interests of the Scots. Further injury was done to Scottish trade by doubling the export duty on their coal, in spite of energetic protests; worst of all was the scandal of the copper coinage.

Scotland, where the people still resorted to barter in many transactions, was perpetually short of small coin. The King had therefore granted to the Earl of Stirling the right to mint copper tokens. This patent was to serve a double purpose: the coins were to solve the problem of small change in Scotland and the profits made by Stirling were to be written off against a considerable debt which Charles had incurred towards him. Stirling was suspect in his native land because he belonged to the large group of courtier Scots who had followed their King southward and associated their fortunes with his, to the neglect of their own country. A poet, a scholar and nothing of a financier, he so managed the copper coinage as to create a noticeable inflation, to bring the quality of the King's money into disrepute and yet not to cover his own debts. The King, who had no other means of paying him off, remained deaf to repeated protestations from the Scots, and left Stirling, year after year, to bedevil the currency of Scotland.

William Noy had died in 1634, leaving his taxation schemes for others to operate. He had claimed to be a lawyer rather than a financier, and it is possible that if the King had had a Treasurer who was also something of a statesman and an administrator, Noy's ingenuity might have become the basis of an effective policy. A man who controlled and organized the collection of taxes so that the maximum came in to the King, and kept the scheming and corruption of Court speculators within bounds, could have given the King's government a steady income. A man who could develop the elements of policy embedded in the King's financial plans might have saved the King's government. No lack in the King's Council was more disastrous than the lack of a clever man at the Treasury.

C. V. WEDGWOOD: from *The King's Peace* (1955).

27

Out from London

Before he wrote his autobiography, Over the Bridge, which attracted thousands of new readers to his work besides winning him a prize of £1,000, Richard Church's novels and poems had given him a less extensive popularity. Here he describes the beginning of a boyhood summer holiday at a time when no ordinary family dreamt of possessing a car which would make it possible for them to escape from city streets whenever they wished. A country excursion was then rare and was therefore looked forward to and valued as an exciting and delightful adventure.

RICHARD CHURCH

THE TERM ended; the small garden filled with upstanding balsams and sunflowers, waiting to flower. The jasmine bower once again was white-starred with perfume that set me longing for I knew not what. The July day came when I ran home from school at midday, fished out the back-door key from behind the water-closet pan, let myself into the house, started the midday meal cooking, and realized that for a month the everydayness of life was to be broken.

Mother came in, and I ran to meet her in the shady tunnel of the jasmine. In my sense of freedom, of exaltation, I flung my arms round her and buried my face in her neck. She staggered and protested.

'Oh, don't, dear! I'm so tired!'

My excitement collapsed. I looked at her, as she preceded me into the house. She was bent, and the nut-
brown, silky hair hung in wisps. She dropped the great
blank handbag to the floor and sat down at the table,
resting her elbows on it and her head in her hands.

I was frightened. . . . But I knew what to do. I warmed
a little milk on the gas-stove, poured it into a breakfast
cup, and added a tablespoonful of rum. She sipped this,
breathing wheezily; and gradually the dear identity
returned. She smiled, and talked to me about the forth-
coming holiday and the problems of packing.

We had the afternoon to ourselves, and after dinner we
sat in the yard, our backs to the cycle-shed, looking into
the forest of annuals contained in the flower-bed beyond
the drooping foliage of the sycamore tree. I found a
shawl and put it round Mother's shoulders, then set up
my fort at her feet, and staged a battle among the lead
soldiers, which included a company of the Coldstream
Guards, who looked rather incongruous among so many
dressed in this drab khaki which had dimmed the British
Army since the Boer War. My artillery consisted of one
field piece, which fired india-rubber shells a quarter of
an inch in length; but they were lethal among the leaden
campaigners.

Behind this slaughter, however, and the momentary
excitement it engendered, my mind was at work on its
own and more unique concerns, chief among them being
my sense of foreboding as I watched my mother, furtively, from time to time. She seemed content to sit
there doing nothing; and I was startled by so uncharac-
teristic a mood. But she was cheerful enough, and we
filled the afternoon with happiness and anticipation.
The heat came down on the concrete at our feet, and

the hot air stirred the nasturtiums and jasmine flowers, teasing our instincts with hints of something larger, wilder, more open and free than could be contained in this Battersea environment of suburban backyards, and the tiny continent of our bread-winning days.

The heat-wave deepened during the following few days while Jack and I lazed about in the house and yard, wearing ragged shirts and discarded garments, because the more presentable were being packed by Mother. She was obviously not strong enough to cycle down to Hampshire, where Father and Jack had been one week-end, to see and rent a cottage at Ropley, near Alresford. From this prospecting journey Jack had returned with half a dozen photographs taken with a plate-camera which he had made for himself, the aperture being a pin-hole. This was only one of his many ingenious artifacts. I had studied the pictures, which included a church that leaned backwards, in the hope of finding that perpetually teasing certainty which we look for when about to take some adventurous step into the unknown. But Ropley remained unreal.

The heat became a torture over the river flats. We watered the concrete in the yard, conjuring a temporary purity and freshness into the air. But this had to be repeated again and again to make the hours endurable, as we fretted and gloomed, in the irritation of boyish impatience, while Mother bent over the tin trunk and the smaller boxes and baskets, pausing from time to time to rest, and ease her breathing, so harassed by the oppressive heat.

Father had not been idle meanwhile. Deciding that Mother could not face the journey by road, he found a second-hand trailer, which he fitted to his solo bicycle. It looked like a bath-chair, being made of wickerwork with padded leather upholstery and a small square of oil-cloth at the feet. A long iron bar secured it to the saddle-pin of the bicycle. The combination was of vast length and had to be assembled out in the street, the process causing several gangs of boys to gather round, some of them being from Surrey Lane School, and therefore superior in all respects to the rest, the anonymous ones.

Father had rehearsed in the street, for in all matters of this kind he was a good soldier. He left nothing to chance. Every nut, every link in the chain, of his steed was scrutinized, tightened, oiled, tested. By the morning of our departure the junior tandem shone like the accoutrements of a crack regiment.

A luggage carrier was fitted to the tandem, on which we were to carry the food for the journey. The great tin trunk was to go by train, with Mother. Father took all the rest, loading up the trailer and roping all safely under a groundsheet. The trailer was so full that no room could be found in it even for the water-melon which Father had brought home the previous evening on his way from the Post Office. So he carried it in a string bag, slung from the handlebars of his bicycle.

On the eve, we slept but little. The heat held through the night, and Jack and I tossed about under a single sheet whispering to each other incoherently. Dawn came as a relief, with a gesture of coolness, and we tumbled out of bed, almost sick with excitement.

It was raining!

We stood at the scullery door, studying the sky beyond the sycamore tree. The clouds rumbled over, but their ruggedness assured Father that they would break, and he pretended to jeer at us because of our downcast vis-ages. He had the confidence and energy of a god that morning. The trunk was corded and addressed to the

Ropley cottage, Father's copperplate calligraphy standing out like a public notice. He dragged the trunk down
to the front door, then had to pull it back a little way so
that the door could be opened. This waste of power only
increased his reserves. He undertook to cook the breakfast, so that Mother could have time to herself, to dress
at more leisure and take stock of all the luggage, the
locking up of the house, the final arrangements about
the cat being left to the care of the next-door neighbour, and a hundred other minor responsibilities any
one of which, being neglected, would have lain under her
holiday like the rose petal under the mattress of the little
princess.

The odour of eggs and bacon filled the house, while
Father stood at the gas-stove squinting up at the clouds
with one grey eye, making meteorological pronounce-
ments calculated to reassure every member of his family.

'Pah! Pride of the morning!' he cried, cracking another egg into the pan and easing up the others with the
flat of a knife. 'Rain before seven, fine before eleven!'

So confident was he that we started off before the milk
and post arrived. Mother pleaded with him to wait, fear-
ing that her boys would catch chills: but Father brushed
her anxiety aside as he brushed away the steady down-
pour of rain—as though it were morning dew. This was
his great day, marred only by the defection of his wife;
but he promised himself, and her, that to compensate for
this he would take her for rides in the trailer while we
were at Ropley.

We put on mackintosh capes over our cycling outfit,
the trailer was attached to Father's machine, Mother
came to the front door to see us off, receiving a smack-
ing kiss and an admonition to 'take it easy, old girl',
and then we were off.

The rain beat against us as we pedalled south-west, past the candle factory. Father led the way, steadily chugging along, the trailer with its covered load gliding behind him like a faithful dog. We followed, sometimes dropping back because so long a procession could not be maintained unbroken on the public highway. I was now almost as expert as Jack at pedalling and economizing my strength. With our legs hidden by the wide-spread capes, we had the sensation of being propelled by magic.

As we drew out of the inner suburbs towards Kingston the clouds broke and the rain ceased. We stopped on the Portsmouth road to discard our dry mackintoshes and to eat some raisins. But excitement would have carried us on without the help of other nourishment. This was my first great journey by road. I was now deemed to be cured of my stomach trouble, and indeed I believed so too. I needed no urging from Father.

The sun came out. The wet roads steamed, and the beams of golden fire combed the wet grass like hair, raising it up, and raising also a plague of flies that buzzed about our sweating heads, our foreheads granulated with salt as the sun dried the exuding pores.

Steadily round and round moved Father's calves, clad in stockings and spats. No variation in speed broke their rhythm. Jack and I plugged away. The tandem was in fine fettle; perhaps a few more ounces in weight than when we started an hour and a half earlier.

From time to time Father broke into song: 'Marching with the Deathless Army', 'I'll Sing Thee Songs of Araby', and the piece that in modern times would have been called his signature tune:

'Oh merry goes the day
When the heart is young.'

He had been born afresh that morning: not a care in the world. He broke off songs recklessly, like a prince squandering alms, to point out interesting features on the road: pubs where he and his Post Office pals had stopped; corners where on former rides he had hesitated, or had a puncture. . . .

The traffic thinned out, the suburbs dropped away (for London was smaller fifty years ago), the countryside grew deeper, wider, more lush. We crossed the Surrey commons, and for the first time in my life I heard larks trilling in the sky.

It was impossible to grow weary, or at least to acknowledge it. Jack too was a different person, if it was possible for so pronounced a character to change overnight. He caught some of Father's enthusiasm, and even cracked a laconic joke or two with me, as he pedalled in front, with my legs and feet shadowing his. There were no complaints from him, as yet, that I was not pulling my weight, or dragging on the up-pedal (the great crime).

In 1904, bicycles were the fastest vehicles on the roads. Father and his trailer were eyed suspiciously by policemen when we passed through Guildford, for this long combination of bicycle and demented bath-chair wriggled its way round the sober horse-traffic like a salmon slipping upstream. The roads were plain macadam, an inch deep in dust of many colours, the tints varying with the nature of the road metal used by the local councils. But the over-all hue was cement-grey; a fine, choking powder that gradually settled along the creases of our skin, our garments, and on every plane surface. By the time we reached Guildford we were three millers, and the trailer gave the appearance of a load of limestone.

On we pushed, though by now I was faint with hunger

and Jack was beginning to grow irritable. 'We'll stop on the Hog's Back,' said Father. 'A grand view from there over the Devil's Punchbowl.'

A minor adventure befell us almost as he spoke. We were bent over our handlebars, at the bottom of a sharp rise. Behind us rode a young man, alone, who had attached himself to us as we left Guildford, using us as pace-makers, perhaps. Jack was annoyed, for he hated collections of people, as being conspicuous demonstrations.

'Can't you let him go, Dad?' he said, urging Father to slow down. But Father had everything timed, and reduced to an economic output. His pace did not vary for some passing flipperdigibert of the road. He replied that we should be stopping soon for our midday meal, and that would enable us to shake off the stranger.

Suddenly we heard a cry of alarm. I raised my bemused head, and saw a stout woman on a tricycle, tearing down the hill with her feet off the pedals, which were flickering up and down, as it seemed, faster than the eye could follow. An instant later there was another cry from the stout woman, and a crash alongside us. The young man had pulled out, intending at last to pass our slow cortège. But he chose the wrong moment, for the tricyclist went slap into him. Machines and human bodies appeared immediately to multiply, and to be scattered all about us, amid a cloud of white dust, and groans and cries.

Jack and Father now both showed a common characteristic, for the bicycle with trailer, and the tandem, calmly slowed and stopped, the drivers dismounting and looking round in mild surprise. I had jumped clear, with a jolt that shook my bones, and I stood trembling, my eyes refusing, for a moment, to focus on the dreadful scene of carnage.

Father strode over to the mound of humanity in the middle of the road, lifted her up as though she were merely an inflated balloon, and assisted her to the side of the road.

'Now stay there!' he said, allowing her to relapse into tears and hysteria, while he returned to pick up the youth, who was kneeling within the frame of his bicycle, while the front wheel spun round, as an afterthought.

The ball of his thumb was grazed and bleeding. That was the only damage, apart from shock. Father whipped the young man's handkerchief out of his pocket, spat on the wound, wiped and bound it. The poor fellow, a weedy creature, sat on the bank, growing paler and paler, his teeth chattering.

'Pull yourself together, lad!' cried Father. 'Your machine's not damaged. I've straightened the pedal, so you can push along before there are any questions asked. Wrong of you, y' know, turning out like that!'

His brusque warning acted like a pail of well water on the youth, who was obviously about to faint. Shaking himself, he stood up, took a deep breath, that brought the colour back into his hollow cheek.

'No fault of mine,' he muttered ungraciously, and stumbled off, walking his machine up the hill, examining it as he went.

Meanwhile Father was directing the tonic of his personality at the stout woman.

'Now, Ma'am!' he cried. 'Is nobody with you?'

She was still incoherent, but we could detect references to her poor husband, and demands for the police, and denunciations of that monster of ungallant depravity who had brought her to this pretty pass. 'It's nobody's fault,' said Father, brushing away at her garments, and flicking her face and hands with her own handkerchief. 'You lost control. Should never do that, you know. Might have ruined your machine.'

By this time the poor husband approached down the hill on a bicycle of rare vintage, the back wheel being about two-thirds the size of the front one, and the chain encased in a honey-coloured, transparent gear-case square at both ends. The handlebars towered up, with grips of cork at least six inches long.

He was a small, nervous man, and he looked at my father beseechingly, like a spaniel.

'I will take charge,' he said. Though that was unbelievable, we left him and his runaway spouse, remounted and rode on.

I was still shaken when we stopped by the roadside before entering Farnham. But the cool deep grasses of the verge soon persuaded me into a calmness that restored my appetite. I looked about me while I devoured hard-boiled egg and bacon sandwiches. The sun was now beating down from a cloudless sky, over a rain-washed landscape every feature of which stood out in hard outline. The only blurred thing was the film of dust on my eyelashes. I blinked, wiped my eyes, and then all was crystalline.

'Ah,' exclaimed Father, 'the melon!'

He cut it in halves, scooped out the seeds, divided one of the halves and passed the quarters to his sons. We dipped our sweating faces into the fruit as though we were playing mouth-organs, while Father worked at his half with his clasp-knife, shovelling the dripping flesh into his upturned mouth and mumbling with pleasure. When all the flesh was scooped out, he split the empty gourd almost to a division, and clapped it, like the Tarn-

helm, on his head, fixing it there with the huge handkerchief that had recently succoured the stout lady of
the tricycle. With his fine Roman nose, his clear grey
eyes, black moustache, surmounted by the white-bound
helmet of gold, he looked like a Crusader. That is how
he rode on, during the fierce afternoon, to the wonder of
townsfolk and villagers as we trundled along through
Farnham and Alton, past lovely parks, pine woods, farm-
steads, over streams and round hillsides, further and
further from London, and from our familiar selves, the
world growing stranger and wilder, and we with it, until
at last, as dusk fell, we stumbled off our machines in the
tiny lane before the meadow-fronted cottages, fabulous
beings no longer in command of our limbs, or our wits.
But we recognized the Mother who awaited us, cool and
serene, the last daylight glinting on her gold spectacles,
and behind her an interior of candlelight and a huge
hearth full of shadows.

RICHARD CHURCH: from *Over the Bridge* (1955).

28

A Thames Night Swim

*In the essay on pages 14-21 Max Beerbohm recollects
London as he used to know it; Iris Murdoch's first novel,*
Under the Net, *includes episodes in which the characters
move about London as it now is. Her book is a characteristic specimen of English fiction in the 1950s, inasmuch
as it passes through various changes of mood—from
grave to gay, from lively to severe—and the people in it
are not set up as models of correct behaviour. The
passage here is the conclusion of a comic unrewarding
search around a number of London City taverns for a
friend of the men who plunge into this unique exploit.*

IRIS MURDOCH

It was a bit later again, it must have been some time
after two, when Finn expressed a desire to go swimming.
Lefty had been talking to Dave, and I was just getting
my second wind. The night was faultlessly warm and
still. As soon as Finn suggested this idea it seemed to
all of us except Dave an irresistible one. We discussed
where to go. The Serpentine was too far away and so
was Regent's Park, and the St. James's Park area is
always stiff with police. The obvious thing was to swim
in the Thames.

'You'll get swept away by the tide,' said Dave.

'Not if we swim when it's on the turn,' said Finn. This
was brilliant. But when was it on the turn?

'My diary will tell us,' said Lefty. We crowded round while he struck a match. High tide at London Bridge was at two fifty-eight. It was perfect. A moment later we were climbing the wall.

'Watch out for police,' said Lefty. 'They'll think we're going to rob a warehouse. If you see one, pretend to be drunk.'

This was rather superfluous advice.

Across a moonswept open space we followed what used to be Fyefoot Lane, where many a melancholy notice board tells in the ruins of the City where churches and where public houses once stood. Beside the solitary tower of St. Nicholas we passed into Upper Thames Street. There was no sound, not a bell, not a footstep. We trod softly. We turned out of the moonlight into a dark labyrinth of alleys and gutted warehouses where indistinguishable objects loomed in piles. Scraps of newspaper blotted the streets, immobilized in the motionless night. The rare street lamps revealed pitted brick walls and cast the shadow of an occasional cat. A street as deep and dark as a well ended at last in a stone breakwater, and on the other side, at the foot of a few steps, was the moon again, scattered in pieces upon the river. We climbed over on to the steps and stood in silence for a while with the water lapping our feet.

On either side the walls of warehouses jutted out, cutting our view and sheltering the inlet where the river came to us, thick with scum and floating spars of wood, full to overflowing in the bosom of London. There was a smell as of rotten vegetables. Finn was taking off his shoes. No man who has faced the Liffey can be appalled by the dirt of another river.

'Careful,' said Lefty. 'Keep well down on the steps, then no one can see us from the street. Don't talk aloud, and don't dive in. There may be river police around.' He pulled his shirt off.

I looked at Dave. 'Are you coming in?' I asked him.

'Of course not!' he said. 'I think you are all mad.' And he sat down with his back to the breakwater.

My heart was beating violently. I began to undress too. Already Finn was standing pale and naked with his feet in the water. He was thrusting aside the flotsam with his foot and walking slowly down the steps. The water reached to his knees, to his buttocks, and then with a soft splash he was away and the wood was knocking upon the stone as the ripples came back.

'What an infernal row he's making!' said Lefty.

My stomach was chill and I was shivering. I pulled off my last garment. Lefty was already stripped.

'Keep it quiet,' he said. 'I don't want to be copped for *this*!'

We looked at each other and smiled in the darkness. He turned to the river and began edging awkwardly down, his body diminishing into the black water. The night air touched my body with a touch which was neither warm nor cold, only very soft and unexpected. My blood buzzed behind my skin with a nervous beat. Then without a sound Lefty had followed Finn. The water took my ankles in a cold clasp. As I went down I could see from the corner of my eye Dave crouched above me like a monument. Then the water was about my neck and I shot out into the open river.

The sky opened out above me like an unfurled banner, cascading with stars and blanched by the moon. The black hulls of barges darkened the water behind me and murky towers and pinnacles rose indistinctly on the other bank. I swam well out into the river. It seemed enormously wide; and as I looked up and down stream

I could see on one side the dark pools under Blackfriars Bridge, and on the other the pillars of Southwark Bridge glistening under the moon. The whole expanse of water was running with light. It was like swimming in quicksilver. I looked about for Finn and Lefty, and soon saw their heads bobbing not far away. They came towards me and for a while we swam together. We had caught the tide beautifully upon the turn and there was not the least hint of a current.

I was easily the best swimmer of the three. Finn swims strongly but awkwardly, wasting his power in unnecessary movements and rolling too much from side to side. Lefty swam with neatness but without vigour. I guessed that he would soon tire. I swim excellently, giving myself to the water, and I have an effortless crawl which I can keep up indefinitely. Swimming has natural affinities with Judo. Both arts depend upon one's willingness to surrender a rigid and nervous attachment to the upright position. Both bring muscles into play throughout the whole body. Both demand, over an exceptionally wide area of bodily activity, the elimination of superfluous motion. Both resemble the dynamism of water which runs through many channels to find its own level. In fact, however, once one has learnt to control one's body and overcome the primeval fear of falling which is so deep in the human consciousness, there are few physical arts and graces which are not thereby laid open to one, or at any rate made much easier of access. I am, for instance, a good dancer and a very creditable tennis player. If it were possible for anything to console me for my lack of height, these things would console me.

Now the other two had gone back to the steps. I swam to one of the barges, and clung on to the cable for a

H

while, throwing my head back to scan a panorama of blue-black sky and black and silver water, and stilling my body until the silence entered me with a rush. Then I climbed up the cable until I was free of the water, and clung to it like a white worm. Then I let go with my feet, and clambered down hand over hand lowering myself noiselessly back into the river. As my legs broke the surface I could feel a gentle and continuous pull. The tide was beginning to run out again. I made for the steps.

IRIS MURDOCH: from *Under the Net* (1955).

29

A Day in A.D. 44

Through his broadcasts Sir Mortimer Wheeler has prob-
ably done more than anyone else to stimulate popular
interest in archæology—i.e. digging up the past—a branch
of historical study which previously attracted only a
limited number of scholars. Maiden Castle, the great
ancient British hill-fortress in Dorset, is one of the most
important prehistoric strongholds that archæologists have
investigated, and what is now known of it comes princi-
pally from the excavations by Sir Mortimer and his team
in the 1930s. The earthen triple ramparts enclosing a
camp of some twelve acres were raised probably not later
than 2000 B.C., and the site was alternately occupied and
long deserted by various tribes up to the time that
fugitives, no doubt fleeing before the invading Romans,
took refuge there, only to suffer annihilation in the battle
so vividly imagined here.

SIR MORTIMER WHEELER

MAIDEN CASTLE has two formidably guarded entrances.
That on the west is screened by no fewer than seven
ramparts; that on the east is sufficiently elaborate but is
of less gigantic proportion. The latter, therefore, we
chose for detailed examination, and the gradual recovery
of its varied and intricate evolution occupied much of
my time during three of our four seasons. As a structural
problem it was the most complicated and entertaining

within my experience, but this is not the context in which to retrace the laborious processes of ratiocination which led eventually to the reconstruction of its history. I am concerned here with one day only in that history, a day which may be dated within the year 44 of our era, and I will recall it primarily not as a sequence of events but as a sequence of discoveries.

The eastern, like the western, entrance is exceptionally provided with two gateways ('in' and 'out'), which open on to a crescentic forecourt. On both sides of the forecourt approaching roads wind upwards from the flanks of an outer court and outer defences. In the crescentic court we began to find ash and the post-holes of burnt huts. Here and there amongst the ash lay the iron heads of Roman catapult quarrels. As we dug on we came upon rough hollows filled with earth and ash, and in each hollow lay a human skeleton, sometimes two. The skeletons emerged, as our work proceeded, in all manner of contortions and orientations, with all the semblance of having been slung carelessly into their crude graves. Then two or three further features shaped the problem.

First, the dead had met a violent, sometimes savagely violent end. The skulls of many of them had been hacked viciously at the time of death; one of them bore no less than nine deep cuts. The victims had been struck variously on the top, front or back of the head—in other words, the wounds were battle-wounds, as indeed their repetition suggested, rather than the mark of methodical execution. And in confirmation of this, one skull showed the square piercing of a quadrangular Roman ballista-bolt, whilst another skeleton—most vivid relic of all—had an iron arrow-head embedded deeply in a vertebra. This last unhappy warrior, as he lay grievously wounded, had been finished off by a cut on the head.

Secondly, the skeletons were those both of men and of women; twenty-three men and eleven women were identified. The women had stood shoulder to shoulder with their menfolk in the final *mêlée*.

But, thirdly, for all the disorderly aspect of the cemetery, the dead had been buried by their friends with a measure of propriety. Most of the burials included bowls or, in one instance, a mug for the traditional food and drink. In two cases the dead held joints of lamb in their hands, joints chosen carefully as young and succulent. Amidst all the evidences of massacre and distraction, this final attention was not the least touching feature of the scene as it lay uncovered before us.

It was now easy enough to reconstruct the succession of events. Before the close fighting began, the regiment of catapults or *ballistæ*, which habitually accompanied a legion on campaign, put down a barrage across the gateway, causing casualties at the outset. Following the barrage, the Roman infantry advanced up the slope, cutting its way from rampart to rampart, tower to tower. In the innermost bay of the entrance, a number of huts had recently been built; these were now set alight, and under the rising clouds of smoke the gates were stormed. But resistance had been obstinate and the attack was pushed home with every sort of savagery. The scene became that of a massacre in which the wounded were not spared. Finally, the gates were demolished and the stone walls which flanked them reduced to the lowly and ruinous condition in which we found them, nineteen centuries later.

The sequel was no less apparent. That night, when the fires of the legion shone out (as we may fairly imagine) in orderly lines across the valley, the survivors crept forth from their broken stronghold and, in the darkness, buried their dead as nearly as might be out-side their tumbled gates, in that place where the ashes of their burnt huts lay warm and thick upon the ground. The task was carried out anxiously and hastily and without order; many of the dead were still in rigor mortis, contorted as they had fallen in the struggle; in any event, the living were in no condition for the niceties of ritual. Yet from few of the graves were omitted those tributes of food and drink which were the proper perquisites of the dead. The whole war-cemetery as it lay exposed before us was eloquent of mingled piety and distraction, of weariness, dread and darkness but yet not of complete forgetfulness. Surely no poor relic in the soil of Britain was ever more fraught with high tragedy, more worthy of brooding comment from the presiding Spirits of Hardy's own *Dynasts*.

SIR MORTIMER WHEELER: from *Still Digging* (1955).

30
Knowledge and Wisdom

In the first half of this century knowledge was gained at a faster pace than at any other time in the history of the world. When the second half of the century began, however, no one remained in doubt that knowledge had brought grave perils as well as great benefits, and that for the good of mankind—perhaps, indeed, for its very survival—knowledge must be directed and controlled by something better than itself. Few men of his time have possessed stores of knowledge equal to those of Bertrand Russell, and few have been more deeply concerned than he to seek a means of balancing knowledge with an equivalent gift of wisdom.

BERTRAND RUSSELL

MOST PEOPLE would agree that, although our age far surpasses all previous ages in knowledge, there has been no correlative increase in wisdom. But agreement ceases as soon as we attempt to define 'wisdom' and consider means of promoting it. I want to ask first what wisdom is, and then what can be done to teach it.

There are, I think, several factors that contribute to wisdom. Of these I should put first a sense of proportion: the capacity to take account of all the important factors in a problem and to attach to each its due weight. This has become more difficult than it used to be owing to the extent and complexity of the specialized knowledge required of various kinds of technicians. Suppose, for example, that you are engaged in research in scientific medicine. The work is difficult and is likely to absorb the whole of your intellectual energy. You have not time to consider the effect which your discoveries or inventions may have outside the field of medicine. You succeed (let us say), as modern medicine has succeeded, in enormously lowering the infant death-rate, not only in Europe and America, but also in Asia and Africa. This has the entirely unintended result of making the food supply inadequate and lowering the standard of life in the most populous parts of the world. To take an even more spectacular example, which is in everybody's mind at the present time: You study the composition of the atom from a disinterested desire for knowledge, and incidentally place in the hands of powerful lunatics the means of destroying the human race. In such ways the pursuit of knowledge may become harmful unless it is combined with wisdom; and wisdom in the sense of comprehensive vision is not necessarily present in specialists in the pursuit of knowledge.

Comprehensiveness alone, however, is not enough to constitute wisdom. There must be, also, a certain awareness of the ends of human life. This may be illustrated by the study of history. Many eminent historians have done more harm than good because they viewed facts through the distorting medium of their own passions. Hegel had a philosophy of history which did not suffer from any lack of comprehensiveness, since it started from the earliest times and continued into an indefinite future. But the chief lesson of history which he sought to inculcate was that from the year A.D. 400 down to his own time Germany had been the most important nation and the standard-bearer of progress in the world. Perhaps one could stretch the comprehensiveness that constitutes wisdom to include not only intellect but also feeling. It is by no means uncommon to find men whose knowledge is wide but whose feelings are narrow. Such men lack what I am calling wisdom.

It is not only in public ways, but in private life equally, that wisdom is needed. It is needed in the choice of ends to be pursued and in emancipation from personal prejudice. Even an end which it would be noble to pursue if it were attainable may be pursued unwisely if it is inherently impossible of achievement. Many men in past ages devoted their lives to a search for the philosopher's stone and the elixir of life. No doubt, if they could have found them, they would have conferred great benefits upon mankind, but as it was their lives were wasted. To descend to less heroic matters, consider the case of two men, Mr. A and Mr. B, who hate each other and, through mutual hatred, bring each other to destruction. Suppose you go to Mr. A and say, 'Why do you hate Mr. B?' He will no doubt give you an appalling list of Mr. B's vices, partly true, partly false. And now suppose you go to Mr. B. He will give you an exactly similar list of Mr. A's vices with an equal admixture of truth and falsehood. Suppose you now come back to Mr. A and say, 'You will be surprised to learn that Mr. B says the same things about you as you say about him', and you go to Mr. B and make a similar speech. The first effect, no doubt, will be to increase their mutual hatred, since each will be so horrified by the other's injustice. But perhaps, if you have sufficient patience and sufficient persuasiveness, you may succeed in convincing each that the other has only the normal share of human wickedness, and that their enmity is harmful to both. If you can do this, you will have instilled some fragment of wisdom.

H*

I think the essence of wisdom is emancipation, as far as possible, from the tyranny of the here and the now. We cannot help the egoism of our senses. Sight and sound and touch are bound up with our own bodies and cannot be made impersonal. Our emotions start similarly from ourselves. An infant feels hunger or discomfort, and is unaffected except by his own physical condition. Gradually with the years his horizon widens, and, in proportion as his thoughts and feelings become less personal and less concerned with his own physical states, he achieves growing wisdom. This is of course a matter of degree. No one can view the world with complete impartiality; and if anyone could, he would hardly be able to remain alive. But it is possible to make a continual approach towards impartiality, on the one hand, by knowing things somewhat remote in time or space, and, on the other hand, by giving to such things their due weight in our feelings. It is this approach towards impartiality that constitutes growth in wisdom.

Can wisdom in this sense be taught? And, if it can, should the teaching of it be one of the aims of education? I should answer both these questions in the affirmative. We are told on Sundays that we should love our neighbour as ourselves. On the other six days of the week, we are exhorted to hate him. You may say that this is nonsense, since it is not our neighbour whom we are exhorted to hate. But you will remember that the precept was exemplified by saying that the Samaritan was our neighbour. We no longer have any wish to hate Samaritans and so we are apt to miss the point of the parable. If you want to get its point, you should substitute Communist or anti-Communist, as the case may be, for Samaritan. It might be objected that it is right to hate those who do harm. I do not think so. If you hate them, it is only too likely that you will become equally harmful; and it is very unlikely that you will induce them to abandon their evil ways. Hatred of evil is itself a kind of bondage to evil. The way out is through understanding, not through hate. I am not advocating non-resistance. But I am saying that resistance, if it is to be effective in preventing the spread of evil, should be combined with the greatest degree of understanding and the smallest degree of force that is compatible with the survival of the good things that we wish to preserve.

It is commonly urged that a point of view such as I have been advocating is incompatible with vigour in action. I do not think history bears out this view. Queen Elizabeth I in England and Henry IV in France lived in a world where almost everybody was fanatical, either on the Protestant or on the Catholic side. Both remained free from the errors of their time, and both, by remaining free, were beneficent and certainly not ineffective. Abraham Lincoln conducted a great war without ever departing from what I have been calling wisdom.

I have said that in some degree wisdom can be taught. I think that this teaching should have a larger intellectual element than has been customary in what has been thought of as moral instruction. I think that the disastrous results of hatred and narrow-mindedness to those who feel them can be pointed out incidentally in the course of giving knowledge. I do not think that knowledge and morals ought to be too much separated. It is true that the kind of specialized knowledge which is required for various kinds of skill has very little to do with wisdom. But it should be supplemented in education by wider surveys calculated to put it in its place in the total of human activities. Even the best technicians should also be good citizens; and when I say 'citizens',

I mean citizens of the world and not of this or that sect or nation. With every increase of knowledge and skill, wisdom becomes more necessary, for every such increase augments our capacity of realizing our purposes, and therefore augments our capacity for evil, if our purposes are unwise. The world needs wisdom as it has never needed it before; and if knowledge continues to increase, the world will need wisdom in the future even more than it does now.

BERTRAND RUSSELL: from *Portraits from Memory and Other Essays* (1956).

31

Mending a Bird

Though collecting is an almost universal hobby, few people are fortunate enough or bold enough to collect animals in the wilds as Gerald Durrell does. His experiences have enabled him to give many fascinating talks on sound radio and television, and his books are not less entertaining; indeed they last longer and are therefore more satisfying. In this story of how he and his wife dealt with a wounded South American bird, they are seen as a skilful and patient animal doctor and nurse-assistant.

GERALD DURRELL

ONE MORNING we received an addition to the collection, which we could hear arriving when it was still a good half-mile down the road. I saw an Indian trotting rapidly towards the camp clearing, endeavouring with moderate success to keep his large straw hat on with one hand while with the other he tried to prevent something from climbing out of a rather frayed wicker basket. The thing, whatever it was, kept complaining about its confinement in a series of rich, bass honks which sounded like someone trying to play a complicated Bach fugue on an old bulb motor-horn. The Indian dashed up to me, laid the basket at my feet, then stood back, doffing his big hat and grinning broadly. . . .

I wondered what species of bird could possibly produce that complicated series of organ-like brays. The
basket lay on the ground, shuddering, and more of the
wild cries broke out. Looking down, I found myself
staring into a cold, fish-like eye of pale bronze colour
that glared through the wicker-work at me. I bent down,
undid the lid of the basket, and lifted it a trifle, so that
I could see the occupant; I caught a brief glimpse of a
tumble of tawny feathers, and then a long, green, dagger-
shaped beak shot out through the crack, buried itself half
an inch in the fleshy part of my thumb, and was immediately whipped back into the basket again. Drawn by
my yelp of pain and resulting flood of bad language,
Jacquie appeared on the scene and asked resignedly
what had bitten me this time.

'A bittern,' I said, indistinctly, sucking my wound.

'I know, darling, but *what* bit you?'

'I was bitten by a bittern,' I explained.

Jacquie stared at me blankly for a moment.

'Are you being funny?' she inquired at length.

'No, I tell you I was bitten by this blasted bird . . . or
rather I was pecked by it. . . . It's a tiger bittern.'

'Not a jaguar bittern?' she asked sweetly.

'This is no time for silly jokes,' I said severely; 'help
me get it out of the basket . . . I want to have a look
at it.'

Jacquie squatted down and eased the lid off the basket,
and once more the green beak shot out, but this time I
was ready for it and grabbed it adroitly between finger
and thumb. The bird protested deafeningly, and kicked
and struggled violently in the basket, but I managed to
get my other hand inside and to grab him firmly by the
wings and lift him out.

I don't know what Jacquie was expecting, but the sight

of him made her gasp, for a tiger bittern is definitely one of the more spectacular of the wading birds. Imagine a small, rather hump-backed heron, with sage-green legs and beak, and clad entirely in plumage of pale-green colour spotted and striped with a wonderful, flamboyant pattern of black and tiger-orange so that the whole bird seems to glow like a miniature feathered bonfire.

'Isn't he lovely?' said Jacquie. 'What gorgeous colouring!'

'Here,' I said, 'just hang on to his feet a second—I want to look at his wing. It seems to be hanging in a rather peculiar fashion.'

While Jacquie held on to his green legs, I ran my hand down the underside of his left wing, and half-way down the main bone I found the ominous swelling of the muscles that generally denotes a break. I probed the swelling with my fingers, and manipulated the wing gently: sure enough, there was a break about three-quarters of the way down, but to my relief it was a clean break, and not a complicated mass of splintered bone.

'Anything wrong with it?' asked Jacquie.

'Yes, it's broken fairly high up. Quite a clean break.'

'What a shame! He's such a lovely bird. Isn't there anything we can do about it?'

'Well, I can have a shot at setting it. But you know how damn stupid these creatures are about bandages and things.'

'Let's try, anyway. I think it's worth it.'

'O.K. You go and get the money, and I'll try to explain to Daniel Boone, here.'

Jacquie disappeared into the house, while I explained slowly and tortuously to the Indian that the bird's wing was broken. He felt it and agreed, shaking his head and looking very sad. I went on to explain that I would pay him half the value of the bird then, and the other half should it still be alive in a week's time. This was a fairly complicated explanation that taxed my primitive Spanish to the extreme. Also, I find it helpful, when attempting to speak a language other than my own, to use my hands lavishly, for a gesture can explain something when a limited vocabulary would let me down. Clutching the infuriated bittern to my bosom, I could not indulge in gestures to help me out, for one hand held the bird round the body, while the other clasped his beak; in consequence I had to repeat everything two or three times before the Indian got the hang of it. At length he grasped my meaning and nodded vigorously, and we both smiled at each other and gave little bows and murmured, ' *Gracias, gracias.*' Then a thought struck the Indian, and he asked me how much I was going to pay; this simple question was my undoing. Without thinking, I let go of the bittern's beak, and lifted my hand to show him the requisite number of fingers. It was the opportunity the bird had been waiting for, and he did what all members of his family do in a fight. He looked upwards and launched his beak in a murderous lunge at my eyes. By sheer luck I managed to jerk back my head in time, so that he missed my eyes, but I did not jerk it back far enough; his beak shot squarely up my left nostril, and the point embedded itself briefly somewhere near my sinus.

Those who have never been pecked in the nose by a tiger bittern can have little idea of the exquisite agony it produces, nor of the force of the blow. I felt rather as though I had been kicked in the face by a horse, and reeled back, momentarily blinded by the pain and stunned by the force of the thrust. I managed to keep my head well back to avoid a second stab from the beak, while my nose gushed blood like a fountain that splashed all over me, the bittern, and the Indian, who had rushed forward to help me. I handed the bird over to him and went to the house in search of first-aid; Jacquie busied herself with wet towels, cotton wool, and boracic, scolding and commiserating as she did so.

'What would have happened if he'd got you in the eye?' she asked, scrubbing at the crust of dried blood on my lips and cheeks.

'I dread to think. His beak's at least six inches long, and if he'd got a straight peck, with that force behind it, he'd have gone right through into my brain, I should imagine.'

'Well, perhaps that will teach you to be more careful in future,' she said unsympathetically. 'Here, hold this cotton wool to your nose; it's still bleeding a bit.'

I went outside again, looking like one of those lurid anti-vivisection posters, and concluded my bargain with the Indian. Then I put the bittern into a temporary cage and went to collect the necessary medical appliances for the operation on his wing. First, I had to carve two splints out of soft white wood and pad them carefully with a layer of cotton wool held in place by lint. Then we prepared a large box as an operating table, and laid out bandages, scissors, razor-blade. I put on a thick gauntlet glove and went to fetch the patient. As I opened the door of his cage he lunged at me, and I caught him by the beak and pulled him out, squawking protestingly. We bound his feet with a bandage, and dealt in the same way with his beak. Then he was laid on the table, and, while Jacquie held his feet and beak, I set to work. I had to clip off all the feathers on the wing; this was not only in order to make it easier to fix the splint, but also to take as much weight off the wing as possible. When the wing was almost as bare as a plucked chicken, I manœuvred one of the flat splints under the wing, so that the break lay in the centre of it; then came the delicate and tricky job of feeling until I located the two broken ends of bone, and then twisting and pulling them gently until they lay together in a normal position. Holding them in this position on the splint with my thumb, I slid the other splint on top, and held the break firmly, trapped between the two slats of padded wood. Then the whole thing had to be bound round and round with yards of bandages, and the finished product tied firmly against the body with a sort of sling, so that the weight of the bandages and splints did not drag the wing down and pull the broken ends of bone out of place. This done, our patient was put back in his cage, and supplied with a plate of chopped meat and some fresh water.

For the rest of the day he behaved very well, eating all his food, standing in one position, not attempting to interfere with his wing, and generally behaving as though he had been in captivity for years. Most wild creatures have the strongest possible views about bandages, splints, and other medical accoutrements, and no sooner do you put them on, than their one ambition in life is to get them off again as quickly as possible. I had had a number of irritating experiences in the past with both birds and mammals over this vexed question of first-aid, and so I was surprised and pleased when the tiger bittern seemed to take the whole thing calmly and philosophically. I felt that at last I had found a bird who was sensible and who realized that we were strapping him up for the best possible reasons. However, I was a bit premature in my judgement, for next morning, when we were checking round the collection, Jacquie peered into the bittern's cage, and then uttered an anguished groan.

'Just come and look at this stupid bird,' she called.

'What's he done?'

'He's got all his bandage off . . . I thought you were being a little too optimistic about him last night.'

The tiger bittern was standing gloomily in the corner of his cage, glaring at us with his sardonic bronze eyes. He had obviously spent an energetic evening stripping the bandages from his wing, and he had made a good job of it. But he had not reckoned with one thing: the inside edge of his beak was minutely serrated, like a fretsaw, the teeth of which were directed backwards, towards the bird's throat. When he caught fish, these little 'teeth' helped him to hold on to the slippery body, and made sure that it only slid one way. This is a very fine thing when you are catching fish, but when you are unwinding bandages you find this type of beak a grave disadvantage, for the bandages get hooked on the serrated edge. So the tiger bittern stood there with some twelve feet of bandage firmly hooked to his beak and dangling down in a magnificent festoon. He looked like an attenuated, morose Father Christmas whose beard had come askew after a hot half-hour distributing presents. He glared at us when we laughed, and gave an indignant and slightly muffled honk through the bandages.

We had to get him out of his cage and spend half an hour with a pair of tweezers stripping the tattered bandage from his beak. To my surprise and pleasure, I found that he had not succeeded in removing the splints, so the wing-bones were still held in the same position. We bound him up once more, and he looked so contrite that I felt he had learnt his lesson. The next morning, though, all the bandages were off and trailing from his beak, and we had to go through the whole laborious re-bandaging again. But it was no use, for every morning we would be treated to the sight of him standing in his cage, heavily disguised under a patriarchal cascade of white beard.

'I'm getting sick of bandaging this bloody bird,' I said, as Jacquie and I cleaned his beak for the eighth morning running.

'I am, too. But what can we do? We're using up an awful lot of bandage; I wish we'd thought of bringing some sticking-plaster.'

'Or even some plaster bandage . . . that would have fooled him. What worries me, though, is that all this messing about isn't going to do the wing any good. For all I know, the bones may have shifted under the splint, and his wing will heal with a damn great bend in it, like a croquet hoop.'

'Well,' said Jacquie philosophically, 'all we can do is to wait and see. We can't do any more than we're doing.'

So, every morning for three interminable weeks, we unpicked, unravelled, and re-bandaged the bittern. Then the great day came when the bones should have healed, and the bandage was removed from his beak for the last time. I seized the scissors and started to cut away the splints.

'I wonder what it'll be like,' said Jacquie.

'Probably look like a corkscrew,' I said gloomily.

But as the splints fell away, they revealed the bittern's wing lying there as straight as a die. I could hardly believe my eyes; it was impossible to see where the break had been, and even when I felt the bone with my fingers I could not have located the break if it had not been for a slight ridge of protecting bone which had appeared at the point where the two broken ends had grown together. The wing-muscles had, of course, grown weak through lack of use, and so the wing dropped considerably, but after a week or so of use he soon regained the power in it, and the wing went back to its normal position. For some time it remained bald, but eventually the feathers grew again, and when he attacked his food-pan with beak snapping and wing flapping, you could not have told that there had ever been anything wrong with him at all. We were very proud of him, not only because he was a good advertisement for our surgery, but also because he was a good example of how worthwhile it is to persevere with even the most hopeless-looking cases.

GERALD DURRELL: from *The Drunken Forest* (1956).

32

Wild Flower

Science fiction was being written by Jules Verne and H. G. Wells before the end of the nineteenth century, and many of Wells's novels and short stories of that kind are within the bounds of scientific possibility. The coming of the nuclear age and the rapid advances in space travel since 1945 have opened up such prospects of new adventure—and also of horror—that writers of science fiction have let imagination leap ahead unchecked, for today's 'impossibilities' may become tomorrow's commonplaces. John Wyndham has written several novels which are science fiction and something more. In addition to providing excitement and stirring the reader's imagination, his characters are always convincing, however futuristic may seem the happenings in which they are caught up. Good science-fiction novels need to be read from beginning to end: no single chapter can fairly or helpfully be taken from the whole. One of John Wyndham's short stories is therefore chosen here.

JOHN WYNDHAM

Not Miss Fray. Not Felicity Fray.

Let others jerk awake to an alarm, scramble from bed, scrub away the clinging patina of sleep with a face-flannel, hunt out the day's clothes, watch the percolator impatiently, urge the toast to pop up more quickly. Let them chew briskly, swallow gulpily, and hurry, arms and legs reciprocating briskly, on their ways. Let these auto-

226

mata, with batteries regenerated, respond with spry efficiency to the insistent eye of the new day's sun, and let them greet the morning with resolution in heel and toe, a high-tensile gleam in the eye, and set off to make their new deals, new conquests . . .

But not Felicity Fray.

For today is part of yesterday. And yesterday and today are parts of being alive. And being alive is not just an affair of the days going clonk-clonk-clonk like the pendulum of a grandfather clock: being alive is something continuous, that does not repeat; something that one should be aware of all the time, sleeping and waking. . . .

It may not last much longer.

There is no savour in hurry; so Miss Fray did not hurry; she did not jerk or bounce into the beginning of her day. About dawn she started to drift from dream through half-dream to day-dream, and lay unmoving, listening to the birds, watching the sky lighten, becoming aware of the day as it became aware of itself.

For more than an hour she lay hovering this and that side of the misty edge of sleep. Sometimes the sounds in her ears were real birds singing, sometimes they were remembered voices speaking. She enjoyed them both, smiling in her half-sleep.

By the time the day began to win her certainly from the night the birds were almost silent. They had done with the greeting, and started on the business of looking for food. She was quite abruptly aware that the world was almost noiseless.

There was an alarming feeling of unreality. She held her breath to listen for some reassuring sound. Supposing it had all stopped, now?—As it might do one day.

Perhaps, even at this moment, there were in some parts

of the world great columns of smoke writhing upwards in Medusan coils, swelling out at the top into cerebral convolutions that pulsed with a kind of sub-life, marking the beginning of the silence that meant the end of everything.

For years now, when she was off her guard, those pillars of smoke had been likely to start up in her mind. She hated and feared them. They were the triumphant symbol of Science.

Science was, perhaps, wonderful, but, for Miss Fray, it was a wonder of the left hand. Science was the enemy of the world that lived and breathed; it was a crystalline formation on the harsh naked rock of brain, mindless, insensitive, barren, yet actively a threat, an alien threat that she feared as un-understandingly as an animal fears fire. Science, the great antibiotic.

So Felicity listened unhappily.

. A bird called, and was answered.

That was not enough.

She went on listening for more reassurance.

In the farmyard several fields away, a tractor coughed, stuttered, and then ran more steadily, warming up.

She relaxed, relieved to be sure that the world was still alive. Then she faintly frowned her ungrateful contempt for the tractor, and pushed it out of her consciousness.

It, too, was a manifestation of science, and unwelcome.

She withdrew among her thoughts. She resurrected stored moments and magical glimpses, and remembered golden words. She landscaped her own Arcady which knew no Science.

The tractor throbbed more briskly as it trundled out of the yard, the sound of it diminished to a purr as it crossed the fields, unheard by Felicity.

There was plenty of time. Enough to take the field-path way to school, and not to hurry over it.

The sun was climbing, a medallion pinned on a deepening blue cloak. Later on, the day would be hot, but now it was fresh, with a touch like a cool, white-fingered hand. Refractile gems still trembled on the leaves and stalks.

Beads from the shaken grass ran down her legs, showered on the white canvas shoes, fell like kisses on her feet.

Cows, coming out from the sheds with their udders relieved, but still slow and patient, stared at her with incurious curiosity, and then turned away to tear the grass, and munch in thoughtless rumination.

A lark, high up, trilled to mislead her from its nest.

A young blackbird, looking puffy and overfed, eyed her cautiously from the hedge.

A light draught of summer wind blew through her cotton frock, caressing her with cobweb fingers.

Then there was a muttering in the sky; then a roaring that rumbled back and forth in the vault; then a shrieking over her head, a battering at the ears and the senses, not to be shut out. The present assaulting her, bawling unignorably, frighteningly through its jet-mouths; Science on the wing.

Felicity put her hands to her ears and rocked her head. The outrage hurtled close above, sound-waves clashing together, buffeting, and reeling back.

It passed, and she uncovered her ears again. With tears in her eyes she shook her fist at the fleeing shriek of the jets and all they represented, while the air still shuddered about her.

The cows continued to graze.

How comfortable to be a cow. Neither expecting nor regretting; having no sense of guilt, nor need for it.

Making no distinctions between the desirable and undesirable works of men; able to flick them, like the flies, aside with the swish of a tow-ended tail.

The shriek and the rumble died in the distance. The shattered scene began to re-integrate behind it, still for a while bloom-brushed and bruised, but slowly healing.

One day there would be too much bruising; too much to recover from.

'Imitations of mortality,' said Miss Fray, to herself. 'So many little deaths before the big one. How silly I am to suffer. Why should I feel all these pangs of guilt for other people? I am not responsible for this—I am not even much afraid, for myself. Why do I have to be so hurt by fear for all and everything?'

A thrush sang in the spinney beyond the hedge.

She paused to listen.

Unguent, sweet notes.

She walked on, becoming aware again of the silk-fringed zephyrs on her cheeks, the sun on her arms, the dew on her feet.

As Felicity opened the door the hive-murmur beyond sank into silence.

The rows of pink-cheeked faces framed in long hair, short hair, plaits, some of it morning-tidy, some of it already waywardly awry, were all turned towards her. The bright eyes were all fixed on her face.

'Good morning, Miss Fray,' they all said, in unison, and silence fell as completely as before.

She could feel the suppressed expectation in the air as they watched her. There was something she must respond to. She looked for it. Her glance went round the familiar room till it reached her desk. There it stopped, where a small glass vase held a single flower.

The rows of eyes switched from her to the desk, and then back again.

She walked slowly across and sat down in her chair, her gaze never leaving the flower.

It was something she had never seen before; she was quite unable to classify it, and she looked at it for a long time.

It was more complex than the simpler field flowers, yet not sophisticated. The colours were clear, but not primaries. The shape was comely, but without garden-bred formality. The ground-colour of the petals was a pale pink, flushing a little at the over-rolled edges, paling to cream further back. Then there was the flush-colour again, powder-stippled at first, then reticulated, then solid as it narrowed into the trumpet, but split by white spurs of the centre veins. There was just a suggestion of orchis about it, perhaps, but it was no kind of orchis she had ever seen, alive or pictured. The petal curves were sweet natural roundings, like limbs, or water cascading, or saplings bent in the wind. The texture was depthlessly soft.

Felicity leaned closer, gazing into the velvet throat. Little crescent-shaped stamens faintly dusted with pollen trembled on green, hair-like stalks. She caught the scent of it. A little sweetness, a little sharpness, a little earthiness, blended with a subtlety to make a perfumer's art vulgar and banal.

She breathed in the scent again, and looked into the flower hypnotized, unable to take her eyes from it, loving it in its brave delicacy with a sweet, longing compassion.

She had forgotten the room, the eyes that watched her, everything but the flower itself.

A fidgeting somewhere brought her back. She lifted

her head, and looked unhurriedly along the rows of faces.

'Thank you,' she said. 'It's a beautiful flower. What is it?'

Seemingly, no one knew.

'Who brought it?' Felicity asked them.

A small, golden-headed child in the middle of the second row pinked a little.

'I did, Miss Fray.'

'And you don't know what it is, Marielle?'

'No, Miss Fray, I just found it, and I thought it was pretty, and I thought you'd like it,' she explained, a trifle anxiously.

Felicity looked back to the flower again.

'I do like it, Marielle. It's lovely. It was very kind of you to think of bringing it for me.'

She loitered over the flower a few seconds more, and then moved the vase decisively to the left of the desk. With an effort she turned her eyes away from it, back to the rows of faces.

'One day,' she said, 'I'll read you some William Blake —"To see a World in a Grain of Sand, And a Heaven in a Wild Flower . . ." But now we must get on, we've wasted too much time already. I want you to copy out what I write on the board, in your best handwriting.'

She picked up the chalk and thought for a moment, looking at the flower. Then she went over to the black-board, and wrote:

'Their colours and their forms were then to me an appetite; a feeling and a love . . .'

'Marielle. Just a moment,' Felicity said.

The child paused and turned back as the others streamed out of the room.

'Thank you very much for bringing it. Was it the only one?' Felicity asked her.

'Oh, no, Miss Fray. There were three or four clumps of them.'

'Where, Marielle? I'd like to get a root of it, if I can.'

'On Mr. Hawkes's farm. In the top corner of the big field, where the aeroplane crashed,' the child told her.

'Where the aeroplane crashed,' Felicity repeated.

'Yes, Miss Fray.'

Felicity sat down slowly, staring at the flower. The child waited, and shifted from one foot to the other.

'Please, may I go now, Miss Fray?'

'Yes,' said Felicity, without looking up. 'Yes, of course.'

Feet scuttered out of the room.

Felicity went on looking at the flower.

'Where the aeroplane crashed.' That had been almost a year ago—on a summer's evening when all the world was quietening and settling down for the night. 'Now fades the glimmering landscape on the sight, and all the air a solemn stillness holds.' Then the aeroplane, wheeling its droning flight, destroying the peace. It was a silver-paper cross up in the sky where the sunlight was still bright. Unusually, Felicity looked up. She tried to ignore the noise and her prejudices, for the craft had, undeniably, a silver-moth beauty of its own. She watched it turn, the sunset glistering the undersides of the wings as it tilted. Then, suddenly, amid the silver there had been a flash of rose-red fire, and the silver moth ceased to exist. Pieces of glittering foil were spreading apart and falling. The largest piece trailed smoke above it, like a black funeral plume.

A great crack slapped at her ears.

The pieces twisted and flashed in the sky as they came,

some fast, some slower. The biggest of all seemed to be falling straight towards her. Perhaps she screamed. She threw herself on the ground, arms clutched over her head and ears, willing to sink herself into the earth itself.

There were interminable second-fractions of waiting while the silver wreckage came hurtling down the sky, and Felicity and all the world about her held their breath.

The solid ground bounced under her; then came the crash, and the shrieking of metal.

Felicity looked up, biting fearfully on her hand.

She saw the silver body, a crumpled fish-shape, less than a hundred yards away, and in that moment petals of flame blossomed round it.

Something else fell close by.

She cringed close to the earth again.

Something in the main body blew up. Bits of metal whirred like pheasants over her, and plopped around.

Presently she risked raising her head again. The wreck was a cone of flame with black smoke above. She could feel the warmth on her face. She did not dare to stand up lest something else should explode and send jagged metal fragments slicing into her.

She had been still there, clinging to the earth and crying, when the crash-parties arrived and found her.

Shock, they had said, shock and fright. They had treated her for that, and then sent her home.

She had cried for the destruction, for the fire and smoke, the noise and confusion of it; and, too, for the people who had died in it, for the wanton futility of it, for the harsh, mindless, silliness of a world that did these things and kept on doing them and would keep on doing them until the last two sub-critical masses were brought together for the last time.

They kept her in bed a few days, with instructions to rest and relax; but it was difficult to relax when things kept on going round and round in one's head.

'Oh God,' she prayed, 'won't You stop them? It isn't *their* world to do as they like with. It's Your world, and mine—the heart's world that they are destroying with their brain's world. Please, God, while there is still time —You destroyed their presumption at Babel, won't You do it again, before it's too late?'

Felicity remembered the prayer as she sat at her desk, looking at the beautiful flower.

They had put a fence round the place where the aeroplane had crashed, and set guards, too, to keep people away. Inside it, men in overall suits prowled and prowled, searching, listening, watching counters.

Cobalt was the trouble, they said. She had wondered how that could be. But it was not the artist's cobalt they wanted: the scientists had taken even the deep blue colour of the sea, and had done something deadly to that, too, it appeared.

Though not altogether, not necessarily deadly, Miss Simpson who taught science at the High School had explained to her. The aeroplane had been carrying some radio-active cobalt intended for a hospital somewhere in the Middle East. In the crash, or perhaps in the first explosion, the lead box that kept it safe had been broken open. It was extremely dangerous, and had to be recovered.

'How? Dangerous?' Felicity had wanted to know.

And Miss Simpson had told her something of the effects of gamma rays on living matter.

Several weeks passed before the searching men were completely satisfied, and went away. They had left the fence, no longer guarded, simply as a mark to indicate the piece of ground that was not to be ploughed this season. The ground had been left free to grow what it would.

And out of the noise, the destruction, the fire, the deadly radiations had sprung the lovely flower.

Felicity went on looking at it for a long time in the silent room. Then she raised her eyes, and glanced along the rows of desks where the bright faces had been.

'I see,' she said, to the emptiness and the unseen. 'I'm weak. I have had too little faith.'

She had a disinclination to revisit the site of the crash alone. She asked Marielle to come with her on Saturday and show her where the flowers grew.

They climbed by a cool path through the woods, crossed a stile and the pasture beyond it. When they came to the enclosure, its fence already pushed flat in several places, they found a man already within it. He wore a shirt and blue jeans, and was engaged in unslinging a heavy cylinder from his back. He laid the thing carefully on the ground and pulled out a large spotted handkerchief to wipe his face and neck. He turned as they approached, and grinned amiably. Felicity recognized him as the farmer's second son.

'Hot work carrying three or four gallons on your back this weather,' he explained apologetically, wiping the handkerchief down his arms so that the golden hairs stood up and glinted in the sunlight.

Felicity looked at the ground. There were five or six small clumps of the flowers growing in the weeds and grass, one of them half crushed under the cylinder.

'Oh,' said Marielle, in distress. 'You've been killing them—killing the flowers. They're what we came for.'

'You can pick 'em, and welcome,' he told her.

'But we wanted some roots, to grow them,' Marielle told him woefully. She turned to Felicity unhappily. 'They're such pretty flowers, too.'

'Pretty enough,' agreed the man, looking down at them. 'But there it is. Can't have this lot seeding all over the rest, you see.'

'You've poisoned them all—every one?' Marielle asked miserably.

The man nodded.

''Fraid they're done for now, for all they still look all right. 'F you'd 've let me know . . . but it's too late now. But they'll do you no harm to pick,' he explained. ''Tisn't poison in the old way, you see. Something to do with hormones, whatever they are. Doesn't knock 'em out, as you might say, just sends 'em all wrong in the growing so they give up. Wonderful what the scientific chaps get hold of these days. Never know what they'll bring out next, do you?'

Felicity and Marielle gathered little bunches of the doomed flowers. They still looked as delicately beautiful and still had their poignant scent. At the stile Marielle stopped and stood looking sadly at her little bunch.

'They're so lovely,' she said mournfully, with tears in her eyes.

Felicity put an arm round her.

'They are lovely,' she agreed. 'They're very lovely—and they've gone. But the important thing is that they came. That's the wonderful thing. There'll be some more—some day—somewhere. . . .'

A jet came shrieking suddenly, close over the hill-top. Marielle put her hands over her ears. Felicity stood watching the machine shrink among the scream and

I

rumble of protesting air. She held up her little posy of flowers to the blast.

'This is your answer,' she said. 'This. You bullies, with your vast clubs of smoke—this is greater than all of you.'

Marielle took down her hands.

'I hate them—I hate them,' she said, her eyes on the vanishing speck.

'I hate them, too,' agreed Felicity. 'But now I'm not afraid of them any more. I have found a remedy, an elixir:

> *It is a wine of virtuous powers;*
> *My mother made it of wild flowers.'*

JOHN WYNDHAM: 'Wild Flower', from *The Seeds of Time* (1956).

33

The Musical Seal

It is a fact that seals are attracted by music, though we cannot confidently say that they 'love' it. We have no means of knowing what sensations animals feel when listening to sounds that give pleasure to us. Some cats are affected when anyone whistles a tune or when music is broadcast: a cat known to the editor of this anthology would jump on his lap and put a paw reprovingly over his lips when particular notes were whistled. The same cat would sit apparently enraptured by most radio classical music, but would run angrily from the room when certain pieces were played. But the ways of Rowena Farre's seal were stranger than those of any cat, for it was not only attracted by music but was also determined to become a performing instrumentalist itself.

ROWENA FARRE

LORA'S MUSICAL talent came out early. Whenever Aunt Miriam or I struck up on the piano the other animals would take no notice. Not so Lora. She would wriggle over to the instrument, lean against it or (more inconveniently) the player's legs, and listen with an expression of intense concentration and joy which was quite flattering, swaying now and then with her whole body to the music. When the music stopped she would sit quietly for several minutes, still under its spell. Her reactions to my singing, however, can only be described as humiliating.

A relation had sent me a mouth organ and book of songs for a birthday present. Thumbing through the book, I decided that I would do a little singing practice each day. For the first session I chose a time when Aunt was out picking wild raspberries and there was not an animal within sight. After a preliminary scale or two, I started off on 'Men of Harlech'. To my annoyance, I heard a loud groan beside me. Looking down, I saw Lora and continued singing. Whereupon she broke into a roar. Seals have perhaps the largest vocal range among mammals. Their repertoire includes grunts, snorts, barks, peculiar mewing, hisses, and a wail which often rises from a deep bass to a treble. The roar turned to a hiss. I still took no notice but my reedy efforts were soon outclassed. Then I had the idea of letting her sing on her own to my accompaniment. During the practice sessions which followed, when I played a simple tune at a fairly slow pace with bars of steadily ascending and descending notes, she made valiant efforts to follow the music in a tuneless wail. A sudden high or low note, or a piece played too quickly, plainly annoyed her, for she would start to grunt and beat about with her fore-flippers—a habit of hers when angry. Within a week she was able to get through 'Baa-baa Black Sheep' and 'Danny Boy' without a break, and was beginning to learn 'Where my Caravan has Rested'.

She began to pester me for a mouth organ. I was playing it outside the croft one afternoon and, growing weary of the grunts and whines and a heavily whiskered nose pressed against my face every so often as she attempted to wrest it from me, I finally acknowledged defeat and placed it in her mouth. From that moment she considered the mouth organ to be hers. Having gained possession of it, she found to her annoyance that it emitted no sound in spite of being gnawed with vigour. So she started tossing it up into the air and catching it as though it were the ball, and then, her annoyance increasing, rolling on it. All to no effect. Taking the instrument in her mouth once again she gave a loud sigh of desperation. This produced a blast of noise from the mouth organ and galvanized Lora to fresh efforts. I set off for a walk. When I returned in about an hour there were most curious sounds coming from the rear of the croft. Lora had learned the blow-suck method and there she was, blowing and sucking feebly, in a state of almost complete exhaustion, for she had been doing this, apparently, ever since I had left her. She made no protest when I took the mouth organ from her. From that day onwards it became her favourite toy, replacing in her affections the rubber ball which she shared with the dog and otters. I do not think Mr. Larry Adler would have approved of her playing, but it certainly gave her a good deal of pleasure.

I happened to mention in a letter to an elderly relation of mine that Lora was developing into a remarkable seal and could sing and play the mouth organ. Aunt Felicity was a staunch defender of all animals, wild and domesticated, and sat on numerous committees which saw to their protection and well-being. The merest suspicion in her mind that an animal was being badly treated roused her fighting spirit. Her letter in reply to my own left me in no doubt that she considered I was committing heinous crimes against the hapless Lora.

'Dear Rowena, I was shocked and ashamed to learn from your letter that you of all people, whom I have always considered to be a lover of animals, should be capable of mistreating one so,' she began. Then, her anger increasing, she continued—' Zoos are an abomination, circuses are worse . . . yet by keeping that seal confined to a croft and only allowing it brief swims in a small loch you prove yourself to be no better than a zoo keeper; and by training it in such unnatural antics as singing and playing on a mouth organ you have sunk to the level of an animal trainer at a circus. . . . *Don't* go telling me in your next letter that you teach the creature by kindness as I know for a fact that only long hours of forced practice could make it perform such tricks.'

I did not mention Lora in my next letter, writing only about such safe subjects as the weather—variable as ever up in these parts—and our amateur attempts at making raspberry jam. Aunt Felicity, though facts were against me no doubt, was quite wide of the mark where Lora's freedom and musical practice were concerned.

At nights Lora slept on her couch in my room. The door of the bedroom was left ajar and the front door was also kept open in the summer so that an animal could get out should it wish to. Most mornings, when breakfast had been eaten and cleared away, and the other animals had long since been out and about, Lora, a late riser, was still dozing on the couch. So it was a surprise when I was woken up very early one morning—it could not have been much later than half-past five—by her flopping off the couch and going into the parlour. The silence was shattered a moment later by hideous blow-suck noises. Her mouth organ had been left on the carpet the night before and it seemed she had decided to put in a little practice on it. Snarls and growls from Ben and the otters proved that they were finding early morning music as uncongenial as I was.

'Take that thing away from her at once!' shouted Aunt Miriam.

I did as I was bidden and placed the mouth organ on the mantelpiece. The whines which followed at having her plaything taken from her were almost as aggravating as the previous cacophony. Eventually she took herself off to the lochan. By then it was time to get up anyway.

A young friend of mine, after visiting us, sent her a toy trumpet. Lora soon learnt to render ear-splitting blasts on this when it was held for her. Another admirer sent her a small xylophone complete with beater. She would hold the beater in her front teeth and bang any note to which I pointed. Her self-imposed practising on these various instruments drove us almost to distraction at times. It became necessary to put them out of her reach and allow her to play them only for short periods in the evenings. An unfortunate result of the singing lessons I had given her was that now, whenever Aunt or I began to play the piano, Lora, were she in the vicinity, would immediately lift her head and wail fortissimo. It is well nigh impossible to struggle through a Brahms sonata with a seal singing at the top of its voice. So most of our playing had to be done when she was in the lochan.

Pessimistic friends and relations had all predicted that our stay at the croft would be a short one. 'Mind you come and see us directly you get back to civilization,' was the tone of the letters we received on arrival at the croft. When a year had passed and it became evident that we were in no hurry to return to civilization the tone of the letters changed, and many a harried, town-dwelling friend wrote saying she envied us the peace and quiet of our lives. Peace we had certainly found, but a musical seal, two boisterous otters and other fauna do not make for the quietest of lives even in remote Sutherland.

ROWENA FARRE: from *Seal Morning* (1957).

34

England Saved

Philip of Spain differed from later would-be invaders of England—Napoleon Bonaparte and Adolf Hitler—since he took active steps towards achieving his aim, whereas they got no further than threatening from across the Channel. But the intention of all three was identical: namely to land an army in England, and Philip's great Armada was to serve as a naval covering force for that operation. How the Armada was defeated by the English navy and the English weather is one of the immortal stories that never stale by retelling.

ELIZABETH JENKINS

THE ARMADA that was being assembled carried tiers of guns, but it was built primarily for the transport of troops with their horses and stores. The ships were to sail up the Channel to the Flemish coast and convoy Parma and his 17,000 troops in their barges across to the Thames estuary. The fighting would be done on land; the expedition was to be, essentially, not naval but military.

Its setting out was delayed for a year because in April 1587 Drake made a lightning raid, burning the shipping in the harbours of Cadiz and Corunna. The bulk of the Spanish navy was lying in the mouth of the Tagus, but Drake was stopped in his design of burning these also by a pinnace which brought him a message from the Queen. She was still trying to make a treaty with Parma in the Netherlands. Drake came home disappointed but bringing with him the vast and richly loaded *San Philip*, one of the largest of the treasure-ships ever to fall into English hands.

In spite of Walsingham's efforts to convince her that the task was hopeless and a waste of valuable time, Elizabeth, alone, kept the stubborn hope that war might be avoided by negotiation; the government meanwhile prepared as for a certainty. Plans to contend with a landing army were made, for barricading roads and destroying bridges, and a chain of beacons was set up whose lights would summon the contingents of the militia to their posts.

The City of London, when called upon for their contribution to defence, asked how many men and ships they were expected to provide. The Council told them, 5,000 men and fifteen ships. The aldermen asked for two days to consider, and then announced that they would provide 10,000 men and thirty ships. Lord Howard of Effingham, the Lord High Admiral, Drake, the Vice-Admiral, and Hawkins, Treasurer and Controller of the Navy, were all satisfied with the seaworthy condition of the Queen's ships, thirty-four in number. Plymouth harbour was crowded and Hawkins had had four of the largest vessels riding in the Sound during an 'extreme and continual storm' and they had felt it 'no more than if they had ridden at Chatham'. Howard wrote to Burleigh: 'I do thank God that they be in the state that they be in; there is never a one of them knows what a leak means.' Dr. Allen did not share the Lord Admiral's opinion; he told Philip the English Navy was so riddled with dry rot, not four ships in it were seaworthy.

Allen, who had been made a Cardinal, now addressed *An Admonition to the Nobility and People of England.*

They must support the invasion, he told them, for it was a crusade to restore the Catholic religion, and to rid them of Queen Elizabeth, that monster of impiety and unchastity, who, he said, 'cannot be tolerated without the eternal infamy of our whole country, the whole world deriding our effeminate dastardy, that have suffered such a creature almost thirty years together to reign over our bodies and souls'. The explanation of these astonishing remarks was to be found at the foot of the *Admonition*: 'From my lodging in the Palace of St. Peter, Rome.' Allen's view of the English Queen, like his opinion of the English fleet, had been formed at a distance.

Elizabeth's unfounded optimism over the prospects of a peace treaty with Parma had a result that Walsingham and the naval commanders found both dangerous and infuriating. She had allowed the whole naval strength to be made ready in December, but only for six weeks, by which time she hoped to have concluded a peace. She had had no experience of a full-scale war and of the methods it demanded, but her experience of the incompetence and the flagrant peculation during the campaign in the Netherlands had so alarmed and angered her that she determined not to see the like again. Instead of giving plenary powers to Howard and Hawkins, as she might safely have done, she kept the administration of supplies in her own hands. She demanded explanations of every charge and she would only allow crews to be taken on and stores bought in for very short periods at a time. No one appeared to understand or really to care for the shocking outpourings of the Netherlands campaign, where she had found the Crown's treasury bleeding to death for lack of capable and honest supervision. She could not make them see the dangers of letting money drain away at so terrifying a rate; nor could Howard and Hawkins make her see the dangers of keeping her ships without their full complement of men, munitions and stores. 'Sparing and war have no affinity together,' said Howard. Such words only increased her agonized resistance, and in the end the English sailors did their work on short rations and fell back on powder captured from the enemy.

The land forces were divided into an army of 30,000 under Lord Hunsdon based on Windsor, whose task was to defend the Queen, and 16,000 who were to prevent an attack on London. These were to be encamped at Tilbury under Leicester.

Mid-July of 1588 was fraught with storms, its nights were moonlight. On July 19 at 3 p.m. watchers on the Lizard saw, at last, the great nightmare, rising above the horizon's rim and creeping over the sea towards them. 'The Spanish Armada,' said Camden, 'built high like towers and castles, rallied into the form of a crescent whose horns were at least seven miles distant, coming slowly on, and though under full sail, yet as the winds laboured and the ocean sighed under the burden of it.' The Spaniards anchored at nightfall outside Plymouth, and when the moon rose at two in the morning they saw that the English ships had come out behind them. The first engagement showed the amazing speed and power to turn of the low-built English ships; the Spaniards said they had never seen ships so handled or that flew so fast. When Lord Howard's flagship was rammed and brought to a standstill, surrounded by galleons who expected to make her their prey, the flagship's boats towed her head round and she then sailed out of their reach at such a pace, 'though the swiftest ships in the Armada pursued her they seemed by comparison to be at anchor'. Three engagements on the 23rd, 24th and 27th inflicted heavy damage on the Spanish Fleet, but by July 28th they had struggled up the Channel and were anchored in Calais roads not far from where Parma expected to embark. On the night of the 28th they were dislodged by fire-ships sent among them on a favouring wind, and the next day when they reassembled the fearful battle was fought off Gravelines. Sixty English were killed, but the slaughter of the close-packed Spanish soldiers under a fire they could not avoid or return was ghastly; as one ship heeled over, blood was seen pouring from its lee scuppers. The ships fled up the east coast of England and the pursuing English ships passed the bodies of the mules and horses the Spaniards had thrown into the sea. They made for the north of Scotland and on to the west coast of Ireland. Storms, wrecks and savage inhabitants continued the chain of their disasters and sufferings, and of 30,000 men embarked for England, less than 10,000 returned to Spain.

ELIZABETH JENKINS: from *Elizabeth the Great* (1958).

35

The Dorobo and the Buffaloes

The author who here describes one of her many adventures in Kenya was born in that East African territory and had her schooling there. She therefore knows the Africans and the country and its wild animals not as a mere visitor but as one who has been familiar with them from childhood. Untravelled Europeans might suppose that lions and leopards are the great sources of danger in East Africa, but far more dangerous is a disturbed herd of buffaloes such as the child saw in the instance recounted in what follows.

ELSPETH HUXLEY

ONE MORNING I surprised two dikdiks in the glade, standing among grass that countless quivering cobwebs had silvered all over, each one—and each strand of every cobweb—beaded with dew. It was amazing to think of all the untold millions of cobwebs in all the forest glades, and all across the bush and plains of Africa, and of the number of spiders, more numerous even than the stars, patiently weaving their tents of filament to satisfy their appetites, and of all the even greater millions of flies and bees and butterflies that must go to nourish them; and for what end, no one could say.

In the middle of this field of silver splendour stood the two dikdiks with their tiny heads lifted, their nostrils dilated and their unwinking eyes, as bright as black-berries, looking straight into mine. I never ceased to marvel at the delicacy and brittleness of their legs, slender as reeds; it seemed impossible that the dikdiks should not break them as they bounded over tufts or hummocks, even with their leaf-light weight.

These dikdiks had the charm of the miniature. They were perfectly made, not a single hair or sinew less than immaculate; little engines of muscle and grace, more like spirits than creatures. One always saw them in pairs. So long as I stood still, so did the dikdiks; I wondered what would happen if I never moved at all. Would they stand and stare all day? Should we all be there at evening, still motionless? But it was hopeless to try to out-stare the dikdiks; after a while I took a step forward and, with a movement of superb ease and elegance, the little buck sprang away to melt into the trees.

I then became aware, as one so mysteriously does, that I was being watched. I looked round, saw nothing, and stepped forward to sit on a fallen log. A current of watching still trembled in the air. After a while I saw a stirring in the dark undergrowth, and a brown furry figure stepped forth into a shaft of sunlight, which awoke in his fur pelt a rich, rufous glow, and twinkled on his copper ornaments.

He was a small man: not a dwarf exactly, or a pygmy, but one who stood about half-way between a pygmy and an ordinary human. His limbs were light in colour and he wore a cloak of bushbuck skin, a little leather cap and ear-rings, and carried a long bow and a quiver of arrows. He stood stock-still and looked at me just as the dikdik had done, and I wondered whether he, too, would vanish if I moved.

'Jambo,' I ventured.

His face crinkled into a smile. It was a different face from that of a Kikuyu, more pointed, lighter-skinned, finer-boned; it wore something of the watchful and defensive look of an animal, with an added humour and repose.

He stepped forward, raised his hand and returned my greeting.

'The news?' I asked, continuing the traditional form of greeting.

'Good.'

'Where have you come from?'

He threw back his head to indicate the hills at his back.

'The forest.'

'Where are you going?'

'To seek meat.'

He came and stood by me, fingering his bow. We could not speak much, for he knew only about a score of Swahili words. From him came a strong, pungent smell, with a hint of rankness, like a waterbuck's; his skin was well greased with fat, his limbs wiry and without padding, like the dikdiks'. I knew him for a Dorobo, one of that race of hunters living in the forest on game they trapped or shot with poisoned arrows. They did not cultivate, they existed on meat and roots and wild honey, and were the relics of an old, old people who had once had sole possession of all these lands—the true aborigines. Then had come others like the Kikuyu and Masai, and the Dorobo had taken refuge in the forests. Now they lived in peace, or at least neutrality, with the herdsmen and cultivators, and sometimes bartered skins and honey for beads, and for spears and knives made by native smiths. They knew all the ways of the forest animals, even of the bongo, the shyest and most beautiful, and their

greatest delight was to feast for three days upon a raw
elephant.

I knew his arrows would be poisoned. He pulled one
out and showed me the sticky black coating on the
iron head. 'This kills the elephant, the great pig, the
buffalo.'

'There are many buffaloes?' I asked. . . .

'Come with me.' He turned and walked towards the
forest with loping, bent-kneed strides. Where the glade
ended, the undergrowth looked black and solid as a wall,
but he slid into it, and I found that we were on a little
path. That was too strong a word for it; it was rather
a crack in the spiked solidity where other feet had
trodden. The Dorobo stooped, I copied him, and we
procceded slowly like crouching animals, he silently, I
treading on sticks and barging into roots and getting
caught by creepers and scratched by thorns.

We came to a small glade sloping down towards a
stream that could be heard whispering at the bottom,
clouded with reeds and long grass. Near the glade's
margin was a patch of bare, greyish earth.

'See!' exclaimed the Dorobo, pointing with satisfaction: and I looked in vain for a herd of buffaloes.

'I see nothing.'

He loped forward again. When we halted on the edge
of the bare patch, I could observe hoof-marks and cattle-
droppings; the hint of a rank odour, faintly bovine, hung
about the place. It was a salt-lick, trampled by the feet of
many buffaloes.

'They come every night,' the Dorobo said. 'If the
bwana brings a gun early in the morning, he will see
many, many, just like cattle.'

'Where are they now?'

He pointed with his chin to the slopes beyond. 'There

above. They sleep. They eat salt at night, and in the early morning they play.'

We returned along the game-track. 'Where is your house?' I asked.

'In the forest.'

'You have no shamba?'

'The elephant is my shamba. These are my hoes.' He touched the quiver at his side. 'Have you tobacco?'

'No.' I felt ungrateful, and I had no money either. 'I will try to get some.'

'Good. Bring it here, and I will take the bwana to the buffaloes.' He smiled, half-raised his hand, twitched his bushbuck cloak more securely on his shoulder and loped off, leaving his ripe civet smell on the morning air.

I wanted to keep the Dorobo to myself; he belonged to the same world as the dikdik and jasmine and butterflies, but I did not know how to get hold of any tobacco; so I was forced to confide in Dirk. His eye gleamed when he heard about the salt-lick.

'That is how to get them, man,' he said. 'There will be many, big bulls and all. I will find that Kaffir, he will show me the spoor.'

'You must take me with you.'

Dirk merely laughed. 'A *toto* like you?'

'But he's *my* Dorobo!'

Dirk said that Dorobo belonged to anyone who brought them tobacco, and rode up with some next morning to the furrow-head. Although we had made no appointment, the Dorobo appeared, this time with another, even thinner and smaller than himself. They departed carrying the tobacco, having promised to meet Dirk at the forest's edge next morning, before dawn, and guide him to the lick. As for me, I was to be left out, and resentment stung me like *siafu*. I had discovered the Dorobo, and now Dirk was going to have all the fun.

That night I thumped my head four times on the pillow, so as to wake at four o'clock. Probably it was the stir of Dirk's departure that really woke me, the lanterns moving in the darkness, the tapping on the door of his rondavel, and the pawing and snorting of the pony he was taking as far as the furrow-head, because of his leg. I dressed in the darkness, shivering, for these early mornings were chilly and the water in the jug stung the skin. I waited until the pony had gone and the lights vanished, then I crept out like a vole to follow on foot.

This was not nearly so simple as I had expected. Although a half-moon threw black shadows, the path developed all sorts of bumps, holes and obstacles unknown in daylight. The grass was soaking wet and bitterly cold, and the twinkling guide-light soon disappeared, leaving me hemmed in by shapes that leant towards me with a crouching menace: leopards, buffaloes, hyenas, even elephants might be within a few feet, gloating at the prospect of a meal. I wished very much that I had stayed in bed, and with every step decided to retreat, but obstinacy drove my reluctant feet forward. Only the furrow hummed a friendly note with its gentle swishing: at least I could not lose the way, so long as I followed it.

As I approached my glade I could hear Dirk's pony cropping the grass, and the movement of humans; he and the syce were waiting for the Dorobo. I waited also, frightened to reveal myself, shivering, and getting hungry; a rumbling stomach threatened to betray me, and I wanted to sneeze.

Many hours seemed to pass before the Dorobo's arrival. At last I heard low voices, the jingle of a bridle, an order given, and then silence, save for the noises of the pony, who was to be left behind with the syce while Dirk proceeded, limp and all, on foot.

The syce, a Kikuyu named Karoli, was to some extent an ally, and I decided to ask him to help me to follow Dirk into the forest. When I appeared he was at first alarmed, then incredulous and finally discouraging.

'The bwana told me to stay here,' he said. 'I do not wish to be eaten by leopards and trampled by buffaloes. Are you not a *toto*? And should not all *totos* be in bed?'

'I shall wait here until he shoots a buffalo.'

'It is too cold, and the bwana will be angry.'

'I want to stay.'

'Haven't you heard about the savage monster that lives in the forest and eats horses? When it smells one, out it comes. It is bigger than a forest pig, it has teeth like swords, and five arms like a monkey's, and seven eyes. It will eat you up in one mouthful, like a stork eating a locust.'

'You are telling lies.'

All the same, I could not help thinking of the monster, with big pointed teeth and burning eyes, and wondering if there might be a grain of truth in Karoli's tale. I hugged the pony's neck for warmth, convinced by now that bed would, after all, be a much nicer place.

'Why do you not go back to Thika, to your mother and father?' Karoli asked. 'Thika is a better place than this. The maize grows tall, and there are sweet potatoes, and the land is fat.'

'Is Thika your home, also?'

'Very close to Thika; and Kupanya is the chief of my people. But my family will think I have died in this cold place, for my bwana will not let me go home.'

We talked of Thika while the darkness thinned slowly and the stars faded, and the sky glowed with a deep, rich, royal blue. The air was steel-keen, a film of dew lay over everything and a breath of frost passed over the glade, leaving no traces. A rain-bird called; its haunting downward cadence was like a little waterfall, melodious and melancholy.

The gun shot could not now be long delayed. Night was fading so fast that we could see tree-shapes thirty or forty paces distant. Something moved just down the furrow; I watched it fiercely: a leopard on the prowl, a homing forest pig? No, only a bushbuck, his pelt dark with dew, picking his way fastidiously along our glade, his nostrils a-quiver to receive the book of scents from which he could read with certainty the news of the morning.

The crash came and shook the trees: another after it, then a third. These three explosions united to form a hollow echo from the hills, and made the pony plunge and whinny. The sound rolled away into a watchful silence. The bushbuck had vanished, the rain-bird was stilled, only the furrow whispered to itself unchanged. Then from the forest came movement, a muffled crashing, the snap of branches, a thumping of hooves.

'They come towards us,' said Karoli.

The sounds were indeed growing louder as the buffaloes, obsessed by panic, stampeded downhill, abandoning all caution in a frantic flight. At such times their big-bossed horns were used like battering-rams to thrust a way through thickets; in their panic they would plunge ahead with no regard for any object in their way.

'To that tree, quickly!' cried Karoli, tugging at the reins and trying to pull the pony after him; it smelt the buffaloes, threw up its head and bolted. I ran to the big cedar where Karoli cowered; he was sweating and rolling his eyes. The buffaloes went by as if a mass of great black boulders had detached themselves from the hillside and come hurtling down upon us at such a speed that they were gone before I had time even to realize what they were; their hoof-beats made the ground quiver under my feet as if it were a hollow gourd. The boulders vanished, the drumming faded, in a moment only the rank smell remained. Karoli rubbed his head and made chattering sounds. We both sat down on a log to rest our weak knees.

'These buffaloes are bad, bad, bad,' said Karoli. 'They will crush you with their feet as a man steps upon a beetle. Eee—eee, there were a hundred buffaloes, a thousand, more than the cattle of the Masai; they were angry, they were bad.' He went on talking to himself in this vein.

By now the sky in the direction taken by the buffaloes was banded with rose and lemon and the colour of flamingo wings: the path was ready, the sun was on his way. From the forest came three figures led by my Dorobo, whose face was eager as a dog's. Dirk was the last, hampered by his leg. When he saw me he was furious, but had no time for more than swearing; he had wounded a buffalo, and had to find the spoor. Two bulls lay dead near the salt-lick, where he had lain in wait until dawn.

The Dorobo ranged through the glade like hounds casting for a scent, and soon one of them stood rigid and gave a low call. On a leaf-blade was a little crimson bead, which Dirk and the Dorobo bent to examine. By its colour they could tell whether the buffalo had been hit in the body, or in the heart or lungs.

My Dorobo took the lead with his head down and his eyes on the ground, bow in hand. Dirk followed with the rifle. The sun came up proud as a lancer, hurling long golden spears over the dew-white grass and silver cobwebs; a red flame sprang up the trunks of the cedars, the birds fluted, the whole world came alive.

ELSPETH HUXLEY: from *The Flame Trees of Thika* (1959).

36

On the Moon

Throughout the centuries the moon has been a nightly
object of romantic interest to poets and lovers. Now it is
being taken over by the scientists and engineers, and it
seems very likely that before long we shall be able to
compare H. G. Wells's novel The First Men in the Moon,
written in 1901, with descriptions by men who have
actually landed there. For the present, however, we have
to rely on cameras and telescopes and satellites to give
information about the sort of place the moon is and what
we can expect of it. Here are the deductions of a former
Astronomer-Royal, but space exploration moves on so
fast that even two years after this was written his expert
observations had begun to fall behind what men in space
have seen with their own eyes.

SIR HAROLD SPENCER JONES

THE MOON is the only world where we should expect
actually to see clear evidence of life, if any existed.
There is no doubt that if there were a lunar inhabitant
equipped with a powerful telescope, he would be able to
see many signs of human activity on the Earth. He
would be able to watch the growth of greater London;
he would see cities like New York, Sydney, Johannesburg
and Ottawa springing up. He would be able to watch the
formation of new lakes by the impounding of water by
dams. He would see land-reclamation works in progress
and the draining of the water from tracts such as the

Zuyder Zee. The seasonal growth of vegetation and the melting of the snow over vast tracts of land with the advance of summer would be clearly visible to him. In the course of a few years he would undoubtedly obtain clear evidence not only of plant life on the Earth but also of human activity.

So, in a similar way, if the Moon were inhabited by intelligent beings we should expect to find plenty of evidence of their existence. We can find none. The Moon shows no signs of change. There are not even seasonal changes of colouration, such as might be attributed to the growth of vegetation. Some astronomers have claimed, indeed, to have seen slight changes in certain regions, changes mainly of tint such as might be produced by the growth of lichens on rocks. But such changes have not been confirmed and are generally discredited. It seems that the observers have been misled by changes in the appearance of the surface detail with changing altitude of the Sun. No! it is not possible to admit that there is life of any sort on the Moon. It is a world that is completely and utterly dead, a sterile mountainous waste on which during the heat of the day the sun blazes down with relentless fury, but where during the long night the cold is so intense that it far surpasses anything ever experienced on the Earth.

The successful launching by the U.S.S.R. and the U.S.A. of artificial earth satellites during the International Geophysical Year 1957-58, and the launching on January 2nd 1959 by the U.S.S.R. of the *Lunik* rocket, which passed within a few thousand miles of the Moon and has become the first artificial planet or asteroid, have marked the beginning of the age of the exploration of space. It is to be expected that in the not distant future manned rockets will be launched and that possibly human beings may be able to land on the Moon and explore some part of its surface. The problems involved in landing on the Moon are simple compared with those of launching the space vehicle from the Moon for its return journey, of slowing it down to prevent it from burning up on its re-entry into the Earth's atmosphere, and of its landing on the Earth. Before manned flights to the Moon are attempted, it is likely that rockets will be launched to reach the vicinity of the Moon, to make an orbit round it, and then return to the Earth. With the aid of special instrumental equipment installed in such a rocket appreciable additions to our knowledge of the Moon could be obtained.

The explorers who first land on the Moon would be faced with many difficulties and hazards. They would need to be encased in airtight suits, provided with oxygen apparatus to enable them to breathe and with provision for absorbing exhaled carbon dioxide and moisture. Protection against the short-wave radiation from the Sun, from the ultra-violet rays down to X-rays, would be essential. Our atmosphere, and particularly the ozone in the atmosphere, absorbs practically all of these radiations, thereby protecting us against them. Even supposing that they could protect themselves against the great heat by day and the extreme cold at night, a worse fate might be in store for them unless their suits were completely bullet proof. For they would be in danger of being shot by a shooting star. The average shooting star or meteor, which gives so strongly the impression of a star falling from the sky, is a small fragment of matter, usually smaller than a pea and often no larger than a grain of sand. Space is not empty but contains great numbers of such fragments. The Earth, in its motion round the Sun, meets many of these fragments, which enter the atmosphere at a speed many times greater than that of a rifle bullet. The meteor, rushing through the air, becomes intensely heated by friction and is usually completely vaporized before it has penetrated within a distance of twenty miles from the surface of the Earth. Many millions of these fragments enter our atmosphere in the course of a day, but the atmosphere protects us from them. On the Moon, however, they fall to the surface and so great is their number that the lunar explorers would run a considerable risk of being hit.

The difficulties that would have to be encountered by anyone who attempted to explore the Moon—assuming that it was possible to get there—would be incomparably greater than those that had to be faced in the struggle to the summit of Mount Everest. In two respects only would the lunar explorer have the advantage. In the first place movement would be less fatiguing because—as the weight of the Moon is only about one-eightieth of that of the Earth—the gravitational pull of the Moon is not very great. If the Moon had an atmosphere like that of the Earth, a golfer on the Moon would find that he could drive his ball for a mile without much difficulty and a moderate batsman would hit sixes with the greatest of ease and perform feats that even Bradman might envy. The second advantage the lunar explorer would have over the climbers on Mount Everest would be the absence of strong winds to contend against. The Moon having no atmosphere, there can be no wind; nor, of course, can there be any noise, for sound is carried by the air. The Moon is a world that is completely still and where silence, 'a silence where no sound may be', prevails.

SIR HAROLD SPENCER JONES: from *Life on Other Worlds* (1959).

37

The Lost Umbrella

Each day in The Times *newspaper the Court Circular (in which the public engagements of members of the Royal Family are announced) appears immediately after the middle pages of the paper. In the last two columns of this 'Court page' there has been printed daily for years past some account of an interesting and often amusing experience written by unnamed contributors. One of these entertaining pieces is reproduced here—a story of how the tables were turned upon a pair of light-fingered girls whose clothes were more conspicuous than their honesty and manners.*

ANONYMOUS

FOR MANY years I have taken my shoes to be repaired at a little cobbler's shop in a back street. Transactions are conducted almost in dumb-show, for the noise of the traffic through the open door, as great lorries jostle one another almost on to the pavement, coupled with the din of machinery and the tap-tap-tap of shoe-makers' hammers, makes ordinary conversation impossible.

The normal procedure is to hand your shoes over the counter and point to the portion, usually heels, to be repaired. A middle-aged woman in a green overall receives them with a friendly smile, flexes the soles and prods them with her thumb, shakes her head and looks doubtful; you nod, and point to the soles as well, and she makes out a ticket—sole and heel, 16s. 6d.

The exchange can be a little more complicated if you insist that the heels only are to be done, and in very rare cases this can lead to the machines stopping work for a moment to facilitate explanations. However, half the ticket is finally handed to you, and the other half tied to the shoes, while you lip-read the day of the week on which the shoes can be collected.

Often there is quite a queue in the shop, for the work is well done, and the shoes even polished before being returned to you. Sometimes a couple of giggling teen-agers, wearing fluorescent make-up and hooped skirts, drape themselves over ageing bentwood chairs in front of the counter trying to keep bare and somewhat grubby toes that end in chipped, purplish nail varnish clear of the floor, while they wait for snapped stiletto heels to be replaced on cinnamon-coloured pointed court shoes. There is a pervading smell of leather, cobblers' wax, shoe-polish, and petrol fumes, with a hint of cheap scent, and a whiff of frying-oil from a fish and-chip shop near by.

I remember a day that seemed to have settled down firmly for a good steady rain, when I took my leaky second-bests to the shop. I joined the waiting line of plastic-coated and hooded humanity, and was followed by a hennaed cutie robed in transparent polythene, and her platinum-pink companion, both eating chips wrapped in newspaper. I leant my dripping umbrella against the counter, and carried out the usual form of mime, bearing away my half-ticket rather hurriedly because I was already overdue at the office.

My departure must have coincided with a break in the clouds, for it wasn't until I was again at my desk that I realized I had left my umbrella at the cobbler's. For all the years I had been going there, I could not remember its name, and the ticket divulged neither name nor telephone number. There was nothing to do but wait until the following day, for I could not leave the office before the shop closed.

Next lunch-time I went straight to the cobbler's, fully expecting to recover my property, but dumb-show had to be abandoned and work stood still while it was explained to me that no trace of my umbrella had been seen. In view of the puddle it must certainly have made on the floor, this bore witness to the constant flow of custom in the shop. My umbrella, then, must be given up for lost at the very time of the year when I needed it most. As funds would not run to another just then, my plastic hood had to suffice.

It was, perhaps, fortunate for me that it was such a wet month, for when collecting day dawned, it was just such another as that on which I had first deposited my shoes. I paddled down the little back street, trying to avoid towering lorries and splashing taxis, afflicted with near-deafness and blinkered by my modern rainwear. Waiting in the queue at the cobbler's counter, I realized that wobbling before me were the redhead and the blonde who had followed me last time and—yes, there was my umbrella, bedraggled and wet against the counter!

Could I be sure it was mine, and not its mass-produced twin? Surely, because instead of the looped silken cord and tassel it had owned when new, which had parted long ago, was the knotted cord I had put there in its place. But what to do! I felt my cheeks beginning to burn as I puzzled how to recover the thing without actually accusing anyone of stealing.

A glance at the two girls, now collecting a pair of stiletto-heeled pointed lilac T-strappers, convinced me that in any argument I should certainly be worsted by sound and fury. My old friend behind the counter could not even see the umbrella from where she stood, so I could expect no help from her, and even she, bless her heart, if involved, would be likely to say too much rather than too little.

It must have been my lucky day. The colourful pair decided to change the shoes they were wearing for the newly mended ones and leave those they wore for repair, and the machinery came to a stop for the complicated but necessary conversational exchange to be made. At the same time, a heaven-sent thought entered my head. I stepped up to the counter, grasped my umbrella firmly in my hand, and said loudly and clearly, 'How nice of you to bring back my umbrella that you picked up by mistake!'

There was a long moment of complete silence—machinists, counter-hand, customers all staring at the two girls on the bentwood chairs. Then the redhead remarked thoughtfully, her foot half-way into the lilac shoe, ''Course, we was be'ind yer larst week, wasn't we?' To my relief, the machinists roared into action at that moment. I collected my shoes, paid, and left the shop before the two girls had recovered from the shock.

I did not need to go to the cobbler's again for several weeks. When I did I half expected that someone would say something. It happened that the shop was almost empty, and only one machine was working, so conversation was possible. My middle-aged friend's eyes twinkled through her spectacles. She pushed back her thoroughly permed hair and inquired, 'D'you win like that on the pools, too, dear?'

ANONYMOUS: from *The Times* (28 September 1959).

38

What! . . . No Books!

Sometimes when we visit a house we have not been in before, we have the feeling that somehow the place has no heart or soul, even though its occupants may be good kind people with well-furnished rooms. Then we suddenly realize that what is missing is—books. . . . Books not only give colour to a home, they are its heart and soul, for in the pages of books are preserved the feelings, the aspirations, the knowledge, and the wisdom of men and women throughout the ages, always 'on call' at the very moment we are in need of advice or comfort or inspiration, if we have a good stock of well-chosen books IN THE HOUSE. It doesn't do to say, 'Oh, if I want a book I can get it from the Library round the corner': 'round the corner' isn't good enough when you need that book here and now. Milton was not exaggerating when he wrote: 'A good book is the precious life-blood of a master spirit, embalmed and treasured up on purpose to a life beyond life.' Here, to close this anthology, is a brief parable of a household which possessed all present-day conveniences and amenities—'tele', 'fridge', washing machine, car—but had no room for books.

ANONYMOUS

WHEN I saw the 'Small Ad.' announcing, 'Book case with dror, five shillings,' I at once smelled woodworm. At so small a cost, however, the risk was worth taking.

When I rang the bell I heard a woman's cry, 'Dad! Door!' and a few seconds later I was facing a harassed little man.

'Is the book case sold yet?' I asked.

He looked at me as though I were a space-man. Then, having decided that I actually did want a book case, he replied: 'Want to have a dekko? It's outside.'

I followed him, padding along a thick carpet. An open door on the right showed a middle-aged woman brooding over the 'Tele'. He led me through a kitchen equipped with 'fridge', washing machine, and other Ideal Home gadgets. We halted before a brick-built air-raid shelter; inside, behind a barricade of bicycles, I could see the case.

'Got it with the 'ouse,' he apologized.

He levered it out for me. At some period of its history, it had been a bureau, but the flap-lid had been removed, leaving a deep shelf above the 'dror', beneath which were two strong shelves. It was exactly what I wanted.

Like an indifferent woodpecker, I tapped it. No peppery dust sifted down, nor did I see any castor-like perforations.

'Just needs a nice coat of paint,' he cajoled. The walnut was absolutely sound.

'The dror comes out,' he said, demonstrating.

'It *is* five shillings?' I asked. I knew that even as firewood it was worth much more.

''s'right,' he agreed. Then, accepting my two half-crowns, he said, before I could tell him that I would get the book case collected later, 'I'll drop round with it in the car to-night if you'll give me the address.'

Then, as an after-thought, he added: 'You fond of reading?'

K

And picking up from the ground a dusty bundle of women's magazines, he thrust them into my unwelcoming arms.

ANONYMOUS: 'No Room for Books'
from *The Times* (6 June 1960).

BIOGRAPHICAL AND TEXTUAL NOTES

BIOGRAPHICAL AND TEXTUAL NOTES

*The notes in this volume are intended
to serve the needs of overseas students
as well as those of English-born users*

1. THE DAY OUR AGE BEGAN

WINSTON CHURCHILL: Born 30 November 1874; son of Lord
Randolph Churchill and grandson of the 7th Duke of Marlborough; educated at Harrow and Sandhurst; entered the army
in 1895 and served in various campaigns; on active service and
as a war correspondent in the Boer War in South Africa; captured by the Boers on 15 November 1899 and escaped on
12 December, an adventure excitingly told in his autobiographical *My Early Life*. Conservative M.P. for Oldham 1900-1906
and, except for brief intervals, was in Parliament for the rest
of his life, finally for many years as M.P. for Woodford,
Essex. Held a number of Cabinet offices, as Home Secretary,
First Lord of the Admiralty, etc., and as Prime Minister from
1940 to 1945 and from 1951 to 1955, when he retired from
government office but retained his seat in Parliament. Received
the Order of Merit in 1946 and became a Knight of the
Garter as Sir Winston Churchill in 1953, a high honour which
permitted him to remain a member of the House of Commons,
whereas a peerage (which there can be little doubt he was
offered) would have compelled him to go to the House of Lords.
His many historical and other writings have given him as last-
ing a reputation in literature as his public services have given
him as a statesman, and he was awarded the Nobel Prize for
Literature in 1953. His accomplishment as an amateur painter
led to his being elected an Honorary Royal Academician Extraordinary in 1948.

PAGE

2 *the Admiralty:* the official name for the various offices and departments which form the headquarters of the British Navy. Winston Churchill was First Lord of the Admiralty (the Cabinet Minister responsible to Parliament for naval affairs) from September 1939 until he became Prime Minister on this 10th May 1940.

Sir Kingsley Wood: (1881-1943), Secretary of State for Air 1938-40; Chancellor of the Exchequer 1940-43.

Mr. Chamberlain: Neville Chamberlain (1869-1940), Prime Minister 1937-40.

a National Government: one in which responsibility is shared by the various parties represented in Parliament, each party contributing to the Government a number of ministers of State roughly proportionate to its strength in the House of Commons.

Downing Street: No. 10 Downing Street, Whitehall, the official residence of each Prime Minister while he holds that appointment.

Lord Halifax: (1881-1959), Foreign Secretary 1938-40; British Ambassador to the United States 1941-46.

whom he should advise the King to send for: a retiring British Prime Minister may, by custom, name the man he considers most suitable to succeed him. Though not constitutionally bound to do so, the King or Queen usually follows the advice so given and invites the named person to form a new Government. But if a Prime Minister in office is defeated at a General Election, the leader of the new majority party receives the royal invitation to assume governmental responsibility.

3 *Mr. Feiling:* (later Sir) Keith Feiling (1884-   ); Professor of Modern History in the University of Oxford 1946-50; author of the official biography of Neville Chamberlain (1946).

the two minutes: After the end of the First World War it became the national practice, in commemoration of those who had been killed, to stop work and traffic and to stand in silence at 11 a.m. on each 11th of November, the time and date in 1918 when the Armistice was signed ending the war between the Allies and Germany.

3 *the Assembly:* i.e. the House of Commons.

4 *the Zuyder Zee:* the large shallow gulf in Netherlands territory, partly drained and cultivated before 1940, but inundated during the war then begun.

the Queen: Queen Wilhelmina of the Netherlands.

the Schlieffen plan: A plan of attack drawn up by Field Marshal von Schlieffen (1833-1913), Chief of the German General Staff, and intended to be brought into operation in any war against France. The plan provided for a large-scale surprise invasion of neutral Belgium and Holland as a means of out-flanking and encircling the left wing of the French army and capturing the Channel ports. In 1914 the plan was put into partial operation by the invasion of Belgium but not of Holland. It then failed, but the intended objectives were temporarily attained when the whole plan was followed in 1940.

5 *the Mall:* the wide thoroughfare leading from Trafalgar Square to Buckingham Palace; used on State occasions as a royal processional way.

no crowd about the Palace gates: At times of public anxiety (as well as of public rejoicing), when the King or Queen becomes a symbol of national unity, crowds often assemble at the gates of the royal residence watching important visitors come and go and hoping that the monarch will make an appearance to the people from the balcony of Buckingham Palace.

quizzically: humorously teasing.

6 *made no stipulation:* laid down no conditions; did not ask for any pledge.

Mr. Attlee: Clement Attlee (1883-   ), Leader of the Labour Party in Parliament 1935-55; Prime Minister 1945-51; created Earl Attlee on his retirement in 1955.

Mr. Greenwood: Arthur Greenwood (1880-1954), Labour M.P. from 1922; Minister of Health 1929-31; Member of the War Cabinet 1940-42.

6 *Mr. Bevin:* Ernest Bevin (1881-1951), Trade Union leader 1910-40; M.P. from 1940; Minister of Labour and National Service 1940-45; Foreign Secretary from 1945.

Mr. Alexander: Albert Victor Alexander (1885-   ), Labour M.P. from 1922; First Lord of the Admiralty from 1940; Minister of Defence 1947-50; created Viscount Alexander of Hillsborough 1950.

Mr. Morrison: Herbert Morrison (1888-   ), Labour M.P. from 1923; Minister of Transport 1929-31; Home Secretary 1940-45; Deputy Prime Minister 1945-51; created Lord Morrison of Lambeth 1959.

Mr. Dalton: Hugh Dalton (1887-   ), Labour M.P. from 1924; Minister of Economic Warfare 1940-42; President of the Board of Trade 1942-5; Chancellor of the Exchequer 1945-7; created Lord Dalton 1960.

7 *at Bournemouth:* where the annual Labour Party Conference was being held that year.

to lead the House of Commons: Although the Prime Minister is in principle the Leader of the House of Commons, his many duties make it impossible for him to be in constant attendance. It has therefore been customary for another senior Cabinet Minister to be named as Leader, to act as chief spokesman for the Government in the Prime Minister's absence. But as this is not an official appointment, the Leader also holds some recognized ministerial office (e.g. while Mr. Harold Macmillan was Prime Minister, Mr. R. A. Butler was Home Secretary as well as Leader of the House).

Lord President of the Council: i.e., . . . of the Privy Council; as a member of the Cabinet he is usually free to undertake special duties not allotted to the departmental Ministers of State.

the three Service Ministers: the First Lord of the Admiralty (Navy), the Secretary of State for War (Army), and the Secretary of State for Air (Air Force).

immediately dismissed by the British electorate: Winston Churchill's political opponents succeeded in persuading the electorate that while his gifts of leadership were invaluable in wartime, he had not the qualities appropriate for a peacetime Prime Minister. He again held that office, however, after the 1951 General Election and until his retirement in 1955.

2. AN AWFUL PROSPECT

EDWARD MORGAN FORSTER: (1879-   ). Born in London; educated at Tonbridge and Cambridge. His five novels (*Where Angels Fear to Tread, The Longest Journey, A Room with a View, Howards End,* and *A Passage to India*) made him one of the most praised writers of his period, particularly among fellow novelists. He has also written volumes of short stories, essays, biographies, a film script, and an opera libretto.

10 *the Brandenburg Concertos:* six musical compositions for various combinations of instruments, written in 1721 by Johann Sebastian Bach (1685-1750) for the Margrave of Brandenburg. They are the most famous pieces of their kind ever produced.

Dante: (1265-1321) the greatest of the Italian poets; author of *The Divine Comedy* (in three parts: Hell; Purgatory; Paradise), one of the world's foremost masterpieces.

Santa Sophia: built in Constantinople as a Christian church about the year 360 by the Emperor Constantine II and added to and reconstructed later. It is a magnificent example of architecture in the Byzantine style, with wonderful interior wall decorations in coloured marbles and gold mosaics. Under Moslem rule it became a mosque, and is now a museum of Byzantine art.

Faith makes one unkind: The allusion here is to the fact that either religious or political opinions when fanatically held lead to persecution and unbridled cruelty.

Sir Richard Terry: (1865-1938) he did a great deal to help the revival of interest in 16th century English church music while organist at Westminster Roman Catholic Cathedral from 1901 to 1924.

10 *A storm in a cocktail:* a variant of the familiar idiom 'a storm in a teacup', i.e. much ado about little.

Jack Payne . . . Henry Hall: dance band leaders popularized by B.B.C. broadcasts.

11 *thé dansant:* tea-time dancing sessions, a popular type of entertainment in the 1920s and 1930s.

Wurlitzer organ: an electric musical instrument, most widely known through its use in cinemas.

madrigals: originally, unaccompanied part songs for two or three voices; most popular and mainly composed in the 16th and 17th centuries.

Racine: Jean Racine (1639-99), leading French author of tragedies in the formal classical style in which tremendously impressive speeches in fine poetry were the principal feature.

Stravinsky: Igor Stravinsky (1882-   ), foremost Russian composer in the modernistic style; he became an American citizen in 1945.

Cézanne: Paul Cézanne (1839-1906), French post-impressionist painter of highly valued pictures.

Mrs. Leavis: Queenie Leavis, wife of the prominent Cambridge scholar F. R. Leavis; she wrote *Fiction and the Reading Public* (1932).

12 *We have . . . to ferry much old stuff across the river:* i.e. we must prevent what is traditionally valuable from being lost in the currents of changing fashion.

Sinclair Lewis: (1885-1951) American novelist; *Babbitt* (1922) is one of the most entertaining of his novels satirizing the materialism and social pretentiousness of the contemporary middle classes.

13 *the Middle West:* the central area of the United States.

best-sellers: novels which have a very large immediate sale but are (usually) quickly forgotten.

mickey-mice: comic cinema films, of which Walt Disney's Mickey Mouse series is typical.

3. THE FLOWER OF CITIES

MAX BEERBOHM: (1872-1956). Born in London; educated at Charter-house and Oxford. When only twenty-four he published a small book of essays called *The Works of Max Beerbohm* and two years later (1896) a Book of Caricatures. From that time until his death sixty years later he was famous both as writer and as artist. He gained new fame and a much larger company of enthusiastic admirers towards the end of his life through his rare B.B.C. broadcasts.

PAGE

14 *August 1935:* The Italian invasion and ruthless conquest of Abyssinia (Ethiopia) at that time was part of Mussolini's plan to make his country 'great'. It began a period of animosity between Italy and Britain which broke the long-standing friendship of the two nations until after the surrender of Italy in the Second World War.

a country in which I had resided: Max Beerbohm lived for many years at Rapallo, on the Italian riviera (Liguria).

stormy petrel: the petrel is a small sea-bird whose appearance is regarded as the sign of an oncoming storm. The term 'stormy petrel' is applied idiomatically to any person who appears to be the forerunner of some kind of approaching trouble.

Bloomsbury: an area of west-central London in which a number of prominent writers and artists lived between the two World Wars. The best known were Virginia Woolf and her husband Leonard Woolf, Lytton Strachey (author of *Eminent Victorians*), J. M. Keynes the famous economist. The district embraces several of the originally beautiful London 'squares' (such as Bedford Square and Bloomsbury Square), large enclosed gardens with fine houses on the surrounding four sides. Most of the houses are now used as offices or hotels (many have been pulled down), and some of the gardens, formerly reserved for the use of residents, have been turned into public open spaces.

PAGE

15 *omnibuses that passed incessantly:* a main traffic road now runs along the eastern side of the squares.

that Duke of Bedford: Francis Russell (1765-1802), 5th Duke of Bedford. He sacrificed his family mansion and estates in Bloomsbury in order to profit from the rents brought in by the houses he caused to be built around the squares named after him and his titles: Russell Square, Bedford Square, Tavistock Square.

16 *near the rose:* close to the heart of things socially; near the royal Court (the rose is an English symbol of royalty).

the University of London: Bloomsbury is designated as the site for new buildings to constitute the University of London, the colleges of which are still widely scattered. The ' white sepulchre ' was Max's scornful name for the Senate House of the University, built in the 1930s and visible from a distance as a towering white structure of Portland stone.

the dons: senior teachers in a university.

Smith . . . Robinson: Max's pseudonyms for Bloomsbury writers and painters whose books and pictures he did not admire.

dissignifications: one of the Bloomsbury art critics, Clive Bell, in a volume of essays entitled *Art*, introduced the term ' significant form ' in relation to works of art in which the shapes of objects (their form) was in itself significant or expressive of the artist's idea and intention, and thus was free from any reliance upon romantic or story interest, as many Victorian and Edwardian works of art had been. Max, however, was unable to find anything ' significant ' in the art favoured by ' Bloomsbury '.

Bloomsbury has got into inverted commas: the air of cultural superiority which was regarded by their critics as a characteristic of the group led to the use of ' Bloomsbury ' in quotation marks as a general term for intellectual arrogance and snobbery.

17 *very Russian:* a vogue for the stories and plays of Tchekov (1860-1904) and the novels of Dostoievsky (1821-81) was strongly current at that time, as also for the communist

principles of Karl Marx (1818-83) and the psycho-analytical theories of Sigmund Freud (1856-1939).

17 *Periclean:* the great period of Greek art and culture during the rule of Pericles (born about 495 B.C., died 429 B.C.), the greatest of Athenian statesmen.

seen through and discarded: Max is, of course, writing ironically.

almost pre-historic: the world after the war of 1914-18 was so different that to older people the period before 1914 seemed almost as though it belonged to an ancient time.

18 *Giotto:* (about 1266-1337) Italian painter who was an early master of the naturalistic style in which persons and objects were painted as they appear in nature, not in a conventional style dictated by religious doctrine.

The Impressionists: a group of late 19th century artists whose aim was to paint in a manner that gave an impression of the subject as it appeared to them at the moment of painting; they were fascinated by the effects of light upon objects more than by objects in themselves, and one of the leading Impressionists, Claude Monet (1840-1926), painted sets of pictures (one set of a lily-pond, another of the front of a cathedral) showing the same scene under changing light conditions. Edouard Manet (1832-83) was a pioneer of Impressionism in France.

Steer: Wilson Steer (1860-1942), English Impressionist painter.

Sickert: Walter Richard Sickert (1860-1942); he and Steer were the leading English Impressionists, though the subjects they painted were usually dissimilar.

MacColl: D. S. MacColl (1859-1948), art critic, watercolour painter, and poet; Keeper of the Tate Gallery 1906-11; Keeper of the Wallace Collection 1911-24.

Rothenstein: Sir William Rothenstein (1872-1945), English Impressionist painter and author of autobiographical volumes, *Men and Memories,* which give a vivid account of the period and its personalities.

kings before Agamemnon: an allusion to a saying in one of the *Odes* of the Latin poet Horace (65-8 B.C.) which is usually translated as ' heroes lived before Agamemnon ' who was king of Mycenae and leader of the Greeks during the siege of Troy. Max uses the phrase here to emphasize his conviction that ' new ' things are not necessarily better than older things. By the phrase in the preceding sentence to the effect that his painter friends in the 1890s did not suppose Manet ' to have been a phoenix ' he means that they did not take the view that all earlier painting was as worthless as ashes or that in Manet painting was reborn in perfection. In mythology the phoenix is a bird continually reborn young and perfect from the ashes of its former self.

18 *inter-bella period:* 1918-1939, the years between the two World Wars; *bellum* (Latin) war, plur. *bella.*

19 *one of them . . . stood out distinctly:* the person referred to here is probably one who was a familiar figure in the British Museum Reading Room before 1939. Said to have claimed that he was the rightful king of Poland, he was a magnificent-looking man resembling an Elizabethan grandee and was a brilliant talker.

20 *the Old School Tie:* the practice among adults of wearing a tie with the colours of the school they attended in youth arouses the scorn (or sometimes the envy) of many who were educated at a different level and regard the practice as a form of social snobbery. Max bought a Charterhouse School tie to wear as a symbol of revolt against the cult of lack-lustre eyes, drooping cigarettes and muddy shoes of the young who hovered on the fringes of ' Bloomsbury '.

Bayswater: a western district of London formerly inhabited mainly by well-to-do families.

21 *Merrie England:* a term then much in use by romantics who believed the Middle Ages to have been an almost Golden Age in England.

4. COMFORTABLE WORDS

HILAIRE BELLOC: (1870-1953). Born in Paris of a French father and English mother; educated at the Oratory School, Birming-

PAGE

ham, and Oxford. M.P. 1906-10. Wrote novels, poems, biographies, historical and other essays, and travel books of which *The Path to Rome* is outstanding.

22 *philologists:* scholars devoted to the study of the origins, development, and uses of language.

23 *Bounders:* ill-bred, exuberant, 'pushing' males.

Painted Harridans: uncomplimentary colloquial term for elderly women who use make-up clumsily and unsuccessfully in the hope of disguising their age.

Trulls: women of low moral character.

24 *'homely':* this word is not always a euphemism for 'ugly'; it is more often used of women who, while they may lack physical beauty, are pleasant, sympathetic, unassuming and comfortable companions in the home, characteristics more important than dance-hall and party glamour.

Approach: used in such terms as 'the Station Approach', i.e. the road or path leading to a railway station.

25 *A Judge in Chambers:* when he holds consultations in his private apartment as distinct from presiding in open Court.

Chamber Music: compositions for a small number of instruments, originally for performance in a private residence, not in a public hall.

the Upper Chamber: in England the House of Lords; elsewhere the Senate or (under different names in different countries) Second Chamber which acts as a scrutinizing, amending, or rejecting body for legislation passed by the House of Commons or Lower Chamber.

vault: arched roof or ceiling.

camber: the slightly convex form of a traffic road.

camera: originally from the Latin for vault and the Greek for an arched covering.

the outlaw of the Nemi wood: the reference is to a legend associated with the sacred wood of Nemi in Latium, central Italy.

26 *locution:* a form of words.

26 *P. G. Wodehouse:* Pelham Grenville Wodehouse (1881-   ),
English writer of highly humorous novels and short stories,
his most notable creation being Jeeves, the valet who is
expert at getting his employer Bertie Wooster out of scrapes
and dilemmas; (pron. Woodhouse).

loonybin: the word survives as slang for a mental hospital
or lunatic asylum.

5. FIDDLER DICK

HERBERT READ: (1893-   ). Born in Yorkshire; educated in
Halifax and at Leeds University. Served in the First World
War in France and Belgium 1915-18, winning the Military
Cross. Assistant Keeper at the Victoria and Albert Museum,
London, 1922-31; Professor of Fine Art, Edinburgh University,
1931-3; Professor of Poetry at Harvard, U.S.A., 1953-4. Author
of volumes of poetry and many books on art including *The
Meaning of Art* (1931 and later editions). Knighted 1953.

27 *Northallerton:* a town in Yorkshire.

'*For there's nae luck about the house*': the first line of an
anonymous song called 'The Mariner's Wife'.

Mariana: named from a line in Shakespeare's *Measure for
Measure* III, i, 279—'There, at the moated grange, resides
this dejected Mariana'; there are also two poems by Lord
Tennyson introducing her.

28 *had become an angel:* a Victorian euphemism for 'had died'.

'*broken in*': trained to do required work.

natty: neat in appearance.

binder-band: a cord of twisted strands for binding sheaves of
corn.

cat-gut: twisted and stretched intestines of various animals
(but not of cats!), used as strings for instruments of the
violin family.

29 *the War:* i.e. the First World War.

29 *sonata:* a musical composition usually for one or two instruments (e.g. for piano, or for violin, or for piano and violin); mostly in four movements or sections and in a set form.

30 *corolla:* centre; crown.

6. PORTRAIT OF AN ACTRESS

VIRGINIA WOOLF: (1882-1941). Born in London, the daughter of Sir Leslie Stephen, an eminent scholar and writer; educated at home; married Leonard Woolf, essayist and political writer. Her novels (*The Voyage Out, To the Lighthouse, Orlando, The Waves,* etc.) were much praised, though they seem 'difficult' to many readers. Both in her fiction and in her essays on literary and related subjects (*The Common Reader,* two series, and other volumes) she maintained an excellent prose style.

32 *Captain Brassbound's Conversion:* one of Bernard Shaw's *Three Plays for Puritans.* The author wrote the part of Lady Cicely Waynefleet in it for Ellen Terry.

losing her memory: defective memory was in fact a family failing of the Terrys.

the Court Theatre: in Sloane Square, London.

Velasquez: (1599-1660) the greatest of the Spanish painters.

33 *an Academy portrait:* a common term for paintings in which careful 'finish' rather than inspiration or originality is the chief quality.

34 *Walt Whitman:* (1819-92) the most original of the American poets.

an elderly famous painter: G. F. Watts (1817-94); his marriage to Ellen Terry was 'arranged' by a masterful woman friend.

36 *Charles Reade:* (1814-84) English novelist and playwright; his one great work is the historical novel *The Cloister and the Hearth.* He was a sound adviser to Ellen Terry and his name was first on a list of her friends (followed by that of Bernard Shaw) found after she died.

PAGE

36 *Lady Macbeth:* a famous painting of her in this role by John Singer Sargent is in the Tate Gallery, London.

37 *Flaubert:* Gustave Flaubert (1812-80), French novelist who gave exhaustive attention to his search for verbal perfection.

7. SONS AND DAUGHTERS LONG AGO

GEORGE MACAULAY TREVELYAN: (1876-   ). Born at Stratford-on-Avon; educated at Harrow and Cambridge. Regius Professor of Modern History, Cambridge, 1927-40; Master of Trinity College, Cambridge, 1940-51. His historical writings include three books on Garibaldi and the struggle for Italian independence, and others on the history of England during the reign of Queen Anne; most popular is his *English Social History: A Survey of Six Centuries.* Awarded the Order of Merit in 1930.

40 *patrician:* aristocratic; upper class.

private chaplain: in the 17th and 18th centuries a priest or parson was often on the domestic staff of socially important families who possessed a private chapel for religious services.

Huguenot refugee: the Huguenots were French Protestants; many of them took refuge in England in the 17th century when they suffered persecution in their own country.

41 *Whig:* the Whigs were a political party in opposition to the Tories. The two parties roughly correspond to present day Liberals and Conservatives.

Eton, Winchester and Westminster: famous public schools founded in 1440, 1392 and 1561 respectively.

Anne's reign: as Queen from 1702 to 1714.

Harrow: public school founded in 1571.

the reign of George I: from 1714 to 1727.

Molesworth: Robert Molesworth (1656-1725); created Viscount Molesworth in 1719; his son John (1679-1726), British ambassador in Italy, became the 2nd Viscount when his father died, and he was succeeded as 3rd Viscount by his soldier brother Richard (1680-1758) who rose to be Field Marshal in 1757.

41 *battle of Blenheim:* fought in 1704 in Bavaria; the Allies led by the Duke of Marlborough and Prince Eugène defeated the French and Bavarians; Marlborough captured Lille in 1708.

42 *Congreve:* William Congreve (1670-1729), English playwright; his best plays are *The Way of the World* (1700) and *Love for Love* (1695).

Farquhar: George Farquhar (1678-1707), Irish playwright: his best plays are *The Beaux' Stratagem* (1707) and *The Recruiting Officer* (1706).

Steele: Sir Richard Steele (1672-1729), Irish essayist and playwright; he was a pioneer literary journalist, starting *The Tatler* in 1709 (until 1711) and *The Spectator* (1711-12) and other periodicals in collaboration with Joseph Addison. Steele's best plays are *The Tender Husband* (1705) and *The Conscious Lovers* (1722).

at the bar: (idiom) the legal profession.

classical curriculum: Latin (and Greek) subjects studied in the schools.

43 *Bentley:* Richard Bentley (1662-1714), famous as a Latin and Greek scholar; Master of Trinity College, Cambridge, from 1699.

the Letters of Phalaris: Phalaris was a despotic and cruel ruler of Agrigentum, a Sicilian city, in about the first half of the 6th century B.C. A series of Epistles said to have been written by him in Greek was proved by Richard Bentley to have been forged.

Aristophanes: (c.448-c.380 B.C.) Greek comic and satirical dramatist; among his surviving plays are *The Birds, The Frogs, The Clouds,* and the anti-war plays *The Acharnians* and *Lysistrata.*

Horace: (65-8 B.C.) Latin poet; author of famous and much quoted *Odes, Satires,* and *Epistles,* and of a treatise in verse, *The Art of Poetry.*

Hellas: another name for Greece.

Pope's rendering of Homer: Alexander Pope (1688-1744) translated (into English rhyming couplets) *The Iliad* in 1715-

PAGE

20 and *The Odyssey* in 1725-6; both versions were enormously popular and earned him about £10,000.

43 *the 'Gothic' had disappeared:* Gothic architecture is the style used in the great French and English cathedrals built in the Middle Ages. Its distinctive features are the pointed arch, external pinnacles, elaborate stone ornamentation in vaults (ceilings) and window heads, vast stained-glass windows, etc. After the fifteenth century Gothic went out of fashion and was replaced by Classical (round arched) architecture modelled on the great buildings of ancient Rome in which solidity and restraint predominated. In the Victorian period there was a Gothic Revival which led to such buildings as the Houses of Parliament at Westminster, St. Pancras Station and Hotel, and many local churches; this was countered by a less extensive Classical Revival. Neither 'Revival' did more than produce indifferent and mostly inappropriate copies of the original styles.

Robert Pitt: a man of no great distinction who does not appear in the *Dictionary of National Biography*; his father Thomas Pitt, an East India merchant as well as Governor of Madras, concentrated on the acquisition of diamonds, one of which he sold to French royalty in 1717 for £135,000.

44 *Locke:* John Locke (1632-1704), English philosopher; his principal writings are *An Essay concerning Human Understanding* (1690), *Letters concerning Toleration* (1689; 1690; 1692), *On Education* (1693), and two *Treatises of Government* (1690) which have received much attention in our time because they uphold the principle upon which democracy is based—that a Government is properly subject to the will of the People.

Swift: Jonathan Swift (1667-1745), Irish satirist in prose and verse; *Gulliver's Travels* (1726), often abridged as an adventure story for children, is his most famous book, but he wrote numerous other important works.

Burnet: Gilbert Burnet (1643-1715), historian and biographer; Bishop of Salisbury from 1689; his writings include a three-volume *History of the Reformation in England* (1679; 1681;

PAGE

1714) but he is remembered mainly for *The History of My Own Times* (published between 1723 and 1734, i.e. after his death).

44 *Eaton:* i.e. Eton College.

45 *Lady Jane Grey:* (1537-1554) great-grand-daughter of Henry VII. Through the intrigues of the Earl of Northumberland and others she was proclaimed Queen when Edward VI died in 1553, but she reigned only nine days, being captured by the supporters of Mary I, imprisoned in the Tower of London and beheaded. She was an attractive girl of modest character and an accomplished classical scholar.

Queen Elizabeth: reigned from 1558 to 1603, succeeding her half-sister Mary I. Like Lady Jane Grey she was a good classical scholar, as well as a great Queen.

two women . . . : Esther Johnson ('Stella') and Rebecca Dingley, to whom Swift wrote a famous series of letters published after his death as the *Journal to Stella* (1766; 1768); another woman friend Esther Vanhomrigh ('Vanessa') occasioned his poem *Cadenus and Vanessa* (1726).

the Spectator: see note to p. 42 above under Steele.

Rob Roy: historical novel by Sir Walter Scott (1771-1832) published in 1817. Diana Vernon is the attractive heroine.

Melinda: 'a Lady of Fortune' in Farquhar's *The Recruiting Officer*.

46 *Guise:* perhaps John Guise (died 1765); served under Marlborough in Flanders and became General Guise in 1762.

A Cornet of Horse: i.e. a junior commissioned officer in a cavalry unit.

47 *Lady Mary Wortley Montagu:* (1689-1762) born Lady Mary Pierrepont, daughter of the 1st Duke of Kingston; she eloped in 1712 with Edward Wortley Montagu, who became British Ambassador in Constantinople; while with him in Turkey Lady Mary learned of vaccination against smallpox and introduced the treatment to England after her return in 1718; later she travelled widely on the Continent and is most famous now for the letters she wrote from abroad

(first published in 1763 after her death, and in numerous later editions).

8. A PEOPLE SLOW TO ANGER

RICHARD HILLARY: (1919-1943). Born in Sydney, Australia. Educated at Oxford; excelled at rowing and went to Germany as one of a crew that won the Hermann Goering Cup, defeating over-confident Germans. Joined the Royal Air Force when the Second World War started; was shot down in flames on 3rd September 1940 and rescued after three hours floating in the North Sea; he was very severely burned and facially disfigured, but after long treatment in hospital and plastic-surgery operations he returned to flying and was killed when his plane crashed on 7th January 1943. In his will he wrote: 'I want no one to be sorry for me. . . . In my life I had a few friends, I learnt a little wisdom and a little patience. What more could a man ask for.' He took the title of his book (the outstanding masterpiece of the war) from I Corinthians 15:26—'The last enemy that shall be destroyed is death.'

49 *the Carburys and the Berrys:* all the men named in this passage were Royal Air Force colleagues not otherwise commemorated.
Luftwaffe: German air-force.
Lady Cufuffle: an invented name to signify the type of political hostess at whose house-parties Government appointments were discussed.

50 *The wind on the heath:* a familiar quotation from chapter 25 of *Lavengro* (1851), a gipsy novel by George Borrow (1803-81).
Ravenscourt Park: a district on the western edge of London, beyond Hammersmith.

51 *the Dorchester:* a hotel of that name in Park Lane, facing Hyde Park.
Jerry: colloquial collective name for Germans.

PAGE

52 *Home Guards:* set up as a volunteer force for home defence after the surrender of France to the Germans in 1940.

a ' flap ': colloquial term for a scare or panic.

Aryan: originally a name given to a group of languages stemming from Indo-European sources; misapplied in Hitler's Germany to people of Teutonic stock to distinguish them from supposed ' lesser breeds '.

53 *Panzer division:* German tank (armoured car) unit.

9. THE MAKING OF AN ARTIST

JOYCE CARY: (1888-1957). Born in Londonderry; educated at Clifton and Oxford; studied art in Edinburgh and Paris. Government service in Nigeria gave him the insight into the African mind shown in *The African Witch* and *Mister Johnson; The House of Children* is in part autobiographical; among his other novels are *Herself Surprised* and *To Be a Pilgrim,* both of them linked with *The Horse's Mouth.*

55 *Bankside:* the south side of the river Thames in the Southwark area of London.

figures: human figures in paintings and drawings.

a Classic: a follower of the formal academic style in art, as practised around 1800.

the old Water Colour Society: founded in 1804 as The Society of Painters in Water-Colours; it became The Royal Society of Painters in Water Colours in 1881.

Turner: Joseph Mallord William Turner (1775-1851), English painter; until about 1796 he worked in water-colours, but afterwards in oils. He is one of the greatest of English artists, though he was much derided by conventional critics until John Ruskin praised him highly in *Modern Painters* (vol. I, 1843).

Sandby: Paul Sandby (1725-1809), English painter, mainly in water-colours.

PAGE

56 *I wasn't looking:* i.e., he was not seeing with an independent personal vision, but was painting in the style of earlier artists.

Manet: Edouard Manet (1832-83), French painter whose early pictures were in the manner of older masters; later he adopted the Impressionist style (see note to p. 18 above), but it was only towards the end of his life and after his death that his great genius was recognized.

Darwin: Charles Darwin (1809-82), English naturalist; his *On the Origin of Species by means of Natural Selection* (1859), one of the world's great books, put forward theories of evolution which were regarded by leaders in the Christian Churches as antagonistic to the doctrine of Divine Creation based upon the first chapter of Genesis.

the Radicals: ' left-wing ' Liberals who advocated radical (root and branch) measures of political and social reform.

57 *the workhouse:* workhouses were Poor Law institutions for the homeless and destitute where they had to do certain types of menial work in return for maintenance from public funds.

vibrating light . . . floating tissue of colour: effects aimed at by the Impressionist painters and by some earlier artists such as John Constable (1766-1837) and J. M. W. Turner.

58 *the grand style:* painting in imitation of the Old Masters.

against the buffers: a dead end, prohibiting further progress (as when a train reaches the buffers beside the platform at a railway terminus.

Blake: William Blake (1757-1827), English painter, engraver, and poet; among his numerous masterpieces is a series of twenty-one water-colour illustrations to the Book of Job; he afterwards reproduced these as engravings.

59 *the marbles at the British Museum:* the ' Elgin Marbles ', statuary from the Parthenon at Athens, bought from the Turkish occupants of Greece at the beginning of the 19th century by the 7th Earl of Elgin; sold by him to the British Museum in 1816.

bar-lady with a gold fringe: the reference is to Manet's

famous painting *The Bar at the Folies-Bergère*. It can be seen in the Courtauld Institute Galleries, Woburn Square, London.

59 *water-lily pool:* the reference is to a series of Impressionist paintings of this subject as seen under differing conditions of light by Claude Monet (see note to p. 18 above).

laissez-faire: a political theory favoured in 19th-century England by those who held that there should be no Government control of trade and commerce.

Marx: Karl Marx (1818-83) founder of modern Communism.

Persian carpets: the patterns used in these were (and are) much admired by modern painters who regard abstract design as more desirable than the imitation of natural objects.

Raphael's cartoons: a series of large drawings in the Victoria and Albert Museum, London; they were made in 1515-16 by the Italian painter Raphael (1483-1520) as preliminary designs for tapestries to be hung on the walls of the Sistine Chapel in the Vatican, Rome.

painting walls: i.e., making murals (wall paintings).

10. A PENNY FOR THOUGHTS

LESLIE POLES HARTLEY: (1895-   ). Educated at Harrow and Oxford. Author of numerous novels, short stories, and literary articles.

62 *the First Shelter:* covered seats provided on the promenades at seaside resorts are commonly called ' shelters '.

bastions: originally, projecting towers of a fortress or castle from which defenders could launch weapons against an attacking force.

63 *tamarisk:* a kind of feathery shrub which flourishes near the sea and bears white or blue flowers.

beetling: overhanging.

PAGE

67 *temporized:* delaying an answer in order to gain time.

the roar of the cataract: (metaphor) the immediate approach of the ordeal he dreads.

68 *not taking offences:* his misquotation of the idiomatic phrase 'Don't take your fences before you come to them', i.e. deal with difficulties when they arise, don't worry about them beforehand; ('fences' in the idiom refers to the obstacles that have to be jumped over by horses and riders in the hunting field or in steeplechase racing.

70 *Zena Dare:* (1887-   ) a popular English actress successful in both musical and nonmusical plays from 1899.

Mt. Pelée: a volcano on the island of Martinique in the West Indies. An eruption in 1902 killed about 40,000 people and desolated the surrounding country.

11. BOBBIE'S ENGLISH CLASS

FRANCIS DOWNES OMMANNEY: (1903-   ). Educated at Aldenham School (Hertfordshire) and the Royal College of Science, where he studied Zoology. Has engaged in Polar Research and particularly in deep-sea fisheries research; Director, Singapore Fisheries Research Station 1952-7; taught Marine Biology at Hong Kong University 1957-60. Author of official publications on deep-sea fishery research, and in *South Latitude* and other books has written of his own experiences and adventures. *The House in the Park* deals with his early life at home and school while members of his family lived at the White Lodge in Richmond Park.

73 *filling my imaginary tanks:* i.e., working out problems in arithmetic (mensuration) relating to the quantity of liquid required to fill tanks of given dimensions.

H. G. Wells: (1866-1946) English novelist, short-story writer, etc.; the 'early romances' referred to were such examples of science fiction as *The Time Machine* (1895), *The Invisible Man* (1897), *The First Men in the Moon* (1901), and others.

73 *Jules Verne:* (1828-1905) French novelist; now regarded as the creator of science fiction; his stories include *Round the World in Eighty Days* (1873), *Twenty Thousand Leagues Under the Sea* (1870), *From the Earth to the Moon* (1865), etc.

Rider Haggard: Sir Rider Haggard (1856-1925), English novelist, best known by the books and characters named by F. D. Ommanney here. *King Solomon's Mines* was published in 1885, *She* in 1887.

74 *asymmetrical:* lopsided.

76 *Gibbon:* Edward Gibbon (1737-94), author of the greatest historical work in English, *The Decline and Fall of the Roman Empire* published in six volumes (1776; 1781; 1783; and the final three volumes in 1788).

Thomas Carlyle: (1795-1881) Scottish historian and essayist; wrote a *History of the French Revolution* (1837), *Sartor Resartus* (1833), *Heroes and Hero-Worship* (1841), *Past and Present* (1843), and other works. He was much influenced in thought and language by German philosophy.

77 *the Elysian Fields:* in ancient mythology, the place to which blessed spirits go.

balderdash: utter nonsense.

impis: plural of *impi*, a gathering of Zulu warriors.

78 *Matthew Arnold:* (1822-88) English poet and essayist and an Inspector of Schools 1851-86. His narrative poem *Sohrab and Rustum* (1853) is a story of the Persian national hero Rustum who engages in single combat with the leader of a Tartar enemy force and slays him, only to be told that the dying man is his own son whom he had not seen for many years.

79 *the host of Heaven:* the moon and stars.

12. PICNICS AND BEDTIMES

OSBERT SITWELL: (1892-   ). Born in London; educated at Eton; served in the Grenadier Guards 1912-19. Author of poems, short stories, novels, and an autobiography in five volumes beginning with *Left Hand! Right Hand!* He succeeded his father in 1943, becoming then Sir Osbert Sitwell, Baronet.

80 *yet:* even now.

Davis: the Sitwell children's nurse.

Edith: The eldest of the three; later Dame Edith Sitwell, an outstanding poet and writer of numerous prose works.

81 *Stephen Pare:* one of the male servants in the Sitwell household; he went blind.

82 *a footman had suddenly laughed:* domestic servants were trained to appear deaf to the dinner-table conversation of those they served. Henry had therefore committed a *faux pas.*

83 *impalpable:* possessing a quality that cannot be defined.

13. PET MARJORY

DESMOND MACCARTHY: (1877-1952). Born in Plymouth; educated at Eton and Cambridge. Journalist and essayist. Knighted 1951.

85 *I have been a child myself:* This is a familiar joke which is perhaps more effective when spoken and soon forgotten than when preserved in print.

86 *maunder on:* ramble on in talk.

almost any object will delight a child: Present-day parents appear to take a contrary view to this and seem to believe that children love most the toys that are biggest, showiest, and cost most.

87 *after a blitz:* after an air-raid, when children as well as men and women are mutilated and killed.

Dictionary of National Biography: the standard reference book (in many volumes) for information about the lives of almost all the notable British men and women. It was begun in 1882 and was at first intended to include those who lived and died not later than 1900, but supplementary volumes were added to include those of later dates and new volumes are now added every ten years.

87 *Farnie:* Henry Brougham Farnie published in 1858 *Pet Marjorie: a story of Child life fifty years ago.* Although the author here refers to him as a journalist, Farnie's main work was as a writer of words for many comic operas.

Mr. Esdaile: Arundell Esdaile (1880-1956), Secretary of the British Museum 1926-40; author of numerous books; edited *The Journals, Letters and Verses of Marjory Fleming* (1924), reproduced in facsimile from her original manuscripts in the National Library of Scotland.

Dr. John Brown: (1810-82) Scottish physician and essayist. *Rab and his Friends* is a famous dog story which, like his essay on Marjory (or Marjorie) Fleming was included in his volumes called *Horae Subsecivae* (1858-61), a title meaning ' Odd Hours ', for he wrote in the time he could spare from his doctoring.

Everyman's Library: a famous series of classics of all nations started at one shilling a volume in 1905 by J. M. Dent, a London publisher. The series is still in progress (though the economic consequences of two World Wars increased the price) and Dent's original intention of including 1,000 volumes has been achieved, though not until a long time after his death.

88 *Frank Sidgwick:* edited *The Complete Marjorie Fleming: her Journals, Letters and Verses* (1934).

Walter Scott: Sir Walter Scott (1771-1832), Scottish poet and historical novelist. He was for a long time reckoned almost as great as Shakespeare, but is now less read.

89 *plaid:* a length of patterned woollen cloth forming part of the traditional Scottish Highlanders' dress.

Gill Morrice . . . Baron of Smailholm: two of the traditional *Border Ballads* from the collection called *Border Minstrelsy* which Sir Walter Scott gathered and published in three volumes (1802-3).

I will instruct my sorrows . . . : the lines quoted are from Shakespeare's *King John*: III, i, 68-73.

PAGE

90 *Sonnet:* These lines have been given here in the way that
Marjory Fleming wrote them, not as Desmond MacCarthy
copied them.

91 *Stevenson:* Robert Louis Stevenson (1850-94), Scottish novelist,
short-story writer, essayist, and poet. *Treasure Island* (1883),
Kidnapped (1886), and *The Strange Case of Dr Jekyll and
Mr. Hyde* (1886) are probably now his best known fictional
works; he also wrote many fine letters to his friends—these
have been published in several volumes since he died.

14. 'OLD SLOWCOACH'

FLORA THOMPSON: (1877-1947). Born at Juniper Hill, Bucking-
hamshire, and educated there at the village school. She started
work at the age of fourteen as assistant to the postmistress in a
nearby town. Thereafter she had further post-office experience
in Surrey and after marrying lived in Bournemouth, where she
added greatly to her knowledge and pleasure by drawing constantly upon the resources of the Public Library. She wrote
in order to pay her children's school fees, and when they were
started on successful careers she produced the books which
made her famous and will keep her so. The first of these, *Lark
Rise*, was followed by *Candleford Green,* and then by *Over
to Candleford*—the three being afterwards issued in one volume
as *Lark Rise to Candleford.* Her books are delightful and also
important, for they embody a firsthand record of English
village and country-town life unequalled by any other writer.
In them we are introduced to a kind of life which Flora
Thompson and her neighbours lived towards the end of the
last century, a kind of life that has now disappeared for
ever: a hard life, yet one which brought satisfaction and
happiness such as few people now know in these easier and
prosperous times. *Still Glides the Stream* was Flora Thompson's last book, similar in substance and a worthy epilogue to
the Lark Rise trilogy.

PAGE

93 *undercutting:* stone carvings on the columns and walls and vaults (ceilings) of cathedrals and churches are often given a three-dimensional effect by having the undersides and backs of the figures or foliage as carefully worked as the outer parts which are always visible. This treatment is called undercutting, and no good and conscientious mason would fail to give his work this perfect finish.

94 *these competitive times:* when work is done as cheaply and hastily as possible to prevent its being given to a competitor at a lower price.

tracery: the openwork carvings in the window heads or arches of churches.

keystone: the large wedge-shaped stone at the centre top which keeps an arch from collapsing. Keystones usually project slightly from the main surface of the arch and are often carved with human or animal faces or other ornamentation.

95 *young feller-me-lad:* a colloquial form of address which may be spoken either jocularly, or as a rebuke from a serious elder to a frivolous youth.

come day go day: colloquial phrase indicating that no interest is taken in work done, apart from its being ' all in the day's work ' for a day's pay.

96 *setting grates:* fixing fireplaces.

billycock hat: colloquial name for an earlier form of bowler hat, lower and rounded in the crown. Originally from ' bully-cock ', since such hats were worn, cocked on one side, by bullies in the eighteenth century.

Charity: Charity Finch is the chief character in the book.

15. HAPPINESS

FREYA STARK: (1893-   ). Educated privately in Italy, and later in London at the School of Oriental Studies. From 1939 to 1945 she was on government service in the Middle East, having in preceding years travelled much in Arabia, distilling her experiences into a series of travel books which include *The Southern Gates of Arabia* and *The Valleys of the Assassins*. She has also written several autobiographical volumes, and among her recreations are mountaineering and embroidery.

98 *Kootenay lake:* in British Columbia, western Canada.

Chippendale chairs: made by (or in the style of) Thomas Chippendale (died 1779), one of England's most famous furniture designers. The pattern book he published, *The Gentleman and Cabinet Maker's Director* (1752), contains many designs which were copied by others.

forced plants: those whose growth and flowering are artificially hastened by being kept in a heated atmosphere (e.g. in a greenhouse).

100 *the war:* i.e. the First World War (1914-18).

Beduin Arabs: those who lead a wandering life in the Arabian desert, moving in search of pasture for their flocks.

Pan-like: in ancient Greek mythology Pan was the god of Nature and country things, and is now regarded symbolically as the personification of joyful paganism.

102 *palpable:* touchable; material.

Mount Carmel: near Haifa in Palestine; a Christian colony of monks and nuns founded there by an Italian in the 12th century started the Carmelites or White Friars.

Beato Angelico: the Blessed Angelico, a title applied to Fra Giovanni da Fiesole, or Fra Angelico (about 1400 or earlier —1455), one of the greatest of the earlier Italian painters.

the van: the forefront.

103 *our Promethean gift:* Prometheus, one of the chief heroes in ancient Greek mythology, stole fire from heaven and was thus able to confer upon humans a gift which brought them the power to challenge Zeus (called Jupiter by the Romans) the chief of the gods. Thus, for us, the ability to *create* (works of art and so on) enables us to share in the powers of the Creator.

104 *the Euganeans:* a range of hills in the Venezia province of

north-east Italy bears their name. One of Shelley's finest poems is ' Lines written among the Euganean Hills '.

104 *castrum:* (Latin) a stronghold; a fortified camp.

the Renaissance: the period which followed after the Middle Ages and is usually dated as beginning in 1453 when, the Turks having captured Constantinople, many scholars fled from there to Italy, taking with them important Greek manuscripts which became the basis of the New Learning that spread throughout western Europe during the next few generations.

Venetian Gothic: a variety of Gothic architecture (see note to p. 43 above) peculiar to Venice.

16. A CAVALIER LADY

LORD DAVID CECIL: (1902-); younger son of the 4th Marquess of Salisbury; educated at Eton and Oxford. Goldsmith's Professor of English Literature, Oxford, from 1948. Author of *The Stricken Deer* (on the poet William Cowper) and of books on Sir Walter Scott, Jane Austen, Thomas Hardy, Lord Melbourne (1779-1848, statesman), etc. Besides the study of Dorothy Osborne, *Two Quiet Lives* contains a long essay on the poet Thomas Gray.

107 *Lady Grey de Ruthin:* the Barony of Grey de Ruthin was created in 1324 and is now held (1960) by the 25th Baron. It is one of the few old-established hereditary peerages which can be held by a woman in her own right, as it was by the lady here mentioned. She married in 1654 Henry Yelverton (later Sir Henry Yelverton) and died in 1676.

Lady Diana Rich: daughter of Sir Henry Rich, 1st Earl of Holland, who fought on the Royalist side in the Civil War after having joined and seceded from the Parliamentary party by whom he was captured and executed in 1649. Dorothy Osborne hoped that her cousin would marry Lady Diana, but she died unmarried.

107 *Chicksands:* Chicksands Priory in Bedfordshire, the Osborne's
family estate. It had previously been a nunnery founded
early in the 12th century.

Cromwell's expulsion of the Parliament: he dissolved the
Long Parliament in 1653.

Mr. Pym: John Pym (1584-1643), M.P. for Tavistock and one
of the five members whom Charles I attempted to arrest at
the House of Commons in 1642. Pym was a leading statesman in the Parliamentary party, but he died a few months
after the Civil War started.

General Monk: or Monck (1608-70), military and naval commander and statesman, serving at different times both the
Cavaliers and the Roundheads.

Lady Anne Wentworth: daughter of Sir Thomas Wentworth,
1st Earl of Strafford, who was executed on Tower Hill in
1641 after having been impeached by the Commons. Lady
Anne married Lord Rockingham.

Mr. Waller: Edmund Waller (1606-87), poet and politician;
played an inglorious part in the struggle between Charles I
and Parliament; he praised Cromwell in a poem written in
1655, rejoiced at his death in another written in 1658, and
welcomed Charles II's Restoration in yet another poem
written in 1660. Yet he is important in English literature as
a narrative poet and as a writer of lyrics.

108 *Lady Isabella Thynne:* born Lady Isabella Rich, sister of
Lady Diana Rich; married Sir James Thynne.

Miss de Mayerne: Elizabeth de Mayerne, daughter of a
famous French physician who settled in London and
became Royal Physician; she married the Marquis de Cug-
nac and died about 1653.

Lord Leicester: Robert Sidney (1595-1677), 2nd Earl of
Leicester; he married in 1616 Lady Dorothy Percy, daughter
of the Earl of Northumberland.

Lady Newcastle: Margaret Cavendish (1624?-74), Duchess of
Newcastle; wrote poems, plays, and essays of very little
merit but is remembered for the biography which she
wrote of her husband William Cavendish, whose second

wife she was. She had many eccentricities, which caused
Samuel Pepys to refer to her in his Diary as 'a mad, con-
ceited, ridiculous woman'; but Charles Lamb, a century
and more later, delighted in her writings.

108 *Bedlam:* general name for a madhouse.

sequestered: secluded; shut away.

fecundity: fruitfulness.

109 *Sir Peter:* Dorothy's father, Sir Peter Osborne (1584-1653),
M.P.; he was a loyal supporter of Charles I and had been
Governor of Guernsey in the Channel Islands.

Temple: Sir William Temple (1628-99), statesman and essayist;
married Dorothy Osborne in 1655; he is one of the masters
of English prose, and among his notable essays are those
entitled 'Upon Health and Long Life', 'Of Ancient and
Modern Learning', 'Of Poetry', etc. For about ten years
from 1689 Jonathan Swift was Secretary to Temple at the
latter's home, Moor Park, Surrey.

110 *Amestris:* this and the three names that follow it were intended by the novelists to have a classical appearance, as
though they were of ancient origin. This was a fashionable
affectation at that time.

punctilios of honour: obedience to formal standards of conventional behaviour when an insult had been offered: e.g.
if a noble or aristocratic woman were wronged by words
or action, her husband (if she were married), her brother, or
her father was bound in honour to challenge the offender to
a duel, a challenge which had to be accepted by the
offender if he were not to be regarded as dishonoured and
disgraced by all who knew him.

Anna Karenina: the tragic heroine of a famous Russian novel
with her name as its title, by Leo Tolstoy (1828-1910).

rhetoric: extravagant, high-flown language.

topicking: discussing current topics.

112 *amorists:* flirtatious, fickle lovers.

the Byronic fashion: in the manner of Lord Byron (1788-1824),
among whose many extravagant observations on love was
that ' 'Tis woman's whole existence '.

17. AN ENGLISH CRICKETER

JOHN ARLOTT: (1914-   ). Born and educated at Basingstoke. Has had varied experience as hospital clerk, detective in the police force, and B.B.C. producer, staff instructor, and cricket commentator.

PAGE

114 *Denis Compton:* (1918-   ) played for Middlesex from 1936 and for England at home and overseas from 1937 until his retirement in 1957; also Association football for Arsenal and England. He made 122 centuries in first-class cricket and took part in 78 test matches. He made the highest aggregate for a season—3,816 in 1947 with an average of 90.85.

Hobbs: Sir Jack Hobbs (1882-   ) played for Surrey (1905-35) and for England at home and overseas (1907-30); made 197 centuries in first-class cricket, still a record; in the 1925 season he made 16 centuries, the record broken by Compton's 18 in 1947.

Tom Hayward: one of Surrey's finest batsmen; his aggregate of 3,518 in the 1906 season was a record not broken until Compton beat it in 1947.

115 *Alan Melville:* captain of the South African team in test matches played in England in the 1947 season.

116 *dog-days:* a metaphorical term for the height of summer, so called from the dog-star (Sirius) which rises at that season. The author here uses 'dog-days' as a term for the period when a cricketer's skill is at its height.

117 *the 'Chinaman':* a kind of 'googly' (see note below) to which the name 'Chinaman' is applied colloquially, probably because the Chinese were popularly supposed (at the time the term was first applied in cricket) to be subtle and deceptive.

Fleetwood-Smith: an Australian cricketer; chiefly a successful bowler.

googly: a type of bowling evolved by a Middlesex cricketer, B. J. T. Bosanquet (1877-1936) about 1903; he played for Eton, Oxford, Middlesex (1898-1919), and England (1903-5).

The googly is bowled with a hand-and-arm action that
leads the batsman to expect an off-break, whereas a leg-
break is actually delivered (or *vice versa*). The origin of the
word is unknown; for some time such a ball was called a
'bosie' (from Bosanquet).

18. PRODUCING A PLAY

GEORGE BERNARD SHAW: (1856-1950). Born in Dublin and educated
at various schools there. He moved to London in 1876 and
failing to establish himself as a novelist he settled to journalism
for the next twenty years, winning a reputation as a music
and drama critic and at the same time training himself as an
effective public speaker on political subjects. His first play
appeared in 1892 and was followed up to the time of his death
by some fifty others which made him the most famous dramatist
of the 20th century. The Prefaces he wrote to the plays are
also famous for the precision and clarity of his prose style,
which is comparable to that of such earlier masters of prose
as Bunyan and Swift. Though all his writings had a serious
aim and did much to call widespread attention to social
injustices of all kinds, their purpose is achieved more by the
power of Shaw's brilliant wit and sparkling humour than by
direct delivery of any message.

119 *should be soprano, alto, tenor, and bass:* Shaw was brought
up in a musical household and learned a great deal of
operatic music in early years, during which he acquired an
enduring love of Mozart's operas. This youthful training
enabled him to become in his thirties one of our great music
critics, and, even more importantly, it benefited his plays
by teaching him to write dialogue which makes it easy for
actors to give variety of vocal tone in the parts they are
playing on the stage. The best example of what may be
called Shaw's 'soprano, alto, tenor, [baritone], and bass'

PAGE

dialogue is the 'Hell scene' in Act III of *Man and Superman*, where Ana represents the soprano, The Old Woman the contralto, Don Juan the tenor, The Devil the baritone, and The Statue the bass.

120 *blue-print:* definite plan.

122 *A play by a great poet . . . may fail hopelessly on the stage:* instances of such stage failures can be found in the works of Byron, Shelley, Browning, and Tennyson, though the last two had some stage success because such great performers as Macready (for Browning) and Irving (for Tennyson) had acting genius which made up for the stage inexperience of the poets.

retortive backchat: dialogue which depends for its humorous effect upon facetious remarks exchanged rapidly between the speakers; such performers were popular on the old-time music-hall stage, when they were called 'cross-talk comedians'.

123 *ad lib.:* ad libitum (Latin), at pleasure; without limit.

124 *Kierkegaard:* Soren Kierkegaard (1813-55), Danish religious philosopher whose writings had their greatest influence long after his death, particularly in the 1930s and onward in various translations.

Ibsen: Henrik Ibsen (1828-1906), Norwegian playwright and poet whose works had a revolutionary influence on European and American drama. Shaw was one of his chief disciples, though Ibsen's plays lack the humour which Shaw's combine richly with seriousness and 'message'.

Edipus complex: (usually spelt Œdipus) a term—derived from the writings of Sigmund Freud (1856-1939) the Austrian psycho-analyst—used to signify the existence of a morbid passion between a son and his mother. In ancient Greek mythology and in plays based on the myth, Œdipus, having been cast out as a baby, grows up without knowing who his parents are. When a young man, he quarrels with and kills a stranger whose wife he then marries, discovering later that they are his father and mother. His mother thereupon commits suicide and Œdipus, having blinded himself, becomes a guilt-stricken homeless wanderer. Since Freud's theories became popular (though often without being fully understood) the term 'Œdipus complex' has become a cliché. Among the cases to which it has been loosely applied by some is that of Hamlet and Gertrude his mother, especially in Act II, Sc. iv.

124 *'Pleecemin', 'Reel and Ideel', 'Mariar Ann':* Shaw imagines the producer noting mispronunciations of 'policeman', 'real and ideal', 'Maria Ann'.

When the play is by Shakespeare . . . : This passage relates to the difficulties and problems arising from passages in *Macbeth* (II, ii, 64), *Hamlet* (II, i, 56), *Henry V*, and *Othello* (V, ii, 2). The 'green fields' or 'green frieze' passage comes in *Henry V* (II, iii) when the Hostess describes the death of Falstaff. In modern editions she is made to say 'his nose was as sharp as a pen, and a' babbled of green fields', though an earlier version 'his nose was as sharp as a pen on a table of green frieze' is thought by some scholars to make better sense, since a table is an appropriate place on which to lay a pen, and green frieze (a kind of woollen cloth) is suitable material for a table covering.

125 *Copyright:* The Copyright Act protects all authors against any unauthorized use of their writings. It is an offence against the law to perform or read to a public audience any modern play unless permission has first been applied for and given in writing by the author or his publisher or his agents. A fee will be payable for the right to perform the play. This is thought by some amateur actors to be unjust, but a play is something made by the author with his mind and at least as much hard work and experience have gone into its making as into the making of anything else which no one expects to get for nothing. So it would be just as dishonest to try to cheat an author as to try to avoid payment for printing programmes, hiring costumes, or hiring a hall or theatre.

126 *ingénue:* (French) stage term for a young actress who plays unsophisticated girl parts.

126 *utility:* stage term for small-part players who fit in usefully
as required.

127 *Tartuffes:* characters resembling Tartuffe, the hypocrite in
Le Tartuffe, a satirical comedy by the great French playwright Molière (1622-73).

Malvolio: the Countess Olivia's steward in Shakespeare's
Twelfth Night.

Lady Wishfort: an elderly, scheming, abusive character in
The Way of the World, a comedy by William Congreve
(1670-1729).

Edmund Kean: (1787-1833) the leading English tragic actor of
his period.

Frederick Robson: (1821-64) a gifted and popular actor and
singer.

Gustavus Brooke: (1818-66) a much-travelled English actor
whose drinking habits ruined the genius he displayed for a
while in London as a player of Shakespearean tragic parts.

a patent theatre: from the Restoration (1660) until 1843 (when
the Theatre Regulation Act was passed) Shakespearean and
other plays regarded as classics, such as those of Goldsmith
and Sheridan, were not allowed to be performed anywhere
in London but at Drury Lane and Covent Garden, the only
two theatres to which the Royal Patent (or charter or licence)
had been granted by Charles II. In 1766 a limited Patent
for the summer seasons only was granted by George III to
the Haymarket theatre for the lifetime of its manager
Samuel Foote (1720-77). Although the Patent system ceased
in 1843, the three theatres named still have the traditional
right to the title Theatre Royal.

128 *antiquarian:* dealing with ancient things.

Euripides: (480-406 B.C.) Greek tragic playwright.

Aristophanes: (about 448-380 B.C.) Greek comic and satirical
playwright.

proscenium: the arched opening at the front of a stage.

wings: side-pieces of scenery.

flats: pieces of scenery consisting of a flat wooden frame
covered with painted canvas.

PAGE

128 *sock:* the soft shoe worn by comic actors in ancient Athenian (Greek) plays.

busken: (usually spelt *buskin*) the thick-soled boot worn by tragic actors in ancient Athenian plays to make them appear taller and more impressive.

hierarchic: priestlike.

the Unities: a theory derived in part from a treatise on poetry and drama—*The Poetics*—by the Greek philosopher Aristotle (384-322 B.C.), and in part from the practice of French 18th-century classical playwrights (chiefly Jean Racine, 1639-99). The Unities—of Time, of Place, and of Action—set a limit to the imagined period covered by the action of the play, confined it to one imagined place, and allowed only a main plot (i.e. with no sub-plots). Some plays fit comfortably within these restrictions, but Shakespeare is among the great dramatists whose works usually ignore all the Unities (see, for example, *The Merchant of Venice*).

129 *Oberammergau:* the village in Bavaria where the Passion Play has been performed every ten years since 1633 by local amateur actors.

the prompt side: at the left of the stage from the actor's viewpoint, the side where the prompter usually sits.

130 *Ristori:* Adelaide Ristori (1822-1906), famous Italian actress.

' *the Bastard of England*': Roman Catholics regarded Elizabeth I as illegitimate because their refusal to recognize the divorce of Henry VIII from his first wife Katherine of Aragon made his marriage to Anne Boleyn (who became Elizabeth's mother) doctrinally illegal.

megalomaniac: a sufferer from a form of delusion which makes the person think himself of supremely great importance.

the grey mare is often the better horse: English proverb implying that a female is often better than a male.

19. A GENTLEMAN PRETENDING

JOHN BOYNTON PRIESTLEY: (1894-   ). Born in Bradford; educated there and at Cambridge. His best-known novel is *The Good Companions*; his numerous plays include *Dangerous Corner*, *Time and the Conways*, and *The Linden Tree*; and he has written many essays and several autobiographical volumes. During the great depression in the 1930s he travelled around the country gathering material for a report on the state of the people, published as *An English Journey*, and during the war he gave many uplifting broadcast talks, some of which he printed as *Postscripts*.

PAGE

132 *the 'Bradford Pioneer'*: a Yorkshire local newspaper published in Bradford.

Shavians: the name given to admirers and disciples of Bernard Shaw.

G.B.S.: he first became well-known by these initials, used as his signature to his early critical articles on music and drama in newspapers and periodicals.

The Ancient of Days: a phrase first used in the prophet's vision in the Old Testament Book of Daniel 7 : 9. Priestley applies it to Shaw as a very old, wise and good man.

Jaeger-type Mephistopheles: Shaw wore woollen garments which, at least in his young manhood, were of the kind invented by a Dr. Jaeger and advocated as specially beneficial to health. The reference to Mephistopheles, another name for the Devil, was applied to the young Shaw because the cut of his beard gave him an appearance resembling that of the stage Mephistopheles in *Faust*.

133 *Chesterton*: G. K. Chesterton (1874-1936), poet, essayist, novelist, and biographer who wrote one of the earliest and best critical studies of Shaw in 1909. He disagreed with most of Shaw's ideas but admired and praised his intellectual and moral courage.

charlatan: impostor; mountebank.

133 *Wells:* H. G. Wells (1866-1946), novelist and writer on political and social topics.

Belloc: Hilaire Belloc (1870-1953), poet and essayist.

Bennett: Arnold Bennett (1867-1931), novelist, diarist, and critic.

134 *polemically:* controversially; argumentatively.

disingenuous: insincere.

dubious: vague; doubtful.

Stalin: Josif Dzhugashvili (1879-1953), called Stalin, Russian Soviet leader. Shaw spoke in praise of Stalin and the Soviet system after a visit to Russia in 1931.

Edwardian: the period of the reign of Edward VII, 1901-10.

135 *Strindberg:* August Strindberg (1849-1912), Swedish playwright and novelist. Many of the women characters in his writings are cruel and ruthless.

kittens: colloquial term for irresponsible and frivolous young women.

Cleopatra: in Shaw's *Caesar and Cleopatra* (1901).

Orinthia: in Shaw's *The Apple Cart* (1929).

orchestrated: adapted it for several voices in his plays.

Mozartian: by or in the style of Wolfgang Amadeus Mozart (1756-91), Austrian composer, whose music Shaw greatly admired and loved.

136 *Chekhov:* (frequently spelt Tchekov in English translations), Anton Chekhov (1860-1904), Russian playwright and short-story writer.

Saturday Review: a weekly periodical in which Shaw wrote his still-famous essays on plays and acting, 1895 to 1898.

Wilde: Oscar Wilde (1854-1900), Irish playwright, essayist, and poet.

George Moore: (1852-1933), Irish novelist.

Yeats: W. B. Yeats (1865-1939), Irish poet and playwright.

'A.E.': pen-name used by G. W. Russell (1867-1935), Irish poet and essayist.

137 *James Stephens:* (1882-1950) Irish poet and novelist.

Gaev: a character in Chekhov's play *The Cherry Orchard* (1904).

137 *cautionary:* with a moral warning.

V.I.P.: common (and usually satirical) term for one who is regarded (or regards himself or herself) as a Very Important Person.

Grand Canyon: a vast gorge of the river Colorado in Arizona, U.S.A.

Bertrand Russell: (1872-   ) 3rd Earl Russell, a title to which he succeeded, but refused to use, on the death of his brother the 2nd Earl in 1931; philosopher, mathematician, essayist, and anti-war propagandist.

iconoclast: originally one who smashed *icons* (religious images); now applied to anyone who attacks conventional beliefs.

'*date*': become old-fashioned, stale, and out-of-date.

20. YOUTH AMONG THE RUINS

ROSE MACAULAY: (1881-1958). Born in Cambridge; educated at Oxford. She became famous as a humorous and satirical novelist with *Told by an Idiot*, *Orphan Island*, and others, though one of her finest books is a historical novel of the 17th century, *They Were Defeated*.

139 *Gresham Street:* This and nearly all the other places mentioned can be found on a map of the City of London.

Haberdashers' Hall: The City Companies formed as Trade Guilds in the Middle Ages built beautiful halls as meeting places for their members and officials. These Company Halls were among the finest buildings in the City, but many of them were destroyed either by fire or by German bombing. Those readers of this extract from Rose Macaulay's novel who live near enough will find it fascinating as well as instructive to explore the surroundings of St. Paul's Cathedral and discover the streets, churches and Company Halls mentioned. (It must be pointed out that when we speak of present-day 'City companies', usually operating

PAGE

with huge financial resources in the interests of share-holders, something different is meant from the bodies that established the Company Halls, for they, properly known as The Livery Companies of the City of London, were concerned more particularly with maintaining standards of manufacture and trading principles and the welfare and conduct of members of their particular craft.)

141 *two great fires:* the Fire of London in 1666 and that started by the German air-force in their massive raid in December 1940.

' *We saw the fire grow . . . the cracking of houses at their ruin':* This is a quotation from the long eye-witness account of the great Fire of London written by Samuel Pepys (1633-1703) in the Diary he kept from 1 January 1660 to 31 May 1669. The passages about the Fire are in the entries dated 2 to 7 September 1666.

probity: honesty.

142 *impressionistically:* showing the total effect of the scene as she saw it at a glance, not in realistic detail.

Dies Irae: (Latin) Day of Wrath or Day of Judgment. The Latin words begin a hymn which is part of the Roman Catholic Mass.

wharf rats: colloquial term for the human waterside prowlers and thieves.

143 *whey-faced:* pale; resembling the appearance of *whey* from milk.

spivs: (slang) those who live in various mean and cheating ways, instead of by honest work.

144 *the maquis:* country covered with bushes and undergrowth in which it is possible to hide. During the German occupation of France in the second World War, French patriots who formed the anti-German Resistance became known as *Maquis* because they had to use secret hide-outs. It was because Raoul and Barbary had grown up at the time that the *Maquis* were working for France that they felt at home among the areas of wilderness in London.

145 *kimkam:* (an old dialect word not now in common use) awry: crookedly.

21. POETRY ON THE STAGE

THOMAS STEARNS ELIOT: (1888-   ). Born in the United States; educated at Harvard, the Sorbonne (Paris), and Oxford. Received the Order of Merit in 1948 and the Nobel Prize in the same year. His most famous poems are *The Waste Land* and *Four Quartets;* his plays include *Murder in the Cathedral* and *The Cocktail Party;* and he has also written important volumes of criticism.

PAGE

149 *monologuists:* makers of long speeches.

M. *Jourdain:* the character in the French satirical comedy *Le Bourgeois Gentilhomme* by Molière (1622-73) who exclaims: ' Par ma foi! il y a plus de quarante ans que je dis de la prose sans que j'en susse rien.' (' Good gracious! then I have been speaking prose for over forty years without knowing it.')

150 *highfalutin:* pretentious; in an artificial and extravagant style.

sardonic: bitterly satirical; cynical.

22. A VIEW OF MARLOWE

KENNETH TYNAN: (1927-   ). Born in Birmingham and educated there and at Oxford. After experience in the theatre as actor and producer he concentrated on dramatic criticism, mainly for *The Observer*, with an interval in the United States writing on the American theatres for the *New Yorker*. His books are on drama and on bull-fighting.

156 *Christopher Marlowe:* (1564-93) born at Canterbury, Kent, and educated at the King's School there and later at Cambridge. His plays are: *Tamburlaine* (about 1587), *Faustus* (about 1588), *The Jew of Malta* (about 1592), *Edward II* (about 1593), *The Massacre at Paris* (published about 1600), and in collaboration *The Tragedy of Dido* (published in 1594). His non-dramatic poems include *Hero and Leander*

PAGE

(left unfinished) and the famous lyric 'Come live with me and be my love'.

156 *the Latin Quarter:* the bohemian district of modern Paris; the term is also applied to the area in any town where artists and writers and their hangers-on congregate and live in (sometimes voluntary or affected) penury and squalor.

gigantic emperor: Tamburlaine.

157 *Ingram Frezer:* Marlowe's murderer; his surname is variously spelt, as Frazer, etc.

facile: easily produced.

brassy leer: hard sly glance.

heresies: Marlowe was an atheist.

high-flying in the upper air: Marlowe was a master of magnificent rhetorical language.

corporal: bodily; physical.

riposte: thrust.

the straitjacket inertia of usualness: the bonds of conformity or conventionality.

some lewder Elizabethan Chelsea: some more disorderly district in 16th-century London corresponding to the present-day 'Latin Quarter' Chelsea.

158 *Jonson:* Ben Jonson (1572-1637), the leading English playwright of the 17th century after Shakespeare died. In his satirical comedy *The Poetaster* (1601) Tucca is a cowardly bully.

for whom a wild boar's head is best served as a pork pie: i.e. they prefer dead and well-cooked conventional ideas to adventurous living ones that may be dangerous.

idées reçues: (French) *literally,* received ideas; generally accepted conventional opinions.

high-tea of warmed-up platitudes: feast of stale clichés.

épater les bourgeois: (French) *literally,* flabbergast the middle classes; shock the conventional.

Flaubert: Gustave Flaubert (1821-80), French novelist whose extreme care for style and determination always to find the exactly right word made him a slow producer of his few novels, of which *Madame Bovary* (1857) is the most famous.

PAGE

158 *Max du Camp:* Maxime du Camp (1822-94), French novelist and journalist; friend of Flaubert and his companion on journeyings in the Near East.

say boo to a goose: ' He can't say *bo* to a goose ' is an English proverb applied to anyone who has so little courage that he fears to oppose or defy anyone at all.

159 *Tamburlayne:* alternative spelling of Tamburlaine.

160 *to ride in triumph through Persepolis:* a famous line in *Tamburlaine* (Part I, 757).

the doctrine of the four elements: the belief held in the Middle Ages that the universe is governed by spirits embodying the four elements—Fire, Water, Air and Earth.

Calor: (Latin) heat.

phoenix: a mythical creature supposed to be eternally reborn from the ashes of the fire in which at intervals it consumes itself.

jeu d'esprit: (French) a clever trifle.

161 *a Jew for his hero:* there was much popular illwill towards the Jews in England then.

162 *yardstick:* standard of measurement by which other things are tried.

aglot: aglet, a corded ornament.

hubris: (Greek) arrogant self-confident pride which, in ancient Greek philosophy, is certain in the end to lead to downfall and ruin through excess.

prototype: original; the first form.

Puttenham: Richard Puttenham (about 1520-1601), probable author of *The Arte of English Poesie* (1589), published anonymously.

23. REVOLUTION THE BRITISH WAY

ALFRED CHARLES WARD: (1891-   ). Born and educated in London. Author of *Twentieth Century Literature*, an *Illustrated History of English Literature* (Chaucer to Shaw, 3 vols; also one-volume edition without plates), *Enjoying Paintings*, etc.

164 *Women's Suffrage campaign:* The prolonged fight for 'Votes for Women' organized by the Women's Social and Political Union was interrupted by the outbreak of war in 1914, and any need for a resumption of the campaign afterwards was avoided by the post-war extension of the Parliamentary franchise to women.

endemic: of regular occurrence.

Karl Marx: see note to p. 59 above.

the Paris Commune: the revolutionary Communist uprising after the disastrous defeat of France in the Franco-Prussian War in 1870.

H. M. Hyndman: (1842-1921), English journalist and socialist leader.

William Morris: (1834-96), English poet, artist-craftsman, and socialist; he mastered and practised many crafts and decorative arts—printing, dyeing; designing fabrics, wall-papers, stained glass, furniture, etc., in co-operation with others.

protean: from Proteus who, in ancient Greek mythology, was able to assume many different forms.

Radical: see note to p. 56 above.

165 *bogy-word:* any word which arouses fear, often without reference to its true meaning and intention.

Fabian Society: a movement for political education on socialist lines founded in 1884.

166 *a bloodless social revolution:* the Welfare State was brought into being by legislative changes, not by revolutionary direct action.

167 *zealotry:* fanaticism.

sacerdotal: working through a priesthood.

crony: close friend.

Established Church: The Church of England 'as by law established'.

Rationalism: the conviction that Reason should be the governing factor in human affairs, not faith or superstition.

agnosticism: the conviction that nothing can be known except what is apparent to the senses and intellect, and that there-

PAGE

fore it is impossible to have knowledge of the existence or of the non-existence of God.

167 *atheism:* total disbelief in the existence of God.

blasphemy laws: legislation which made it a punishable offence to speak offensively of any Christian belief.

ratiocination: formal reasoning based on logic.

168 *centering on Moscow:* centuries ago Russians began to claim that Moscow was 'the third Rome', i.e. the leader of the world in succession to (1) Rome of the ancient Empire (2) Rome of the Catholic Popes.

169 *Utopia:* a State ruled on ideal lines; the word derives from the description of such a State in *Utopia*, written in Latin in 1515-16 by Sir Thomas More (1478-1535). The English translation of *Utopia* (by Ralph Robynson) did not appear until 1551.

24. CREATION AND CRITICISM

CHRISTOPHER FRY: (1907-   ). Educated at Bedford Modern School. Actor; schoolmaster; director of Repertory companies at Oxford and Tunbridge Wells. His plays began with *The Boy with a Cart* (1939) followed by *A Phoenix Too Frequent* (1947), but he first became famous with *The Lady's Not for Burning* (1948).

170 *pinchbeck:* an alloy of copper and zinc (base metals) used as an imitation of the precious metal gold. The word is extended to anything sham.

170-1 *the dams of form:* attention to form in writing and the other arts slows down the otherwise rapid and perhaps undisciplined working of the imagination.

171 *facility:* easy, carefree production.

bacchic: from Bacchus, the god of wine in ancient mythology.

172 *relevance:* the bearing of one thing upon another or others; appropriate relationship.

tensionless: without strain; free from anxiety.

172 *The Way of the World:* a comedy by William Congreve (see note to p. 42 above).

before I produced it . . .: Christopher Fry was for a time the Producer at the Oxford Repertory Theatre.

173 *some . . . other part of the forest:* a stage direction used in modern editions of Shakespeare's *As You Like It.*

174 *a man's reach has exceeded his grasp:* lines in 'Andrea del Sarto' (a poem about the Italian painter with that name) by Robert Browning (1812-89) run: '. . . a man's reach should exceed his grasp,/Or what's a heaven for?' *temeritous:* rash; over-bold.

John Gay: (1685-1732) English poet and playwright; best known as the author of *The Beggar's Opera* (1728) and for his *Fables* (1727 and 1738). *The Rehearsal at Goatham* (1754), an unacted farcical comedy.

175 *Prince of Egypt:* see Exodus chapter 2.

176 *clairvoyant:* possessed of second-sight, the ability to visualize mentally or to know things that are happening elsewhere or in the minds of others.

reflex-action: automatic response, not under the control of the conscious will.

25. THE COMPLETE MAN

PRINCE PHILIP, DUKE OF EDINBURGH: (1921-   ). Son of Prince Andrew of Greece and Princess Alice of Battenberg. Educated in England and Scotland; entered the Royal Navy in 1939 and served on H.M.S. *Valiant* in the battle of Cape Matapan. Married Princess Elizabeth, daughter of George VI, in 1947. President of the British Association for the Advancement of Science in 1951.

177 *the classics:* the ancient literature of Greece and Rome (in Greek and Latin).

178 *mobility:* ease of movement.

180 *making compromises:* adjusting oneself to prevailing conditions and possibilities.

26. THE KING'S MONEY SPINNER

CICELY VERONICA WEDGWOOD: (1910-   ). Born in Northumberland; educated privately and at Oxford; author of histories, biographies, and essays on literary subjects, including *The Thirty Years' War*, *Oliver Cromwell*, *William the Silent*, and volumes on the English Civil War period (*The King's Peace* and *The King's War*).

PAGE

183 *extra-Parliamentary revenue:* funds not voted by Parliament.

patent: a royal licence to manufacture or trade in certain specified things.

projectors: they would now be called company promoters.

185 *Colbert:* Jean Baptiste Colbert (1619-83), chief adviser to Louis XIV of France. He initiated a number of successful economic reforms, improved transport facilities, and took a hand in other national developments.

étatisme: (French) State socialism.

the fens: the low-lying areas of certain English eastern counties.

Berkhampstead: a town in Hertfordshire.

186 *Vintners' Company:* the medieval City Company or Trade Guild of wine merchants.

Star Chamber: a court of justice held in a part of the Palace of Westminster where the ceiling was ornamented with gilt stars. Originally founded in the 14th century as 'a poor man's court', by the 17th century it had become oppressive and much hated and was abolished in 1641.

Abell: William Abell; imprisoned by the Commonwealth for having supported Charles I's taxation demands, and for other offences; after his release settled in Holland in 1655.

187 *tax farmer:* a person who paid for the privilege of collecting taxes, from which his own profits came. The system produced many abuses—of unjust treatment of taxpayers and of theft from sums collected—and was at length abolished and replaced by a civil service department with salaried officials as inspectors and collectors.

PAGE
189 *plaiding:* manufacturing a particular kind of woollen cloth.
inflation: reducing the value (i.e. the purchasing power) of
money by increasing the total currency.
190 *bedevil:* spoil; create a confused state of affairs.

27. OUT FROM LONDON

RICHARD CHURCH: (1893-   ). Born in London and educated
there at Dulwich Hamlet School. Author of many novels,
volumes of poetry, and various other books, including a con-
tinuation of *Over the Bridge* called *The Golden Sovereign.*

192 *field piece:* a cannon that can be moved forwards or backwards as troops advance or retreat.
193 *Battersea:* a south-west London district in which the extensive Battersea Park alongside the river Thames is a prominent feature.
Jack: Richard Church's elder brother.
artifacts: objects made by humans, as distinct from natural
ones.
the river flats: low ground beside a river.
195 *Pride of the morning:* colloquial term for early morning
showers.
Rain before seven, fine before eleven: a common English folk-
saying.
197 *macadam:* roads surfaced with layers of broken granite or
other hard stone pressed down by a steam roller to form a
level and durable traffic way. Named from the inventor
John Loudon McAdam (1756-1836).
198 *Hog's Back . . . Devil's Punchbowl:* famous beauty spots in
Surrey.
flipperdigibert: (usually spelt *flibbertigibbet*) empty-headed
frivolous young person.
200 *a bicycle of rare vintage:* from the description this was probably an early 'safety' model, an improvement on the
'penny-farthing' kind, so called because the front wheel
was very large and the back wheel very small.

PAGE

200-1 *Tarnhelm:* in Germanic mythology a headdress which enabled the wearer to become invisible.

201 *fabulous:* the original meaning of the word was 'belonging to fable or legend', but it has become one of the most threadbare of present-day clichés through its daily misuse by advertisers of 'fabulous bargains' and a hundred and one other 'fabulous' things. Richard Church uses the word here in the allowable sense of 'scarcely human-looking'.

28. A THAMES NIGHT SWIM

IRIS MURDOCH: (1919-   ). Born in Dublin; educated in London, Bristol and Oxford; Assistant Principal at the Treasury 1942-4; served with the United Nations Relief Organization in Belgium and Austria 1944-6; Lecturer in Philosophy, Oxford, from 1948.

202 *the Serpentine:* the lake in Hyde Park and Kensington Gardens.

203 *pitted:* with indentations, made in this case by flying fragments during air-raids.

the Liffey: the river which runs through Dublin, the capital of the Irish Republic.

204 *river police:* part of the London police force safeguards shipping and performs other duties on the river Thames; it has its own patrol boats.

copped: (slang) arrested.

205 *Judo:* a form of Japanese wrestling.

dynamism: indwelling energy.

29. A DAY IN A.D. 44

MORTIMER WHEELER: (1890-   ). Director of the National Museum of Wales, 1924-6; Keeper and Secretary of the London Museum, 1926-44; has undertaken much archæological excavation at home and abroad. His extraordinary wealth of knowledge has been shown in many broadcast and television programmes, and in his writings on Roman Britain and on archæological subjects relating to France, India and Pakistan. *Still Digging* is an autobiography largely concerned with his experiences as an archæologist. Knighted 1952.

208 *ratiocination:* see note to p. 167 above.
    crescentic: crescent-shaped.
    quarrels: heavy short arrows.
    orientations: compass directions.
    ballista: a war machine for catapulting stones or other missiles at enemy fortifications.
    vertebra: a single segment of the backbone.
210 *rigor mortis:* (Latin) temporary stiffening of a corpse soon after death.
    Hardy's . . . Dynasts: The Dynasts is a great poetic drama of the Napoleonic Wars by Thomas Hardy (1840-1928), published in three parts (1904, 1906, 1908). Its characters include, besides the human historical characters, groups of Spirits or (as the author calls them) ' Phantom Intelligences ' who act as choruses watching and commenting on the earthly events.

30. KNOWLEDGE AND WISDOM

BERTRAND RUSSELL: (1872-   ). Born in Wales; educated privately and at Cambridge. Author of important books on mathematics and philosophy and has also written numerous volumes on politics and current topics. Received the Order of Merit in 1949 and the Nobel Prize for Literature in 1950. He succeeded his brother as 3rd Earl Russell in 1931 but did not use the title.

212 *the distorting medium of their own passions:* i.e. they were biased and did not give a true account of events and persons.
    Hegel: Georg Wilhelm Hegel (1770-1831), German philo-

sopher. His lectures on *The Philosophy of History* were published after his death.

213 *philosopher's stone:* Medieval alchemists believed that it would be possible to discover a substance that would enable base metal (such as lead) to be changed into the precious metals gold and silver.

elixir of life: It was also believed in the Middle Ages that a draught conferring everlasting life could be invented.

214 *the tyranny of the here and now:* being bound by inability to see beyond our own place and time.

the Samaritan: see the parable of the Good Samaritan in the New Testament, St. Luke 10:30-37.

215 *Henry IV in France:* 'Henry of Navarre', born 1553; after a Protestant upbringing he joined the Roman Catholic Church in 1593, following his accession to the throne in 1589, but by the Edict of Nantes (1598) he granted liberty of worship to French Protestants. He was murdered by a fanatic in 1610.

Abraham Lincoln: (1809-65) President of the United States from 1860 until he was murdered by a demented actor John Wilkes Booth. The 'great war' he conducted was the American Civil War (1861-5) fought to prevent the 'Slave States' of the South from leaving the Union and setting up a Confederation of their own.

31. MENDING A BIRD

GERALD DURRELL: (1925-   ). Born in India; educated privately and in France, Italy, Switzerland, and Greece. Student Keeper at Whipsnade Zoo, 1945-6. His books, mainly about his experiences in search of wild animals, include *The Overloaded Ark, The Drunken Forest, My Family and Other Animals.*

217 *a . . . Bach fugue:* Johann Sebastian Bach (1685-1750), German composer, many of whose works are among the world's greatest music; *fugue:* a type of advanced musical

composition in which two or more melodies or themes are introduced in turn by various instruments or voices and thereafter woven into a complex pattern of sound.

218 *Jacquie:* the author's wife, Jacqueline.

bittern: a marsh bird resembling a heron.

219 *Daniel Boone:* the author confers this name facetiously upon the Indian (whose real name is unknown), perhaps because Daniel Boone (1734-1820), an American frontiersman, no doubt encountered many kinds of birds during his journeyings across the American continent.

tortuously: in a roundabout manner.

220 *sinus:* one of the interior cavities of the head.

223 *attenuated:* extremely thin.

224 *patriarchal cascade of white beard:* a long full beard such as Old Testament patriarchs (Abraham, Moses, etc.) are given in religious art.

32. WILD FLOWER

JOHN WYNDHAM: (1903-   ). Born in Birmingham; educated at Bedales. After trying various occupations he succeeded as a writer, more especially as the author of such outstanding ' science fiction ' novels as *The Kraken Wakes* and *The Midwich Cuckoos.*

226 *patina:* incrustation; coating; used here figuratively to denote the sensation of having a layer of dirt on the skin when waking after sleep.

percolator: a vessel for coffee-making.

227 *a high-tensile gleam:* a look that indicates readiness to cope with the stresses and strains of the day's work.

228 *Medusan coils:* in ancient mythology, Medusa was a monster in human shape whose hair was entwined with writhing serpents.

cerebral convolutions: resembling the coiling and folding surface appearance of the brain.

228 *a wonder of the left hand:* It is an ancient belief or super-
    stition that anything approaching from the left-hand side
    is unlucky or evil; *sinister* comes from the Latin for left
    side.

    antibiotic: used here in the sense of destroyer. Antibiotics
    used in the treatment of disease destroy bacteria.

    Arcady: earthly paradise.

229 *refractile gems:* i.e. (here) gleaming dew; *refractile*, throw-
    ing back light from various angles.

    to mislead her from its nest: larks do not rise vertically from
    their nests, but first run some distance on the ground.

230 *Imitations of mortality:* an intentional misquotation of *In-
    timations of Immortality* from the title of a fine poem by
    William Wordsworth (1770-1850).

    spinney: a group of trees and bushes.

    Unguent: soothing.

231 *reticulated:* with a network of markings.

    orchis: one of a family of English wild flowers.

232 *William Blake:* (1757-1827) English poet, painter, and en-
    graver; the lines quoted are from his *Auguries of Innocence.*

    Their colours . . . a feeling and a love: quoted from ' Lines
    composed a few miles above Tintern Abbey ' by Words-
    worth.

233 *Now fades . . . solemn stillness holds':* quoted from ' An
    Elegy in a Country Churchyard ' by Thomas Gray (1716-71).

234 *sub-critical masses brought together:* the explosion of nuclear
    bombs is caused by the contact of two parts which are safe
    while separate.

235 *Babel:* see ch. 11 of Genesis for the story of the people who
    attempted to build a tower ' whose top may reach unto
    heaven ' and were condemned by God to confusion of
    tongues ' that they may not understand one another's
    speech '; ' Therefore is the name of it called Babel; because
    the Lord did there confound the language of all the earth.'

    Cobalt: a hard white metal, used in the composition of
    alloys and as a colouring ingredient in paints and in
    glass-making; more recently it has been found possible

to use cobalt as an intensifying agent in nuclear weapons.

235 *gamma rays:* a kind of X-rays with great penetrating power; they may cause serious harm to human tissue if the body is exposed to them without expert medical control.

237 *hormones:* substances secreted by the glands of the body; if they are either deficient or present in excess there are harmful effects on growth and general health.

238 *clubs of smoke:* club-shaped clouds swelling out at the top, formed after nuclear explosions.

33. THE MUSICAL SEAL

ROWENA FARRE: She spent her early childhood in India before being sent to Britain, where her Aunt Miriam looked after her and taught her. They lived at first in London and afterwards in Sutherland as described in *Seal Morning*. She has since travelled a great deal and lived among gipsies, as well as doing office work.

240 *Men of Harlech:* a traditional Welsh patriotic song.

241 *Larry Adler:* a popular concert performer on the harmonica, another name for mouth organ.

242 *a croft:* the Scottish name for a small-holding (a portion of enclosed land rented or bought for cultivation or the raising of livestock).

loch: (Scottish) lake.

243 *cacophony:* harsh sounds; discords.

lochan: (diminutive of *loch*) a small lake.

xylophone: a musical instrument consisting of a series of small bars of varying length mounted horizontally on wooden supports; when struck with a special light hammer (beater) the bars vibrate and produce musical notes.

a Brahms sonata: in this case, a piece of piano music by Johannes Brahms (1833-97), German composer. Sonatas are compositions in a particular form for one or two instruments, usually for piano and/or violin.

244 *Sutherland:* the northernmost western county of Scotland.

34. ENGLAND SAVED

ELIZABETH JENKINS: Educated at Letchworth and Oxford. Novelist and biographer.

245 *convoy:* (verb) escort and protect.

Parma: Alexander Farnese, Duke of Parma (1545-92), one of the ablest military commanders and statesmen of his time. Though born in Rome he was brought up in Spain and at length, in the service of Philip II the Spanish king, Parma became Governor-General of the Netherlands which were then occupied and oppressed by Spain. Philip ordered Parma to assemble at the Netherlands ports an immense fleet of boats to carry an army across the North Sea to invade England. The 'Invincible Armada' was sent from Spain to ensure the safe passage of Parma and his troops, but the destruction of the Armada put an end to the invasion plan.

Drake: Sir Francis Drake (about 1540-96), the most famous of the English Elizabethan seamen.

246 *Walsingham:* Sir Francis Walsingham (about 1536-90), one of Elizabeth's principal Secretaries of State.

Lord Howard of Effingham: (1536-1624) he commanded the English fleet against the Armada.

Hawkins: Sir John Hawkins (1532-95).

Plymouth: (harbour and Sound) still a great naval base; on the south coast of Devon.

Chatham: a great naval dockyard until 1960; on the north coast of Kent, in the Thames estuary.

Dr. Allen: William Allen (1532-94) an English Roman Catholic leader, he left Oxford for Flanders in 1561 and founded the English College at Douai in northern France in 1568 for the training of priests to conduct Counter-Reformation activities in England. The Pope made Allen a cardinal in 1587.

PAGE
247 *peculation:* embezzlement; fraudulent misuse of money.

the campaign in the Netherlands: an unsuccessful English expedition led by the Earl of Leicester had been sent to the Netherlands (1585-7) to assist the Dutch against the Spaniards.

plenary powers: authority to decide and act without prior consultation with the Queen or her Ministers of State.

248 *Lord Hunsdon:* (1524?-96) served Elizabeth as diplomat, State official and military commander.

Leicester: Robert Dudley, Earl of Leicester (1532-88), favourite of Elizabeth, whom he daringly aimed to marry; he was thought to have murdered his first wife, Amy Robsart, and in general his character and conduct were far from irreproachable.

the Lizard: the headland with that name on the south-west coast of Cornwall.

Camden: William Camden (1551-1623), historian and antiquary; after making extensive tours throughout Britain he published a valuable work called *Britannia, a . . . description of . . . England, Scotland, and Ireland from the earliest antiquity.* Later he issued *Annals* of the reign of Queen Elizabeth. The Camden Society founded in his memory in 1838 has brought out many volumes of original documents dealing with the early history and literature of Britain.

249 *Gravelines:* French coastal town on the Strait of Dover.

lee: the sheltered or shoreward side.

scuppers: holes to drain water away from the deck.

35. THE DOROBO AND THE BUFFALOES

ELSPETH HUXLEY: (1907-   ). Born (Elspeth Josceline Grant) in Kenya; educated at the European School, Nairobi, Reading University, and Cornell University (U.S.A.). Married Gervas Huxley 1931. Author of novels, travel books and other writings, mainly about East Africa.

PAGE

250 *Dorobo:* a hunting tribe once enslaved by the Masai (see note below); they are normally small in stature.

dikdik: a very small and delicately formed species of antelopes or gazelles; sometimes they are little more than twelve inches high and weigh only a few pounds.

251 *buck:* used always as singular *or* plural.

rufous: reddish-brown in colour.

Jambo: a common word of friendly greeting in Swahili (properly Kiswahili), the chief African language spoken in the eastern coastal areas and elsewhere in that region.

252 *Kikuyu:* one of the principal African tribes in Kenya and adjacent territories.

threw back his head: Africans rarely indicate direction by pointing with the hand as Europeans mostly do. Instead they make a head movement. See p. 253: 'He pointed with his chin.'

waterbuck: another and larger species of antelope.

Masai: a formerly warlike East African tribe, notorious as cattle raiders.

bongo: a large, striped antelope.

253 *bovine:* like that of an ox.

salt-lick: a place where salt-water pools have dried out, leaving the earth salty enough to attract animals who need salt in their diet to keep them in healthy condition.

bwana: Swahili word for *master,* or *sir.*

254 *shamba:* (Swahili) plantation. He means that he lives by elephant hunting, not by cultivating the soil. Therefore the arrows in his quiver are as useful to him when hunting as a hoe is to a man who tills the ground.

loped off: bounded away.

civet smell: pungent smell similar to that exuded by a civet cat.

man: the word is often used by sophisticated Africans (and latterly, imitatively, by certain classes of whites) simply as an interjection addressed to either sex.

toto: (Swahili) child.

255 *siafu:* (Swahili) a kind of ant which 'attacks all living creatures alike, and bites fiercely'.

rondavel: a round grass-hut.

vole: a creature resembling a mouse.

syce: a servant who takes care of horses.

256 *Thika:* a town on the Thika river, some twenty miles north-
east of Nairobi the capital of Kenya.

257 *steel-keen:* cold and 'cutting' like a sharp knife.

bossed: with knobs or round projections.

258 *flamingo:* a large bird with a long neck and long legs and
beautiful flame-coloured wings.

the spoor: the footmarks and scent by following which
hunters can track wild animals.

259 *a red flame sprang up:* an appearance due to sunlight.

36. LIFE ON THE MOON

HAROLD SPENCER JONES: (1890-1960). Born in London; educated
at Latymer School, Hammersmith, and Cambridge. Astronomer-
Royal 1933-55. Knighted 1943.

37. THE LOST UMBRELLA

265 *a hennaed cutie:* colloquial term for a girl who colours her
hair and dresses showily, hoping to attract male attention.

267 *'Course, we was be'ind yer larst week, wasn't we?':* In spite of
their schooling, many British young people fail to observe
civilized speech habits, often because it has become their
chosen form of snobbery to prefer ugly voices and bad
grammar to pleasant voices and correct grammar. A London
boy whose mother complained of his bad speaking replied:
'Ger, I ain' goan ter talk posh!'—even though his parents
set him a good example. This boy was one of the very many
school-children and adolescents who conspire to debase
their beautiful national language, because they make-

believe that deliberate bad pronunciation proves that they do not belong to the 'stuck-up' classes. But there is no virtue in artificially affected ugliness, and a pleasant voice and good speech should be recognized, even by a cutie, as no less important than the latest fashions in shoes and frocks and hair-styles.